Using Statistics in Sport and Exercise Science Research

Joanne L. Fallowfield, Beverley J. Hale, and David M. Wilkinson

Lotus Publishing
Chichester, England

First published in 2005 by
Lotus Publishing
9 Roman Way, Chichester, PO19 3QN, UK

Cover Design Jim Wilkie
Printed and bound in the UK by Antony Rowe

Acknowledgement
In addition to the gratitude we feel for the continued love and support of our families, we would specifically like to express our thanks to Prof. Terry McMorris, Simon Delves, Richard Harris and Dr Neil Maxwell, for their help at the beginning, middle, nearly the end, and very near to the end (respectively) of this project. We would also like to thank Emma Wiggs and Dominique Lihou for allowing us to use some of their dissertation data in examples presented in the text. Finally, we would like to thank all who contributed to our sample of active researchers (Chapter 12), for their time and their candour – *many a true word is spoken in jest*!
JLF, BJH, DMW (August 2005)

British Library Cataloguing in Publication Data
A CIP record for this book is available from the British Library
ISBN 1 905367 00 7

For Alex, Joseph and Matthew

JLF

For Naomi, Michael and Philip

BJH

For Rhona, Matthew and Katc

DMW

Contents

1

Introduction:

The Purpose

Chapter Objectives

- To introduce the experimental *research process*
- To describe the concepts of *standardisation* and *control*, and their importance in conducting high quality research
- To briefly critique how *experimental control* will impact upon the research findings and our *confidence* in the research conclusions.

Introduction

Conducting research can be both an exhilarating and a frustrating activity – where the quest for new answers and new explanations of phenomena may easily and unwittingly be confounded by inadequate or poor planning and avoidable errors. *Using Statistics in Sport and Exercise Science Research* has been written to guide the novice researcher through the processes involved in identifying a worthwhile and answerable research question, formulating hypotheses, designing a research study, collecting, organising, evaluating, and analysing data, drawing conclusions, and finally presenting your work to the scientific community. Whilst accepting that there are many different approaches to conducting research, this text will primarily focus upon the experimental approach where usually data are collected and then statistically analysed in order to shed light upon a specific research question. With this end-point in mind, *Using Statistics in Sport and Exercise Science Research* will initially examine the preparatory steps of conducting research that will ensure the right data are correctly collected under appropriate circumstances to allow valid conclusions to be drawn. We will then discuss general issues concerning data collection, before providing a very practical review of different approaches to statistically analysing data. This will be followed by a worked example, where a number of the issues raised in the preceding chapters will be addressed within the context of a real sport and exercise science research project. It should be noted that this book does not set out to provide a definitive text on research methods, nor do we claim that it will provide all the answers to your statistical questions; rather we aim to present a practical manual to assist those starting out in research to develop a sound theoretical framework for organising their work. Thus, our primary aim is to develop research confidence through developing a greater understanding of the research process.

Getting it Right From the Start: Standardisation and Control

The watchwords for sound experimental research are *standardisation* and *control*. Standardisation refers to maintaining a prescribed level or condition; keeping conditions as far as possible the same in all *repeated* tests or experimental trials[1.1]. The environment in which research is being conducted should be standardised as far as is possible. This can be relatively easy if the work is being conducted in a laboratory or in an indoor facility such as a sports hall or a gymnasium, where it is possible that ambient temperature and humidity may be quite tightly controlled – especially if the facility has air conditioning – though we cannot assume environmental control will be possible in all indoor facilities. The research environment is much more difficult to dictate when conducting studies out of doors or in real sport and exercise venues where you do not have the luxury of such a level of control (e.g. on a soccer pitch, in a work environment, or on the

---

[1.1] It should be noted that this refers to repeated tests or trials of the same experimental condition. We will examine later how the experimental condition will be modified to address the aims of the research project. However, this will be a systematic change and not the chance variations – or error – associated with poor standardisation.

beach). Here one of the biggest challenges to standardisation is the prevailing weather conditions, which will be beyond your control. If your research is to be conducted outdoors you will need to construct standards of weather – in terms of temperature, humidity, air movement/wind speed, solar radiation (sunshine) and precipitation – which will define the conditions within which it is acceptable to conduct your work. This setting of criteria for outside – and inside – work does not only concern the weather, but also the physical conditions of the research location that may influence the performance of your research volunteers. For example, if your study concerns soccer players performing on a grass pitch, you would need to consider the conditions under foot – Is the pitch soft or hard? How will this be evaluated? What is the effect on performance? What are the permissible standards that are acceptable, and how would these be tightly enforced? When conditions are outside of your predetermined acceptable standards you will have to abort your trial. This is never an easy decision, especially when it takes considerable preparation on your part, and on the part of the volunteers, not to mention expense, to set up each trial. However, in the long run this is the right decision to take to ensure the quality of your research and the integrity of the data.

When discussing standardisation in the sport and exercise sciences we must also consider the volunteers/participants of the research as well as the environment in which the study is to be undertaken. When working with human participants it can often be difficult to truly standardise their status prior to each trial. Obvious issues to address in terms of the exercise sciences include: health status, training status (weekly training/exercise loads in terms of activity mode, frequency, intensity, and duration of exercise); pre-trial resting status or the nature and extent of prior exercise; nutritional status/diet and regular supplementation regimens (including vitamins and minerals); regular intake of prescriptive or non-prescriptive drugs; and, alcohol/nicotine intake. When conducting research in the context of health related exercise, it might additionally be necessary to ascertain relevant information concerning a participant's immediate family. As was the case for the research environment, it is essential to set rules governing participation. These rules will be dictated by the specifics of the research question, but will also reflect the population to which the research findings are ultimately to be applied. Consequently these rules need to be very carefully constructed and then rigorously applied during the recruitment and selection of research participants, and again prior to each experimental trial.

This process of setting rules governing the behaviour of participants and defining the environment within which research takes place is referred to as *experimental control*. Poor experimental control will lead to poor standardisation and a high level of unpredictable variation (i.e. error) between the measurements taken. Whereas with good experimental control the research participants and research environment are standardised as far as is practically and appropriately possible, and this will result in a relatively lower level of unpredictable variation between repeated measurements taken during a trial. In an ideal world, 'tight' experimental control would yield identical data if the same group of participants, under the same conditions, were measured/evaluated in the same way on two or more occasions (i.e. repeated measures). Thus, if the conditions were systematically changed, the same group of participants, measured/evaluated in the same way, would yield different data that would reflect the *effect* of the change. The manipulation of the experimental conditions in this way is known as the *research intervention*.

For example, we might wish to examine whether technological developments in the design of a football can improve shooting accuracy of football players. In this case the *research intervention* would be the new football design, with the current design providing the control (no change) condition. The *repeated measure* would be the shooting accuracy, measured once with the current design and repeated with the new design for each research participant. Before commencing our experiment we must consider any other factors, aside from football design, that might influence this measure. Aside from potential 'environmental factors' as discussed previously in this chapter if the work were to be undertaken out of doors on a soccer pitch, an obvious factor would be the skill level of the players recruited to undertake the experimental trials. In order to control for differences in the skill level of the research participants, we could specify the required playing standard during participant recruitment and players of the same standard would be recruited. Another factor might be the position from which the shot was taken; again this is something that is relatively straightforward to control and standardise in the execution of the data collection. If the *research intervention* (i.e. football design) resulted in an *effect*, we would observe a systematic increase or decrease in shooting accuracy depending upon whether the new ball design improved or impaired the players' shooting performance. Moreover, if the research intervention did not have an effect, the only variation in shooting accuracy would reflect the normal level of (unpredictable) human error in executing this skill.

Unfortunately research is not conducted in an ideal world where there would be no measurement error; it is conducted in the real world! There will therefore always be a degree of measurement variation, especially in the case of the sport and exercise sciences where normally you are working with real people who do not always behave or react in a consistent and predictable way. Through standardising the experimental conditions and exerting a high level of experimental control, the aim is to minimise this degree of measurement variation. This in turn will give us confidence that the effects we can identify in the data are as a consequence of the research intervention. We are able to measure this confidence through the application of appropriate statistical procedures (refer to chapters 5–9), and this will provide a probability[1.2] that the outcome was not as a result of chance but is a real observation.

As a postscript to the above discussion, it is important to remember that any text providing guidance on the research process will describe the best case scenario, where procedures associated with best research practice are readily applied. However, the reality of research may be somewhat different, and it is important to note that, whilst we must strive to attain standardisation and control in our work as far as is possible, there may be situations where this is not possible to the level we would like and we must make judgements on whether a degree of tolerance in our measures is acceptable. Such a situation may be acceptable – or at least preferable to the work not being undertaken at all – but we must be able to document this measurement tolerance, as this will influence our level of confidence in making decisions on the data. Furthermore, it may equally be appropriate and correct to evaluate events and behaviour of our research objective *in situ*, where the variation in the *real* sport and exercise environment (indoors or outdoors) is part of the phenomena we are seeking to explore.

[1.2] *Probability* is a measure of the degree of confidence you might have in the occurrence of an event; measured on a scale from zero (i.e. impossible) to one (i.e. certain).

Overview of *Using Statistics in Sport and Exercise Science Research*

Following on from this introductory chapter, Chapter 2, *Getting Started: The Nature of Research*, helps you to take the first steps into research, through translating an inquiring thought into a research question. Once we have a question, how do we decide whether it is actually worthwhile – does this research question have scientific merit and value? Assuming it has merit and will expand scientific knowledge and understanding, how do we translate a relatively general research question into specific 'testable' hypotheses? Once we have identified our research hypotheses, these will dictate many aspects of the research design. This initial planning stage of *question-hypotheses-design* is fundamental to good quality, valid research; poor planning will lead to poor research and poor conclusions.

Chapter 3, *Experimental Design and Data Collection*, will examine a number of common experimental designs from the sport and exercise sciences, and critique the relationship between research question and experimental design. Whilst we are not suggesting a 'one design fits all' philosophy, a number of general styles/forms of questions asked in the sport and exercise sciences fall into common research designs. This will not prove a definitive list, but we hope to provide the necessary tools to allow the structure of a research question to be identified and the knowledge to translate this into an appropriate research design. This chapter will define the language of research design, and hence allow the new researcher to clearly articulate and understand the process that they wish to undertake. We will also consider some general issues in data collection. Ultimately, the quality of data collection will be determined by the research skills of the investigator. In this context research skills refer to both an understanding of the theories and principles of measurement, and the practical ability (i.e. competency) to undertake the specific measurements required for the project being undertaken. Measurement competency will contribute to measurement variation; a low level of competency will lead to a high level of measurement (i.e. error) variation.

Chapter 4, *Organising and Illustrating Data*, examines different approaches to evaluating raw data. Following data collection, how might we initially examine the data to try and identify any patterns in the data before we commence any form of statistical analyses? Thus, different forms of descriptive statistics will be described as well as different approaches to pictorially presenting data. Too often researchers are tempted to hastily key their data into a sophisticated statistical software package on the computer before trying to see what the *raw scores* have to say for themselves. This can result in a relatively blinkered approach to research, where interesting and novel findings in the data are unconsciously and needlessly overlooked.

The following five chapters – *Introducing Inferential Statistics, Looking at Relationship and Association: The Relationship Between Variables, Using Relationship for Prediction: Regression Analysis, Testing Differences Between Two Groups,* and *Looking at Differences in More Complex Experimental Designs* – provide guidance on analysing and evaluating data based on approaches involving the testing of hypotheses. The different approaches will be described and critiqued within a range of relevant sport and exercise science scenarios. Worked examples will be given to aid understanding, and the reader will be taken through these examples to demonstrate how these different approaches can be applied to appropriate data sets. Some of the mathematics and statistical theory will be given in the form of *technical boxes* and *calculation boxes* for those researchers who wish to understand further the principles behind the different approaches to measuring association and differences.

Chapter 10, *Pulling It All Together: A Worked Example*, draws all the theory and practical advice presented in the preceding sections of this book into a step-by-step example of the research process in action. This is followed by *Presenting Your Findings* (chapter 11), where the different approaches to presenting your research findings to the scientific community are described and discussed. Finally, chapter 12, *Common Problems in Conducting Research: Solutions and Reflections*, presents varied thoughts on the research process from active researchers presently working within the various sub-disciplines of the sport and exercise sciences. Problems encountered whilst undertaking research, and strategies for their solution, are presented. In addition, the highs and lows of the research process will be discussed from the personal perspectives of the active researchers, as well as advice for the novice researcher just starting out on their first investigation.

And Finally: A Short Note on Reporting Accuracy

Throughout this text all examples are defined and explained within their sub-discipline context to illustrate the direct relevance of the chosen research and/or analytical approach to the specific sport and exercise science situation.   Equally we have endeavoured to observe sub-discipline reporting conventions where possible.   Nevertheless, there are a number of examples from the exercise physiology sub-discipline reporting respiratory data where, for clarity, we have not followed the correct reporting convention.   Specifically, this refers to the annotating of the respiratory data of maximum oxygen uptake (VO_{2max}) and maximum minute ventilation (V_{Emax}). In the annotation of these data the 'V' indicates a measure of *volume* in litres, and this volume is expressed over time as a *rate* (i.e. litres per minute, $l.min^{-1}$).   As such, the correct approach to annotate these data is to record a dot over the top of the V (i.e. $\dot{V}O_{2max}$) indicating a rate.

Summary/Key Points

1.   The research process concerns identifying a worthwhile and answerable research question, formulating hypotheses, designing a study, collecting, organising, evaluating, and analysing data, drawing conclusions, and finally presenting your work to the scientific community.

2.   The watchwords for sound experimental research are *standardisation* and *control*.

3.   Through standardising the research environment (outdoors/indoors) and the recruitment/selection of participants, an investigator is able to exert tight *experimental control*.

4.   A high level experimental control is essential to ensure a low level of unpredictable variation (i.e. error) between repeated measures.

5.   Through standardising the experimental conditions and exerting a high level of experimental control, the aim is to minimise the degree of measurement variation. This in turn will give confidence that the effects identified in the data are as a consequence of the research intervention.

6.   We can measure the *probability* that the outcome was a real effect, and not as a result of chance, through the application of appropriate statistical procedures, and this will determine the *level confidence* in which we can draw conclusions.

2

Getting Started:
The Nature of Research

Chapter Objectives

- To describe the domains of human performance
- To understand the *scientific method* in evaluating human performance
- To apply this method in an ethical manner
- To critique approaches to measurement
- To discuss issues informing the generalisation of these measurements.

Introduction

The starting point of research is the inception of an idea and the development of a worthwhile *research question*. This might be viewed, on face value, to be fairly straightforward. However, in practice articulating the 'problem' to be solved can often be one of the hardest parts of conducting research. Similarly, the translation of this 'question' into *research hypotheses* – or suggested testable explanations – and subsequently into an appropriate research design is not without difficulties.

The sport and exercise sciences are concerned with the acquisition of knowledge through observations of sport and exercise, and those participating in sport and exercise either as a performer, a coach, a supporting professional (e.g. official, therapist/sports medic, or administrator), or indeed as a spectator. Kerlinger (1966) described scientific research in terms of a systematic and controlled investigation of the *presumed* relations between natural phenomena. Thus, the sports and exercise sciences are involved in: the systematic acquisition of information; the evaluation of this information; and finally, the application of this information either to explain or predict phenomena. This *decision making process* can be described in terms of: *measurement*, or the act of assessing; *test*, the method by which a measurement is taken; and *evaluation*, a judgement concerning the goodness, quality, merit, value or worthiness of the measurement outcome.

The following chapter will further examine the active research process from a practical perspective. The starting point of research is an observation or a thought concerning the being or behaviour of phenomena (i.e. facts, occurrences or events perceived by our senses) in the world around us. Issues concerning the translation of this observation or thought into a research question will be discussed. Ethics and the development of an ethical framework within which to conduct research will be introduced – how might morals and social values inform the thoughts, actions and behaviour of the investigator, and the subsequent thoughts actions and behaviour of the research participants? In discussing measurement and the generation of data, it is appropriate to examine the nature of the data obtained. This chapter will discuss the *levels of measurement* and describe the nature of *statistics*. The way in which measurement is performed influences the way in which we can use the data obtained. One purpose of experimental research is to relate the findings of a small group of participants (i.e. the sample) to a larger group of similar individuals (i.e. the population) without having to test the population (i.e. to *generalise* the research findings). In this context the term *population* is not used in a geographical sense in relation to a town, a country, or a continent; in discussing the population we are referring to the whole group from which our sample was chosen (i.e. the people who were eligible to take part in our study). This chapter will conclude by considering some of the general issues concerning *data evaluation*. The timing and preferred approach to data evaluation should be considered at the planning stage of any research programme, such that potential difficulties might be addressed and as far as possible avoided. The relationships between observation/thought/perception, research question and research hypotheses are described in figure 2.1.

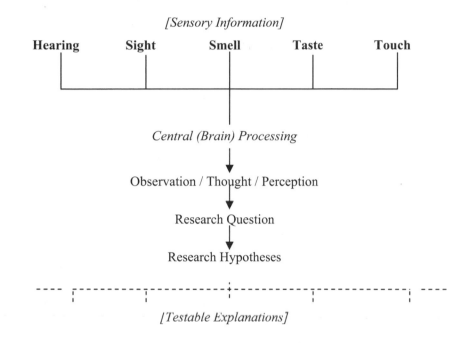

Figure 2.1   Developing a research question and the relationship between
observation/thought/perception, research question and research hypotheses.

Domains of Human Performance

Human activity can be discussed in terms of the cognitive, affective, or psychomotor domains. A domain can be defined as a field or scope of knowledge and/or activity, and we can describe human knowledge and behaviour relative to this conceptual framework. The *cognitive domain* is concerned with objectives of knowledge and mental achievement. The kind of skills that might be evaluated relative to this domain includes: comprehension, application, analysis, synthesis, and evaluation.   From a psychological perspective, these are viewed as reasonably measurable attributes – through questionnaire and/or problem solving type activities – and we might relatively easily assign a score of some description to reflect an individual's cognitive capacity. In contrast, the *afferent domain* is less clear-cut; this domain is concerned with objectives of attitudes and perceptions. An individual's value-base will influence their attitudes towards, and perceptions of, events and the world around them. When performing measurements in the afferent domain we are concerned with obtaining information concerning an individual's approaches to receiving, responding, valuing, and organisation.   This domain appears more diffuse and transitory in comparison with the cognitive domain. It involves an individual's emotions – which are more contextual and less certain, and therefore vary from day to day. Finally, the *psychomotor domain* is concerned with objectives of physiological and psychological performance, and is evaluated through measuring reflex movements, perceptual abilities, physical/physiological capabilities (and capacities), and skilled movements (technique).

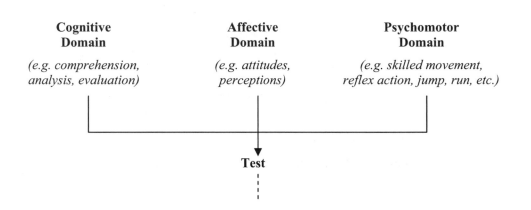

Figure 2.2   Relationship between domains of human performance and test.

Figure 2.2 describes the relationships between the domains of human performance. The domain in which human performance is being assessed will dictate the form of *test* applied, or the way in which a measurement is taken. Unfortunately, in the sport and exercise sciences research questions do not always sit neatly within a single domain, drawing upon an understanding of one or more domains in order to provide a comprehensive and meaningful answer – this is one of the 'joys' of working in the human sciences!

Developing a Research Question

Aside from the fundamental sensory inputs (refer to figure 2.1) to the brain informing this process, a research question may evolve from many different sources:

- practice – either personal experience or organisationally commissioned
- observation
- and/or previous research – either personal or from an awareness of the scientific literature

Due to such a multiplicity of information sources, trying to tie down your question into a manageable form can be a daunting task. In this context the adage 'Keep it Simple…' can never be overstated! You are far more likely to develop a sound experimental design if you are able to break the problem down into manageable chunks. Table 2.1 presents a checklist, and an example from the sub-discipline of sport psychology, of how you might develop a research question from an initial thought.

Action	Example
1. Conceptualise your thoughts into a 'directed' way of thinking…	*In a sporting activity such as officiating (e.g. soccer referee) where decision-making is key to the outcome of the game, the mental alertness (or state of tiredness) of an individual might feasibly influence their performance, where reduced alertness (or increased tiredness) would impair their officiating performance*
2. State your research problem in one sentence; what is the key issue?	*Increasing mental tiredness, due to reduced quantity or reduced quality of sleep, might adversely affect the decision-making ability of sports officials*
3. Can this key issue be reduced to a single question?	*Does sleep deprivation impair decision-making in sports officials?*
4. … Or are there a number of questions?	*This example can usefully be reduced to a single research question, though we may wish to distinguish between differences due to sleep quantity or sleep quality as a follow-up study*
5. If there are a number of questions, are they of equal relevance or importance? (… *the answer to this is usually 'no'*)	*Points (5) and (6) are not applicable in this example*
6. Identify the most important question and order the remaining (if appropriate)…	
7. Review the quality with which this question or framework of questions encapsulates your initial thoughts as described in (1), and has intellectual merit in terms of previous research…	*We are happy that this research question satisfactorily operationalises our initial thoughts, and has both intellectual merit in terms of the research literature and has practical merit in terms of modern professional sport*
8. Abort your research question if there is no intellectual merit or practical significance…	*Continue with research project…*
9. Or if you are confident in the 'worthwhileness' of your research question, modify your research question if necessary…	*No modifications required.*
10. …Or continue…	*Continue…*

Table 2.1   Checklist for developing a research question.

By the end of this process, you should be in a position where you have articulated your initial research thought into an appropriate research question, and reviewed the practical relevance and intellectual merit of this question.

Ethics and Research

Having identified a research question we must then decide whether the question itself, and the methods and procedures required to answer the question, are ethically acceptable. Ethics views human behaviour from a perspective of *good* or *bad*. E*thical directives* prescribe how we should behave in situations we may encounter (Drowatzky 1996). As conducting research is a form of human behaviour, it is governed by a code of practice that determines the right way to conduct research and conversely identifies what is the wrong way. This code of practice is, in turn, informed by a number of internationally accepted conventions, many relating to the natural sciences originated from the war crime trials following the Second World War which investigated alleged unethical research atrocities.

Prior to starting a research programme there is the planning stage, which has partly been discussed in the previous section, the first element of which being the identification of the problem. We must then try to express this problem in a manageable form, normally as a single or series of *research questions*. These questions are operationalised in the development of *research hypotheses*, conjectural statements or explanations about the problem. The next element is to deduce the consequences of these hypotheses. For example, a research question in the sub-discipline of sport biomechanics may be concerned with the relationship between lower limb length in a specified population and performance of the 110 m high hurdle track and field event. The research question may be phrased in terms of:

> *"Does lower limb length influence performance in the 110 m high hurdle event in proficient (i.e. personal best race time of <15 s) hurdlers?"*

Operationalising this research question, we might develop the following research hypotheses:

Null hypothesis

H_o: Lower limb length does not influence the performance of proficient
hurdlers in the 110 m high hurdle event

Alternative (or experimental) hypothesis

H_1:   Lower limb length does influence the performance of proficient
hurdlers in the 110 m high hurdle event

The null hypothesis describes the outcome of no relationship, or in the case of a research intervention no difference or no effect. In contrast, the alternative, or experimental, hypothesis describes the situation where there is a relationship, or there is a difference or an effect. From a practical perspective we can be more precise in defining our alternative hypothesis in that intuitively you would expect that there is an optimum range of lower limb (leg) lengths for performance of this event relative to the height of the high hurdles: if the legs are too short, the athlete would struggle to clear the hurdles without compromising forward sprinting speed; if they are too long, the athlete would easily clear the hurdles but may not have the power and skeletal-muscular architecture for sprinting between the hurdles. In setting out on your research programme you tend to be more concerned with formulating your alternative hypothesis (H_1) – which is associated with a real relationship, or difference or effect – and less concerned with the null hypothesis (H_o). However, it is important to note at this point that in terms of the statistical analyses presented later in this book, we are largely concerned with testing the null hypothesis and to what extent the null hypothesis *may or may not* hold true. Therefore the precise formulation and wording of our null hypotheses is vital in directing our data analyses following data collection. We will return to the process of formulating hypotheses in chapter 3.

Having formulated our research hypotheses, we are now in a position to consider what would be an appropriate *research design* to answer the research question. The design is often a compromise between what we would really like to do and what is ethically and practically possible. The constraints to what is possible include:

1.   *Time* available to conduct the research programme (e.g. in our example research question, how many hurdlers do we need to test, what do we require them to do and how long will each assessment take will define the *required* time allocation, but we may not be able to commit to this period of time)

2.   Appropriate *sample of participants* relative to the specific detail of the research question and the population we ultimately wish to explore (e.g. can we find a group of willing participants who are diverse enough in relevant characteristics to be representative of *all* proficient 110 m hurdlers?)

3.   *Resources*. With respect to the present example, where are we going to test the hurdlers? Will the investigators go to the athletes' training/performance location or will the athletes come to a laboratory/sports facility? Will we be covering any travel expenses? What is the availability of equipment and will all participants use the same equipment?

4.   Research *expertise* (including specific practical skills required for the data acquisition)

5.   Research *ethics*

Whilst *research ethics* is listed at the bottom of this not an exhaustive list, it should be viewed with over-arching importance. If one does not view research from an ethical perspective at all times then the research will be fundamentally and morally flawed. Simplistically put, research conducted in an ethical manner is informed by a system of moral principles governing the actions and practices of the individual. Thus, the final element in the planning stage may be considered to be where the research proposal is scrutinised by a panel of experts to determine its ethical research merit. This review process does not merely focus upon the well being of those involved (in terms of both the participants and the investigators), but will also be concerned with whether the research programme is scientifically sound. For if a project is not scientifically sound, and does not therefore make a valuable contribution to our understanding, it might be deemed unethical to subject individuals to the associated possible risks (especially in terms of personal injury), discomforts, or expense (of time, money, or resources) in conducting the study. If the research question is deemed to be unethical, or if the methods and/or procedures required to test the hypotheses and answer the question are deemed to be unethical or impractical, it will be necessary to either revise the project or indeed to abandon the study altogether.

To return to the example of the 110 m high hurdles, there does not appear to be any ethical issues that would preclude progressing with the research question. The methods and procedures required include standard anthropometric measurements of the lower limbs, and 110 m high hurdles run time. Assuming that normal research participants' rights[2.1] are adhered to, and the measurements are conducted in accordance with accepted codes of practice[2.2], there are no obvious[2.3] ethical reasons why this research project might not continue to the experimental stage. Ultimately the appropriate ethics committee overseeing the work undertaken within a particular organisation or institution will make this decision. Within the sport and exercise sciences, it might be appropriate for a university ethics committee to review your research proposal, or for more clinical work a hospital ethics committee or a regional health trust ethics committee would better undertake this process.

Approaches to Measurement: What Exactly are Statistics?

In order to ultimately make statements or decisions concerning the wider population from research findings (e.g. English professional football players) based upon observations made on a small sample (e.g. twenty professional football players registered with professional football clubs affiliated to the English Football Association), we must first make some measurements and obtain some statistics relating to the research question being addressed. Before we progress any further, is important to be clear what we actually mean by the term 'statistics'. Answer: something to be wary or mistrusting of ...is a common perception! However, *statistics* should be viewed as

---

[2.1] *Research participants' rights* can be defined as: the right to be fully informed of all the experimental details with respect to the conditions under which the study will be undertaken, the measures to be made, and the inherent possible risks and discomforts; the right to privacy or non-participation; the right to remain anonymous; the right to confidentiality; and the right to expect experimenter responsibility (Tuckman 1978).

[2.2] For an example of a *Code of Conduct* appropriate to the sport and exercise sciences you are referred to the *British Association of Sport and Exercise Sciences* website (www.bases.org.uk) and select the Accreditations link.

[2.3] Though there may not be any obvious reasons, there may be some less obvious reasons that relate to the specifics of the research problem and the context in which it is being investigated.

nothing more sinister than pieces of information. In the context of this book, we are dealing with pieces of information that concern the sport and exercise sciences, and hence we can start to see that statistics in themselves can serve many useful purposes in helping us to make sense of phenomena, occurrences, or behaviour. Statistical procedures can be used to summarise vast amounts of information, or data, into a manageable form (i.e. *descriptive statistics* which describe and summarise information concerning the research participants in our sample). Alternatively, statistical procedures can also help us to examine whether relationships or differences we observe in our sample are likely to occur in the population from which our sample was drawn (i.e. *inferential statistics* which are derived from a logical process of reasoning, deduction or calculation). Statistics are derived from numbers and quantities, and are therefore used in the branch of data analyses known as the *quantitative methods*. The different statistical techniques we can use to describe or make inferences about the data we have collected are governed by how these values are measured or obtained. From a statistics perspective, we can describe the measured values or the values obtained in terms of the *level of data*:

1. *Nominal* (or categorical) *Level* – Groups observations into categories. Numbers are used as labels, (for example – we can categorise research participants' gender: 0 = male, 1 = female; or we can categories players' netball position: 1 = Goal Keeper, 2 = Goal Defence, 3 = Wing Defence, 4 – Centre, 5 = Wing Attack, 6 – Goal Attack, and 7 – Goal Shooter). The numbers have no numeric meaning (i.e. of order, magnitude or size); they could equally have been recorded using different numbers to convey the same information (e.g. gender: 1 = male, 2 = female). As a consequence, the numerical values cannot be used for calculation.

2. *Ordinal Level* – Not only categorises data but also places them into a rank order on the basis of some identifiable characteristic. The numbers identify the rank of a data point, but do not represent equal differences between the attributes being measured. For example, teams in a football league are ranked on the basis of points scored – the team with the most points is 1st, the next is 2nd, then 3rd, etc. However, if we were to calculate the actual points difference between team 1 and team 2, team 2 and team 3, team 3 and team 4 etc., we would be unlikely to find them the same. Thus, whilst we

can conclude that team 2 is better than team 4, we would not be in a position to comment on the magnitude of this difference. The ordinal level of measurement might also be used to categorise sports performers into hierarchical groups: 1 = elite, 2 = intermediate, 3 = novice. In this example, the better the skill level of the performer, the lower the category number.

3.   *Interval Level* – Interval level data are ranked, categorised and have equal differences between each value, they therefore allow the size of the difference between observations to be assessed. Interval numbers are used to represent the degree to which a given characteristic is present, and so will not start from zero. Therefore, in light of this fact, values should not be multiplied or divided but addition and subtraction are justified. Shoe sizes are a good example of this, where the difference between a size 4 and size 7 is the same as the difference between a size 9 and size 12 (it is a specific fraction of an inch between each size), but a size 6 is not twice as large as a size 3.

4.   *Ratio Level* – These are measurement scales that have both equal intervals and an absolute zero. Numbers on this scale represent the highest level of measurement available and all calculation procedures are possible. Heights, weights, distances and speeds all fall within this classification of measurement, and for example statements like *4 m is twice as high as 2 m* do make sense.

Different methods of statistical – or data – analysis are available for evaluating data obtained from each of the four *measurement levels*. It would be meaningless to apply methods appropriate for ratio level data to nominal level data; therefore it is essential to be able to identify the levels of your data accurately before considering any form of data analysis.

Computer based statistical software packages are an essential aid to analysing large data sets. Whilst such software speeds up the data handling process immensely, they are no substitute for understanding …computers simply do as they are told by the operator, and will analyse data sets inappropriately and/or inaccurately if instructed to do so. It is therefore essential to understand what you *intend* to measure, and why you *intend* to take the measurements in the way proposed, before you start your study. Following data collection, it is important to look at the raw data and discern whether there are any interesting patterns, trends or differences in the data (refer to chapter 4 for further information on initially exploring your data). Only then, when you have an initial understanding of your data, are you in a position to set up your data sheets on the computer correctly in preparation for appropriate data analyses.

It is important to note that data do not always have to involve quantities and measurement. Often in the sport and exercise sciences we are interested in the feelings of athletes, the opinions of coaches, or the emotions of spectators. These data are often complex and cannot be coded into categories, nor can they be readily measured in any conventional form. Data collected through interviews, observations, journals, or narratives – usually in the natural setting of the research objective – would fit into this description, and they usually have their foundation in words. These data need to be analysed through a different set of techniques known collectively as *qualitative techniques*. Readers are referred to Ritchie and Lewis (2003) in the first instance if further information on qualitative research methods is required.

Issues Concerning Measurement

Objectivity

In conducting research in the sport and exercise sciences, we are required to make observations of specified forms of human behaviour. To make sense or rationalise these observations, we usually make some kind of measurement and assign a score or value to that particular measurement. In the previous section we described the different *levels of measurement*, and cited examples of the ways in which different scores or values might be assigned in different contexts. Though it should be noted that it is not always the case that a score might be assigned; the procedures adopted for recording the observations made will depend upon the specific detail of the research question being addressed. Nevertheless, the process of *measurement* usually involves the assigning of a score or number to some mode of human performance. The scientific approach dictates that this process is as *objective* as possible (i.e. independent of perception, personal or emotional bias). The opposite of objective is *subjective*, where subjective observations will be influenced by individual perception, and personal or emotional bias. Normally sports performance can readily be measured reasonably objectively, for example in terms of race times, distances thrown, heights jumped, goals or baskets scored, and so on. However, there are a number of sports where strict rules have to be applied in order to ensure that the outcome is evaluated objectively; such sports are generally the more aesthetic sports such as diving, gymnastics, or figure skating, where a judge will make a decision on the quality of the performance and translate this decision into a numerical score. Controversy occasionally ensues at these sporting events as to whether the outcome was truly objective and '...independent of perception, personal or emotional bias'.

Validity

The scientific approach also dictates that the process of measurement is valid, where validity is concerned with whether a test is actually measuring what it purports to measure – that is *relevance* – and whether this can be measured consistently – that is *reliability*. Relevance can be discussed in terms of *content validity*, *criterion validity*, and *construct validity*. *Content validity* is sometimes referred to as *face validity*; there is 'a logic' to a chosen approach. For example, if aerobic performance was to be assessed it would be logical to apply a test in which an individual's aerobic abilities would be limiting such as the 12-minute run test (i.e. The Cooper Test). Content or face validity will influence a test's specificity, in that those with high content validity tend to be most specific to the attribute being measured within a particular sporting or exercise context, and therefore will yield the best agreement in terms of the presence of that attribute and the measure obtained.

Criterion validity is where the quality of a test is determined in relation to a gold standard. Criterion validity is discussed in terms of *concurrent validity* and *predictive validity*. *Concurrent validity* is where a measurement instrument is evaluated relative to some criterion that is administered at the same time. For example, a panel of expert judges will score a gymnastic performance against a register of identified technique/skill criteria with associated tariffs of increasing scores to reflect increasing standards of difficulty. A similar approach is taken in other aesthetic sports such as diving, freestyle snowboarding and figure skating, where the scoring matrix combining skill and difficulty provides concurrent validity to the judges' scoring that is taking place simultaneously. Another example would be the application of anthropometric tests, such as measuring the sum of skinfolds, as a means of evaluating body fat percentage. In this example body fat percentage is the criterion to which sum of skinfolds has been correlated and shown to be systematically related. In contrast, *predictive validity* is where a criterion is used to predict future behaviour. For example, a battery of anthropometric assessments, performance ability/aptitude tests, and perhaps psychological profiling might be used to identify talent in young performers in order to predict possible future sporting success. The content of the test battery should be appropriate to evaluate physical and psychological qualities deemed integral to a specified sporting performance (i.e. to be systematically related), and would have been evaluated as having high predictive validity.

Finally, some human attributes are very difficult to identify and objectively measure, such as many of those attributes identified within the afferent domain (e.g. anxiety, intelligence, sportsmanship, creativity and attitude). These are described by Thomas and Nelson (1990) as:

'...hypothetical constructs that carry a number of associated meanings'

(pp. 346).

What this means is that a pattern of behaviour has to be constructed which is consistent with high or low degrees of these attributes. For example, a pattern of physiological and psychological behaviour could be deduced for an individual who was highly anxious (e.g. demonstrating signs of physiological stress in terms of heart rate, perspiration and hormonal profile, in association with specific cerebral electrical activity), and these behaviours would provide a measurable means of evaluating some scoring system for evaluating anxiety. *Construct validity* is the degree to which a test measures a hypothetical construct, and refers to the ability of a test to discriminate. A more explicit example is one in which we wish to examine power from a performance perspective. For example, The *Sargent Jump* Test is reported as a simple method of discriminating between individuals on the basis of lower limb (leg) power. It requires subjects to follow a standardised protocol and jump as high as possible, touching a mark with their chalked fingertips on a reach board. This test therefore yields a score in terms of a height jumped, not a measure of power in watts. Nevertheless, The *Sargent Jump* Test has high construct validity in terms of being able to discriminate between individuals of low leg power (e.g. long distance runners) and individuals of high leg power (e.g. high jumpers or triple jumpers). A commentary on validity is given in table 2.2.

Validity		Commentary
Content		Also termed *face* or *logic* validity
		Measurements have a direct or logical relationship to the abilities, behaviour or events being examined
		Example: *An occupational fitness test should reflect the physical demands of the tasks to be undertaken in the job*
Criterion		Founded on having a true criterion measure available
		Validity is based on determining the systematic relationship between the criterion and other measures used to estimate the criterion
	Concurrent	Measurement taken in <u>same time</u> frame as a criterion measure is taken
		Example: *Skinfolds validly measure percentage body fat – where body fat is the criterion*
	Predictive	Measurement taken <u>now</u> to predict <u>future</u> outcomes
		Example: *Measure body fat, exercise patterns, smoking habits and blood pressure to predict future risk of heart disease*
Construct		Involves procedures used to validate measures that are unobservable but exist in theory
		Information is gathered from a variety of sources, and when viewed collectively provides theoretical evidence for the construct being measured
		Example: *Profile of Mood States Questionnaire (Lorr 1984) – we know that individuals have mood states and that these will vary depending upon the specific situation or environment in which the individual is located. A register of statements describing six different possible mood states, and their positive or negative expression, was developed and evidence was provided to support the constructs linking these statements to particular mood states*

Table 2.2   A commentary on validity.

Reliability, Repeatability and Reproducibility

A test must be <u>both</u> relevant and reliable to be valid. *Reliability* is concerned with the consistency with which a variable may be repeatedly measured. This issue was briefly discussed in chapter 1 in relation to the need for standardisation and control. For any measurement taken, the score obtained will reflect the true or actual score, and an error score.

i.e.   **OBTAINED SCORE = TRUE SCORE** ± *ERROR SCORE*

The error score will reflect the difference between the obtained score and the true score, and will represent an *unknown* value. We can deduce the approximate average size of this error score by evaluating the quality of our measurement approach (this issue will be discussed in further detail in chapter 3), however through careful attention to standardisation and experimental control we should aim to minimise the size of the error score as far as possible. Table 2.3 presents a summary of some of the potential factors that can affect the reliability of a test. A test will be deemed *repeatable* if, for the same set of circumstances on the same day, the obtained score is reported consistently. A measure of repeatability is often cited as a means of demonstrating the quality of a measurement approach. Furthermore, a test will be deemed *reproducible* if, for the same set of circumstances on different days, the obtained score is reported consistently.

The Importance of Reliability

Reliability is important when taking measurements in the sport and exercise sciences as it dictates the size of change or difference that might be detected with confidence. If a measurement approach is very reliable, smaller changes can be detected. This is especially important when evaluating attributes of human performance that may show only small, but 'practically' meaningful, changes over time. For example, the size of physiological adaptation to training diminishes as an athlete becomes fitter, such that elite athletes must train very hard for relatively smaller improvements. However, these small improvements could have important performance benefits (e.g. in terms of race times), and it is therefore important that these changes can actually be detected and measured. The quality of a test will therefore be determined by its ability to discriminate small changes. The relationship between validity and reliability, relative to the domains of human performance, are presented in figure 2.3.

Factor	Increase Reliability	Decrease Reliability
Research Participant		
Participant characteristics/ability	Low variability	High variability
State of rest	Rested	Fatigue
Test proficiency	High skill level/ability Learning Practice	Low skill level/ability No or limited learning No or limited practice
Test Administration		
Time between trial	Decrease time between trials	Increase time between trials
Test conditions	Increased similarity	Decreased similarity
Environmental conditions	Constant climatic conditions (e.g. noise, excessive heat, excessive cold, poor lighting, air movement, etc.)	Variable climatic conditions
Test Specification		
Specific participant knowledge/ability	High knowledge/ability	Low knowledge/ability
Level of difficulty	Appropriate level of difficulty	Too difficult/too easy
Measurement accuracy	Appropriate level	Inappropriate level

Table 2.3   Factors affecting test reliability.

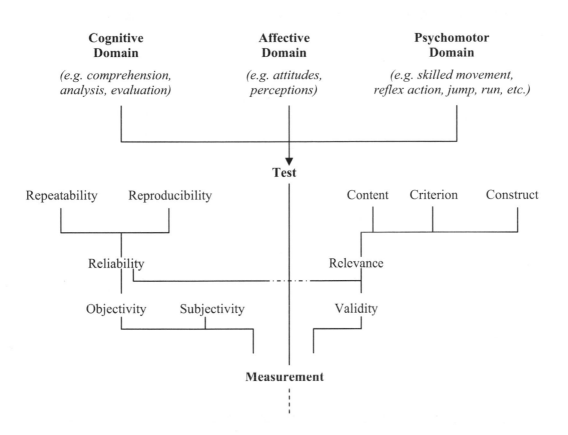

Figure 2.3   Relationship between domains of human performance, test and measurement.

Precision and Accuracy of Measurements

Precision and accuracy are two terms that are used in everyday language but rarely do we stop and focus on what we actually mean by whether a measure is *precise* or indeed *accurate*. These two terms have been schematically depicted relative to circular targets in figure 2.4, where the centre of the target is representative of the true score. Precision is an expression of repeatability and reproducibility, and is depicted on the target as a tight cluster of measurements (refer to target i and iii). Where as accuracy is an expression of agreement between repeated measurements and the actual 'true' score or value. This is depicted on the target as a series of measurements spread more widely over the target (refer to target ii). However, the average reading from this series of measurements is consistent with the true score, and therefore deemed to be accurate.

Error Types		Random	Systematic	Gross
	(i) 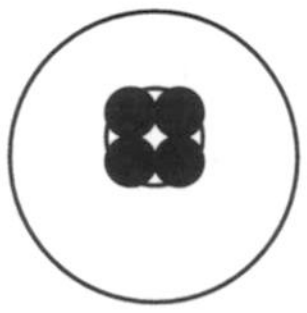	(ii) 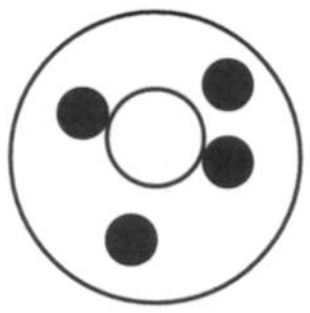	(iii) 	Use The Wrong Target!
Precision	Optimal	Bad	Good	-
Accuracy	Very Good	Good	Bad	-

Figure 2.4   Schematic representation of precision and accuracy.

A measurement may have a high degree of precision – tightly clustered measurements – but have poor accuracy in that the average measurement is not consistent with the true score (i.e. target iii). This might occur if a measuring instrument has been incorrectly calibrated, such that the instrument is measuring consistently but consistently wrong. Such an error is normally relatively easy to correct by following appropriate re-calibration procedures. Conversely, a measurement may have poor precision – a wide spread of measurements – but have good accuracy (i.e. target ii). This situation would be more problematic, as there is greater – and widespread – random variation. In this situation there must be something not very sensitive with the measuring instrument or the operator has poor/incorrect technique. To have a high level of confidence in a measurement it needs to be both precise and accurate (i.e. target i).

Performing repeated measurements, in standardised and controlled conditions, and assessing the distribution of the measurements assesses precision[2.4]. Accuracy can be evaluated in a particular measurement system by comparing measurements to gold standard values, or known values. For example, in exercise biochemistry the accuracy of measurements made on a series of blood samples should be evaluated against a *quality control* (QC) sample. The QC is normally a sample of blood, plasma or serum with a known concentration of the substance (i.e. metabolite, hormone, electrolyte, etc.) of interest. Similarly in exercise physiology, we might evaluate the accuracy of our expired gas analysis system against cylinders of single or mixed gases of known certificated composition. In sport biomechanics and motor control, the accuracy of a force platform or movement analysis system may be evaluated using first principles from the science of physics. Perhaps more problematic is how we might evaluate the accuracy of our approaches to taking measurements in the afferent domain, where we are often limited to the use of questionnaires.

Making Generalisations

In the sport and exercise sciences observations are made on a sample drawn from a prescribed population (e.g. a specified sport, a representative level of participation, or a geographical locality), as it would be impossible to make observations on the whole population! Thus, there are a number of issues that will determine the confidence with which observations made on that sample with reference to a specified research question might be generalised back to the population as a whole.

[2.4] This can be achieved by determining the *coefficient of variation*, which will be described in chapter 4.

Populations and Samples

In statistical language a *population* is taken to mean a whole set of people, things, or events which have a given characteristic in common. For example, returning to our research question example of the 110 m high hurdle event, our population would be all those proficient athletes, of different nationalities, ages, genders and abilities, who compete in this particular track and field event. We may wish to further delimit our population by defining a certain level of performance; for the research question stated we would ideally require a population of elite hurdlers, in order to prevent factors relating to skill level and specific fitness or training history impacting upon performance. A *sample* is a selection made from the population, either randomly or according to a set of prescribed rules, which is representative of the defined population as a whole. For very practical research, requiring subjects to be present at a particular location for measurements to be made, our sample will be necessarily geographically limited. For example, we may be logistically limited to recruiting elite hurdlers within a specified distance from a testing centre. However, with the advent of the Internet with its worldwide coverage, certain research questions may lend themselves to being addressed on a truly global scale. Nevertheless, however we choose or are able to construct our sample of research volunteers/participants, it must be remembered that the quality of the research sample will ultimately determine the meaningfulness of generalisations drawn from the research study and made about the population, and the confidence we can have in these generalisations.

Other Issues: Experimental Design, Effect Size and Statistical Power

Of fundamental importance in making appropriate and valid generalisations are the experimental design, and the precision and accuracy of the measures taken (i.e. our consistency of measurement). However, as discussed previously our confidence in an experiment can be improved through careful consideration of issues concerning the *control* of the experiment, and *standardisation* of the experimental procedures. The generalisability of the research outcome will be enhanced by the nature of the sample group: do the participants reflect the same characteristics (with reference to the research question) as the population as a whole (e.g. height, body mass, body composition, measures of fitness, training histories, lifestyle)? Is the sample size appropriate for the experimental design and the measures being taken? With reference to this latter point, increasingly scientists will discuss the *effect size* and *power* of an experimental design. These concepts will be discussed in greater detail in chapter 3. However, suffice to say at this point that *effect size* is a measure of 'meaningfulness', and reflects the ability to detect differences in data based on the research intervention being tested. That is, if an intervention, such as a nutritional supplement, is associated with a big change in performance times relative to the natural differences between runners, then the effect of the supplement is likely to be observed even if a small sample is drawn from the population. If the supplement is associated with a relatively small change in performance time, you would need to evaluate this intervention in a much larger sample in order to be confident that there has been a *real* effect of the supplement. Statistical *power* is an indication of whether the procedures used are likely to lead to the right decision. For example, if the test detects a difference in a sample group based on the use of a nutritional supplement, we are likely to generalise this to the population and conclude that the nutritional supplement is effective. In so doing, there is always a *chance* that we have made an incorrect decision and have therefore reached the wrong conclusion. It is this chance that is measured by statistical power.

There will always be limitations to experimental designs, and these can often be articulated at the outset. Many of the natural sciences are limited in that they endeavour to reduce phenomenon to the 'law of the single variable', measuring only one thing that may change from individual to individual. This potentially makes for a relatively artificial scenario. Such a reductionist approach removes the 'social context' of human behaviour, which is often at the heart of sporting and exercise experiences.

Evaluating Your Data

The final stage in the decision making process of the scientific approach to conducting research is the *evaluation* of the data collected. This activity will be discussed from a statistical analysis perspective in chapters 5–9, however it is worth considering some of the general issues concerning data evaluation at this initial planning stage in the research process. The scientific method of conducting research requires the researcher to speculate on the outcome of a study before the first piece of data is collected (i.e. to articulate an alternative hypothesis, H_1). This might be viewed as both a strength of this approach and a weakness: a strength in that through careful preparation, many of the potentially hazardous or expensive problems or errors may be addressed at the planning stage; a weakness in that through such a directional approach to researching we may become less open-minded or aware of unpredicted or less conventional explanations for phenomena, introducing human bias from the outset.

Data evaluation requires a judgment to be made concerning the data in relation to the initial research question.   The confidence with which we make this judgement will depend upon the appropriateness of the research design, standardisation of the research participants and the research environment, and experimental control during the execution of the research trials. Evaluative judgements might be made initially or partway through the research project – *formative evaluations* – or at the project's completion – *summative evaluations*. The quality and merit of the data might be evaluated against standards determined from the population – *norm-referenced* (e.g. average race time for a junior 110 m high hurdler is 15 s) – or in relation to a prescribed standard – *criterion referenced* (e.g. world class 110 m high hurdler would be aiming to compete with race times <13 s, current world record is 12.91 s), whilst the value or worthiness of an intervention is normally evaluated against a control (no effect) trial.

To return to the discussion of the *decision making process*, which was introduced at the start of this chapter and underpins the scientific approach to research, it would be appropriate to conclude the chapter by reviewing the inter-relationships between the activities of *measurement* (the act of assessing), *test* (the method by which a measurement is taken), and *evaluation* (a judgement concerning the goodness, quality, merit, value or worthiness). This is presented schematically in figure 2.5.

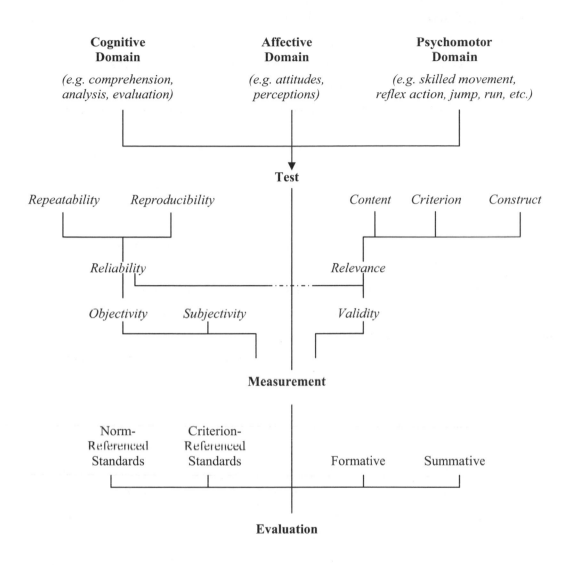

Figure 2.5   Relationship between domains of human performance, test, measurement and evaluation.

Summary/Key Points

1.   Human performance can be discussed in terms of the cognitive (knowledge and mental achievement), affective (attitudes and perceptions), and psychomotor (physiological and psychological performance) domains.

2.   The first stage in the research process is articulating your research thought into a research question.

3.   It is then important to determine whether the question itself, and the probable methods required to answer the question, are ethically acceptable.

4.   The process of measurement involves *objectively* assigning a score or a number to some mode of human performance. The selected *scale of measurement* will be dependent upon the nature of the observations being made, and will be dictated by the specific detail of the experimental design.

5.   This process of assigning a score or a number must be *relevant* and *reliable* in order to be *valid*, and must demonstrate an appropriate level of *precision* and *accuracy* to allow confident decisions to be made about your data.

6.   The *generalisability* of these decisions back to the population will depend upon how well the experimental sample represents the population as a whole, the standardisation of experimental conditions, and experimental control.

7.   This decision making process will also be influenced by the *effect size* (or meaningfulness) of a measure, and the *power* of an experimental design.

8.   There will always be limitations to experimental designs, and these should be articulated at the outset. Nevertheless, such limitations should not preclude research from being conducted, but should be considered when applying research findings back to the target population.

9.   The final stage in the decision making process of the scientific approach to conducting research is *data evaluation*. The preferred approach to data evaluation must be considered at the initial planning stage in the research process, where the scientific method requires the researcher to speculate on the outcome of a study before the first piece of data is collected.

10.　　The data might be evaluated against standards determined from the population – *norm-referenced* – or in relation to a prescribed standard – *criterion referenced*, whilst the value or worthiness of an intervention is normally evaluated against a control trial.

3

Experimental Design
and Data Collection

Chapter Objectives

- To describe some typical models of experimental design

- To describe approaches to forming your research sample

- To critique the practical application of the concepts of *power* and *effect size*

- To discuss approaches to improving your design sensitivity

- To introduce standards of professional practice.

Introduction

Using Statistics in Sport and Exercise Science Research focuses on the use of descriptive[3.1] and inferential[3.2] statistics to assess the effectiveness of various interventions – whether this be a nutritional supplementation regimen in exercise physiology, mental skill training in sport

---

[3.1] *Descriptive statistics* – provide mathematical summaries of data sets, and can describe the pattern or characteristics of the data distribution.
[3.2] *Inferential statistics* – are concerned with making measurements and decisions on a sample, and relating – or generalising – these measurements and decisions to the behaviour of the population from which the sample was drawn.

psychology, movement optimisation in sport biomechanics, a rehabilitation programme in health-related exercise, or an injury treatment intervention in sports therapy. In the previous chapter we have examined the initial planning stage of conducting research, from the inception of a research idea, through the formulation of a research question and testable research hypotheses, to a consideration of measurement issues and the nature of data (information). This chapter will examine how the research hypotheses can be operationalised into a scientifically sound and ethically appropriate research design – the appropriate approach to obtaining and examining data. This will be achieved by examining some of the common *forms* of research question in the sport and exercise sciences through case examples, and then describing the decision making process that ultimately will give rise to the appropriate experimental approach. Central to the process of question-hypothesis-design is the activity of selecting your research sample. The sample is the group of research participants (i.e. volunteers, sports performers, patients, etc.) on which the study is to be conducted. This activity is pivotal to the success of any research study; how closely a sample reflects the characteristics and behaviour of the wider population will determine the confidence with which the study's research findings can be generalised. Leading on from a consideration of experimental design and sampling, we will also consider some of the very practical issues concerning data collection, again to ensure that the process is scientifically sound, but also to ensure that we conform to accepted standards of professional practice.

Experimental Design

In chapters 5–10 we will examine a variety of experimental designs and discuss how different design and analysis approaches are appropriate for different forms of research questions. We will present examples that:

- Compare male and female research participants (*an independent groups design* – a participant can not be both male and female!)
- Compare different therapies for muscle soreness (another *independent groups design* that includes a *placebo control group*, as it is not possible nor ethical to inflict injuries repeatedly over time)

- Examine the effects of sleep deprivation (*a repeated measures design* to control for variability in individuals, as short term sleep deprivation does not require a long time between trials for participants to return to normal patterns of function)

The following section will describe the general forms of these experimental designs and discuss their appropriate application under different circumstances. As discussed previously, *Using Statistics in Sport and Exercise Science Research* has not been written to provide a definitive list of all potential research questions, related experimental designs, and subsequent methods of data analysis. Rather it seeks to provide the necessary knowledge, understanding, and confidence, to examine the research question, to make informed decisions on the most appropriate approach to experimentation, and finally to explore, analyse, and evaluate your research data.

Repeated Measures or Within Subjects Design

There are several considerations we have to make when designing an experiment. The first decision is related to what we are looking to find out. If we are looking to find a *difference* between two (or more) different treatments or conditions, then we are going to want to ensure our standardisation and control are as tight as possible so that we can isolate the effect of the treatment as the main source of variation (difference) between experimental groups. If the treatment is reversible it may be possible to use the same individuals in both treatments in the experiment (i.e. subjects *cross-over* to perform both treatments in two separate trials), and then look at changes in the research participants to evaluate the effect(s) of the treatment. This type of design is known as *repeated measures*, or *within subjects design*. It is looking to reduce potential variation by controlling individual variability. Each research participant is measured more than once (hence *repeated measures*) and the statistical test procedure associated with such a design will look to evaluate change *within* each individual's repeated measurements (hence *within subjects*). This type of design minimises, but does not eliminate, some unexplainable variation (error).

Placebo Controlled Randomised Design

You cannot control for a participant having different motivational levels on one test day or trial compared to the next test day or trial. However, it is possible to control for 'perceived' benefits, or otherwise, of a treatment or condition. For example, if the treatment under investigation is a sports beverage providing additional energy, a research participant undertaking a trial *without* the drink may expect to perform worse than undertaking the trial *with* the drink. To control for the potential influence of a research participant's perceptions of what the outcome *should be*, a drink is administered during both trials; in one trial the energy component of the drink is included, where as in the other trial the energy component is omitted, and any taste or consistency differences between the two treatments is disguised. Thus, in removing the psychological perceived benefit, and assuming good standardisation of all other related aspects across the trials, it would only be the energy component itself affecting the results. The 'dummy' drink, with no active ingredient, is known as a *placebo*. Importantly, research participants will need to provide informed consent regardless of whether they are receiving the placebo or the treatment. In addition to this placebo control, it is usual to *randomise*[3.3] the order in which participants undertake the different trials (in this example, the *without energy* and *with energy* trials). This will control for a potential learning effect across two or more trials, where knowledge and familiarity with the experimental conditions and the requirements of the trials may influence the outcome[3.4]. Randomising the order in which research participants will complete the trials will mean that any benefits to a second, or more, attempt(s) is not apparent for the same treatment. This experimental design is termed *placebo controlled randomised trials*, which simply means that participants receive either an active treatment (e.g. an energy providing sports beverage), or a dummy treatment (e.g. an artificially sweetened beverage) in a non-systematic order.

Independent Groups Design

Having the *same* research participants undertaken *all* trials, as in the repeated measures design of the sports beverage example, is good for controlling individual variation and also maximises the number of participants in each group. As will be discussed later in this chapter, it is not always possible to apply this approach; if the experiment involves a treatment or intervention that is not reversible (e.g. a physical or skill training programme), the same people cannot be in the control

---

[3.3] To *randomise* means to set up or organise the trials with no pre-arranged or planned order.
[3.4] This issue will also be addressed by ensuring that all participants undergo some form of familiarisation to the experimental procedures prior to the start of data collection.

group and the treatment/intervention group. Under these circumstances it is usual to have different groups of participants for the control and treatment trials, and this would be termed an *independent groups design*. The use of a placebo treatment is still useful here for the control (i.e. no change) condition, so that one group does not feel psychologically disadvantaged – or advantaged – in relation to another.

Matched Pairs Design

Independent groups designs are more problematic from a practical experimental perspective, as you need more participants taking part in your study to ensure that each group is representative of the population(s) of interest (refer to the section on Selecting the Sample on page 42). If the groups are randomly assigned, a simple division of the total number of research participants into group A, group B, and so on, is a common approach. However, we would need fairly large participant numbers to be confident of population representation (refer to the section on Maximising Design Sensitivity on page 49). These experimental designs are analysed using statistical techniques that take into account that different people are being compared across the different treatments or interventions. In some situations it is possible to improve this design – in terms of controlling for individual variation that may obscure treatment differences – by matching research participants in relation to affective factors (this will be discussed in greater detail later in this chapter). This design is referred to as a *matched pairs design*, and the approach to statistical analysis is the same as a repeated measures design. This process is only effective though if the matching is good; a 'near miss' on some matches, and the whole experiment is compromised.

Single Blind or Double Blind

It is important to note at this stage that in administering an experimental treatment or intervention, you avoid any form of communication (e.g. oral, written, or body language) or behaviour that might be deemed prejudicial to the outcome of the investigation. That is, you must ensure that your actions, and the actions of others involved in the trials, do not signal – intentionally or unintentionally – to the research participants how they should respond whilst undertaking an experimental trial. Administering the trials either *single blind* or *double blind* can help to reduce prejudicial influences. Single blind describes a situation where the research participants alone are not informed of which trial they are undertaking, and the control and treatment trials are – as far as possible – made indistinguishable. In the case of double blind, this describes a situation where both the research participants and the investigators administering the experimental conditions are not informed of which trial is being undertaken. In the case of supplementation type studies, both single and double blind is normally relatively straightforward to achieve. However, it is not always possible to include this control strategy in your experimental design; some interventions such as physical training, skill/technique training, injury or rehabilitative therapies by their very nature cannot be administered using a blind model.

Selecting the Sample: The First Step on the Way ...Or the First Big Mistake!

Random Sampling

The most commonly described approach to selecting a sample is to adopt some form of *random sampling*. For example, if we wished to form a sample from a population of English Premier Football League players, every player registered to play in the Premier League would randomly be assigned a number. We might then use a random number table, or more commonly a computerised random number generator programmed to operate between one and the total number of Premier Football League players, to select the members of our sample. The sample should be characterised and behave in the same way as the population. Though this is hard to achieve in practice with random sampling, unless the sample is large. The sample size is key to ensuring that our sample is representative; small samples relative to the size of the population present a greater chance of being unrepresentative. Unfortunately in many of the sub-disciplines of the sport and exercise sciences – especially exercise physiology and sports biomechanics – we are often forced to conduct research on relatively small samples due to the nature of the work undertaken, practical issues of conducting the required measurements, as well as financial and resourcing issues. Thus, if the sample is small we must pay particular attention to the way in which it is formed and guard against an unrepresentative sample. Thus, random sampling alone is often not suitable for the task of forming a sample in the sport and exercise sciences.

Stratified Random Sampling

Stratified random sampling is where the population is divided on the basis of a characteristic before random selection takes place. Returning to our football player example, the population will be formed from unequal proportions of defensive players, mid-field players, and attacking players; to be representative, our sample should similarly reflect these positional player proportions. To ensure that this is the case, we would initially divide, or stratify, our population into player position categories and then programme our computer to randomly select from each category in the same proportion that category appears in the population. Stratified random sampling is particularly appropriate for survey and questionnaire based research, where the sample is likely to be relatively large (i.e. several hundred research participants). However, for this approach to work you do need to know the exact size and structure of the population. In our English Premier Football League example this is not a problem, as the membership of the population is accurately recorded. Unfortunately this is rarely the case and often the population cannot be specified sufficiently for stratified sampling to be applied.

Systematic Sampling

Systematic sampling is appropriate for populations that are so large that it would not be possible to consider every potential research participant individually, and hence the processes described above would not be possible. For example, for the purposes of our research question we may need to broaden our football player sample to be representative of every one in the United Kingdom, or Europe, or even the World, who played representative level football. This might theoretically be achieved by collating all the league lists of registered players for the designated geographical area, and then adopting some kind of systematic rule (e.g. every 1000th or 10 000th name, depending upon the population size), in the selection of names from these lists. Nevertheless, due to problems of ensuring the integrity of our systematic rule relative to the sampling process, it is always preferable to endeavour to randomly sample as far as possible. Though equally it is important to be aware that, as inferred above, sampling is rarely truly random in the sport and exercise sciences.

Post Hoc Justification of Sample Representation

Whilst random sampling is the desired goal in forming our research group, it is not always possible to totally achieve the theoretical ideal in practice; as discussed previously, the more technologically demanding and labour intensive sport and exercise science sub-disciplines usually struggle on this front.   When your sample size and composition is constrained by what is practically possible rather than statistically desirable, the best course of action is to provide some form of *post hoc*[3.5] *justification* based on the quality of your research sample. Even though our population may be relatively local and relatively small, such as English Premier Football League players, it would still be very difficult to obtain a true random sample due to player personal, professional and contractual constraints.   The most realistic course of action would be to obtain a sample of 'willing' players, and then to identify population characteristics to which your sample would need to conform (e.g. age, height, body mass, football specific fitness criteria, and perhaps some measure of training/playing history).   Even then, it is often the case that your 'willing players' will not be the elite group specifically required to address your research question.   In this case you will need to build in to your research design measures that will enable you to demonstrate the appropriateness of your sample with reference to your research question, and ultimately to support generalisations that will be applied to the wider population.

As discussed in the section on experimental design, once we have established our research sample we may need to divide this sample into two or more groups depending upon the form of our research intervention.   Research designs require that groups are randomly formed within a sample, or participants are randomly assigned to the various research groups.   This participant randomisation to groups within a sample can be achieved by adopting the same procedures as described previously for selecting a random sample from a population; participants within a sample are assigned a number-name and these are assigned according to a table of random numbers or a computer programme if your sample size is large.   This approach should ensure that

---

[3.5]   *Post hoc* is a term often applied to *research method* and *statistical* operations to identify that these activities take place '...after this', that is at a later point in time.   In the current example, the integrity of the sample is confirmed after the sample has been formed, as opposed to applying sampling techniques that ensure the integrity of the sample simultaneous to its formation.   We will present a modified definition of post hoc in relation to statistical analyses approaches in chapter 9.

the groups are equivalent at the start of the research study, and therefore any differences in behaviour or participant characteristics at the end of the study may be attributed to the research intervention. The best way of ensuring that your research groups are as similar as possible is to use the same people in each group (i.e. repeated measures design). This model will be addressed in more detail later in this chapter.

The Control Group or Control Condition

For most experimental designs we need to identify a control group or a control condition; that is the condition of *status quo*. This is the group or condition that is not subjected to experimental intervention or do not experience any change in circumstances that would influence the variable of interest. The purpose of the control group or condition is for comparison; if we had not experimentally modified the experience or behaviour of our participants, what would be the outcome?

The most straightforward example would be in a *two group experimental design*, where you have selected your sample from the population of interest, and then you have randomly assigned the participants within your sample into either *Group A* or *Group B*. Finally, you randomly assign the groups as either the *Control Group* or the *Experimental Group*. As a 'belt and braces' measure, it might then be appropriate to perform statistical examinations to ensure that the two groups do not differ in characteristics that might influence the research outcomes – though this should not be necessary if the above process was truly randomly performed and the research sample is large. Appropriate tests for examining differences are presented in chapters 8 and 9. Alternatively, if the study is to be conducted using a *cross-over experimental design*, where all participants in the research sample will participate in every experimental condition, one condition will be identified as the control condition. Participants would then be assigned to each of the experimental conditions, including the control condition, in a random order. This makes for a better experimental process, as individual differences between research participants (e.g. body mass, training status, diet, etc.) will have an effect in each condition, and will have the *same* effect in each condition. Though importantly care must be taken to ensure that participants return to a 'normal' baseline status between each condition or trial. In exercise studies this would require sufficient recovery to ensure that residual fatigue does not accumulate over repeated trials. In supplementation studies this would require a 'wash out' period to ensure that functional traces of the supplement are not present over repeated trials. Studies involving learning or skill development are not easily addressed using a cross-over design, as participants will not be able to unlearn or deskill between repeated trials.

Power and Effect Size Revisited

The concepts of power and effect size were briefly introduced in chapter 2, where *power* was discussed in terms of the ability to detect *true* treatment effects and *effect size* referred to the ability to discriminate that two conditions are likely to be different. Power provides a measure of design sensitivity; is the experimental approach appropriate for detecting real changes or differences in data? It has been described from a statistical perspective as the probability of rejecting the null hypothesis when the null hypothesis is false (Cohen, 1988). That is, if a treatment effect or an intervention effect really exists, and is associated with a difference between your experimental groups or conditions – as detected by your statistical test – that is too large to have occurred by chance, then your test is said to have sufficient power. Thus, power is associated with making the right statistical decision or inference based upon the available – sample – data. Figure 3.1 depicts the statistical decision 'errors' associated with a research approach based upon hypothesis testing.

Figure 3.1 describes the decision-making errors as: *Type-I Error* – reject the null hypothesis (i.e. no effect) when it is true – that is, finding differences that are *not* there; and, *Type-II Error* – accept the null hypothesis when it is false – that is, *not* finding differences that *are* there. From a practical perspective, the consequence of a type-I error would be that we might recommend an intervention, (e.g. a training approach, a nutritional supplement, or a rehabilitation programme), when it is in reality ineffective. Similarly, if we consider the practical consequences of a type-II error, a research intervention that results in a real effect would be rejected and an important opportunity would therefore be missed.

		Status of the null hypothesis in the population	
		Null hypothesis true	**Null hypothesis false**
Researcher's decision based on the sample data	**Do not reject the null**	1 – Alpha *Correct Decision*	Beta *Type-II Error*
	Reject the null	Alpha *Type-I Error*	1 – Beta *Power*

Figure 3.1   Power and decision errors associated with hypothesis testing.

Power is most closely associated with beta or type-II error, which is that a real treatment effect occurs but we fail to reject the null hypothesis of 'no effect'. In chapter 5 we will discuss the idea of setting our alpha level to 0.05 or 0.01 (i.e. the *level of significance* or *significance level*), which dictates the confidence we require to accept or reject our experimental hypotheses.   This significance level is set by convention and might be modified depending upon the nature of the experiment being conducted, for example: an exercise physiology performance study reported in the literature, involving very invasive techniques in a relatively small sample, advocated in this case the use of a more liberal significance level of 0.10; conversely, in drug therapy trials, where the consequences of a wrong decision may be much more injurious, we may advocate a more conservative significance level of 0.001.

Unfortunately, we do not have any such scientific conventions to guide our selection of an acceptable level of power. Intuition and experience of the researcher, as well as the fact that power is the *complement*[3.6] of type-II error, should guide the selection of an acceptable level of power. Cohen (1988) provides a more pragmatic approach and recommends 0.80 as a minimal level of power. With experience you may wish to modify this level – accepting a lower or higher level of power in more liberal or conservative experiments or studies – but in doing so you must first calculate the possible human and/or financial cost such a decision would incur.

From the above discussion, it would be the ideal to conduct some form of power analysis prior to commencing data collection. However, this is rarely possible due to the interrelationship of power, effect size, and sample size. For example, power cannot be determined without some previous indication of the associated effect size or your research intervention. Therefore, normally you will need to perform some form of retrospective estimate to ensure that power is at an acceptable level for your research design. Thus, the power of your subsequent data analyses will be influenced by your sample size (larger samples give your data analyses greater power), the level at which data is accepted as being statistically significant and therefore practically important (i.e. the alpha or significance level), and the population effect size for the experimental intervention or condition (Shultz and Sands 1995). When designing a study, we have greatest knowledge and control over the sample size and the significance level, whilst the effect size is more of an unknown.

The effect size provides an indication of how far removed data are from the null hypothesis (i.e. no effect). Alternatively, in chapter 4 we will describe measures of central tendency; effect size refers to the non-centrality of data and the degree to which it occurs at the extremes of the normal 'bell-

---

[3.6] *Complement* refers to one of two parts that make up a whole, or in this case that make 1.0. Thus, the <u>sum</u> of power and type-II error is 1.0 (i.e. power + type-II error = 1.0).

shaped' distribution (refer to chapter 5 for a description of the normal distribution). The greater the estimated or anticipated population effect size, the more likely a true effect or difference will be identified, and therefore the greater power of your experimental design. In the sport and exercise sciences, where sample sizes and population effect sizes tend to be small, studies are often *underpowered* (i.e. there is insufficient power to identify a true difference if one exists), and there is therefore a greater chance of making a type-II error and accepting instead of rejecting the null hypothesis. This is one reason why some researchers have argued to modify the significance level to a more liberal level of 0.10 from the more conventional level 0.05. However, this approach has not been met with uniform acceptance, and if you are hoping to present your findings to the wider scientific community (refer to chapter 11), you may have to continue to work within accepted conventions. Furthermore, it is also imperative to be cautious if finding 'no difference' (i.e. accepting the null hypothesis) supports your research argument, as this is a relatively easy decision to achieve with a research design of low power.

Maximising Design Sensitivity (or 'Upping' Your Experimental Power)

In chapter 1 we described the golden scientific rules of *standardisation* and *control*. You will see from the following sections how we might put these rules into action in order to improve our design sensitivity and hence maximise our experimental power. The sport and exercise sciences repeatedly flaunt many of the preferred ways of conducting research from the statistician's perspective: samples sizes tend to be small (typically much less than 30); we normally study humans, who are infinitely variable and do not behave or react consistently; occasionally our measurements lack exactness as the object of our measurement defies definition (e.g. emotions, perceptions, feelings); and equally our measurements may lack sensitivity, as we endeavour to identify very small functional adaptations in elite athletes which result in important performances changes.

Sample Size: More is Better?

Previously in this chapter we have discussed issues of sampling and commented that to improve power we need larger samples. This is often one of the biggest frustrations in the sport and exercise sciences. By the nature of the research questions we are asking, our participant population is sometimes quite limited. Recruitment is further constrained by geographical location (e.g. if participants need to attend a laboratory or specific assessment venue), time (people naturally change over time and, unless this is a variable of interest, normally data collection should take place over a suitably short time interval in order to improve reliability), and expense (this might be travelling expenses for either the participant or the researcher where physical contact is necessary for the taking and/or recording of measurements). As we will discuss below, effect sizes tend to be small to medium in the sport and exercise sciences, and therefore if we decide to take the approach of increasing sample size to improve our power we would probably need to recruit at least 100 participants in each experimental group! The resources to fund such a study are beyond the budgets of most researchers, and we would therefore be better to invest time and energy in appropriate initial participant recruitment, ensuring good trial standardisation, optimising experimental control, and minimising measurement variance. These issues will be discussed in greater detail below.

Research Participant Heterogeneity

A large portion of the variation in experimental data is due to variation in the participants making up the experimental sample. *Heterogeneity* refers to a lack of relationship, and if a sample were highly heterogeneous the participants would all be very different from each other. The danger in such a situation is that there is greater difference between the participant members of a sample than might result from the intervention of interest, and as a result the intervention effect is lost in the large variation between participants, and a type-II error is made.

One way to overcome a loss of experimental power due to sample heterogeneity is to identify those population variables (i.e. characteristics that can change – or vary – from person to person) that have the potential to impinge upon the outcome measurements, and to control for these variables when forming your sample. For example, in the sport and exercise sciences there are a number of population variables that will impact upon outcome variables to different degrees depending upon the specifics of the experiment or study being undertaken. For most exercise physiology studies gender, age, body mass and/or body composition, training status and training history are all obvious variables to consider in defining your experimental sample. In sports biomechanics body mass and specific measurements relating to the relative length and girth of limbs may be of importance in relation to the execution of sports techniques. In sports medicine training and injury history may be of importance. In sports psychology, personality measures, measures of cognitive/psychometric ability, measures associated with values and feelings, the social context or background of the participants, as well as their representative level of performance or exercise habits may be of interest. This controlling of variables that combine to define a sample will result in the formation of a *homogenous* sample, which is one where the variation between participant members is minimised.

Sample homogeneity is a strength from a statistical analysis perspective as it will enhance the power of your experimental design, ensuring that a 'real' effect in your data can be identified. However, any approach that is controlling or constraining sample formation might compromise the essential randomness of this process, and as such the sample may no longer reflect the population to which we are intending to apply the generalisations generated from our experiment or study. This genuine concern is readily addressed through careful consideration of the specific research question, the experimental design being applied, the objective criteria for participant recruitment and selection, and finally the approach to data organisation and analysis. Careful planning in all these areas needs to be finalised before the first piece of data is collected.

In relation to experimental design there are two obvious design strategies for overcoming problems of participant heterogeneity. First, let each participant serve as his or her own control. This *cross-over design* requires that every participant perform every trial, including a control trial, in a randomised order. Such an approach would result in any variation between participants being cancelled out. Whilst intuitively appealing, this approach is not universally applicable across the many varied research questions in the sport and exercise sciences. As mentioned previously, it would not be appropriate to apply a crossover design to any intervention that has a non-reversible or lasting effect. For example: physiological or psychological training or technique interventions where new abilities and/or new approaches cannot be totally reversed or unlearned; injury treatments and rehabilitation programmes where it would not be possible, and indeed would be highly unethical, to re-inflict the same injury or illness in order to try a different approach; or dietary supplementation interventions with unknown 'wash out' periods for the restoration of pre-supplementation biological levels. In these examples the next best approach would be to match participants on one, or a range, of variables to produce broadly homogenous sample groups. The choice of *matching variable(s)* will depend upon the specifics of the study being undertaken, and will reflect those participant-specific variables thought to influence the outcome variable. In selecting your matching variables remember to be specific to your research question and to keep focussed; the more variables by which you chose to match participants will, on the one hand promote sample homogeneity, whilst on the other hand make it more difficult to obtain a good match across all variables. One negative practical aspect to this design is that if a participant is unable to complete a trial, the data for that participant and their matched pair must be removed from all other trials.

Experimental Control and Maximising Measurement Sensitivity

There would be no point to conducting experimental studies, or observing research participants, if no form of measurement were undertaken. Research is conducted in order to acquire new knowledge or to provide evidence in support of conjecture or anecdotal observations. This knowledge is acquired in the form of manageable pieces of information through a range of appropriate measurement procedures and protocols. These pieces of information are then summarised into statistics. In chapter 2 we discussed issues concerning measurement precision and accuracy, we should also consider measurement scale (relative to effect size) and our ability (or sensitivity) to measure change, measurement reliability and reproducibility, and uniformity of measurement administration (standardisation of timing, measurement device and procedures adopted), as these will all contribute to measurement sensitivity.

From an experimental perspective, we need to be able to measure and evaluate the research intervention; this will provide our *independent variable* (i.e. that part of the experiment manipulated by the researcher; also called the treatment variable). This might refer to a supplementation dose in a sports nutrition study, training volume in an exercise physiology study, type of running shoe or underlying ground conditions in a sports biomechanics study, the nature of visual information in a sports psychology study, or perhaps treatment mode in a sports therapy study.   Measurements taken during an experiment or study will be made on the *dependent variable(s)* (i.e. the effect of the independent variable).   Table 3.1 presents a classification of the independent and dependent variables as described by Morrow et al. (1995).   This provides a useful matrix by which we can readily discriminate between variables, especially in more complex experimental designs.

The Independent Variable	The Dependent Variable
Presumed cause	Presumed effect
The antecedent/initial event	The consequence
Manipulated by the researcher/investigator	Measured by the researcher/investigator
Predicted from…	Predicted to…
Predictor	Criterion
X – axis	Y – axis

Table 3.1   Classification of experimental variables (adapted from Morrow et al. 1995).

As discussed in chapter 2 our dependent measures must be *valid* and *reliable*, however the ideal dependent variable is one that varies maximally in response to the experimental treatment or condition, but is relatively unresponsive to any other possible effectors.   Obviously in the real world this rarely occurs in such a singularly unique way, where most dependent variables will be subject to a range of secondary effectors.   The degree to which changes in a dependent variable reflect changes in the independent variable is termed *measurement sensitivity*.   This sensitivity decreases as a chosen dependent variable is more responsive to effectors other than the experimental treatment or condition.   The optimal dependent variable(s) and their measurement sensitivity can be determined through pilot testing of an experimental protocol.   Often an investigator will intuitively know the measures from which the primary dependent variable(s) will be selected, and in this case the pilot study serves to confirm this intuition and assess the normal *variance*[3.7] of a measure (refer to chapter 4 for a definition of the *coefficient of variation*). However in very complex experimental designs involving multiple variable outcomes – such as might be found in sport psychology – straightforward intuition is not always adequate and a pilot study for evaluating the range of possible dependent variables becomes imperative.

Differences or variation in a measure might result from the experimental intervention or condition, but will definitely occur because of natural differences between participants (i.e. participant heterogeneity) and measurement error. It is hoped that the variation resulting from the experimental intervention or condition will follow some form of discernable pattern (i.e. systematic variation), and thus be readily identifiable. Similarly, whilst participants will infinitely vary on a range of characteristics, again it is hoped that this variation will follow some form of pattern predetermined by the participants' physical or psychological characteristics. In contrast, the variation arising from measurement error is not considered to follow a discernable pattern (i.e. random variation). Though it is important to note that measurement error could be systematic if the researcher repeatedly made the same mistake when taking measurements! Measurement error will normally arise due to: differences within a participant over repeated trials (e.g. in motivation, concentration, and biological variation); differences in the specific procedures adopted in taking measurements (e.g. subtle differences in the way a researcher may discern a measure or score); and differences in the performance of measurement instruments (e.g. the random erratic behaviour of analysers). The focus of experimental control is to minimise measurement error; a tightly controlled experiment will reduce within-participant variation by prescribing the pre-trial activity of participants, by specifically defining measurement protocols and by calibrating all measurement instruments. Thus, by minimising measurement error through experimental control we will be able to discern smaller effect sizes and increase power. Measurement error can be reduced through standardising the administration of experimental trials.

[3.7] *Variance* is a measure of dispersion in data, or the degree to which data are different or divergent; it is determined from the square of the standard deviation and is a mathematical statistical description of the spread of data around the mean. Variance will be discussed in greater detail in chapter 4.

Standardisation and Minimising Procedural Variation

Standardisation of experimental trials or the protocols adopted in observational studies will promote statistical power. Good standardisation requires meticulous planning; every element of your research project must be considered in advance of commencing data collection:

1. Re-consider your research question…

2. Is this reflected in your research hypotheses?

3. Review all elements of your experimental design…

4. What are your parameters against which trial/condition/observation period are standardised? Are these appropriate? Are these adequate?

5. Review parameters defining your research intervention…

6. Are they appropriate? Unambiguous? Reproducible? Repeatable?

7. Review your measurements…

8. Are all measurements appropriate and/or necessary? Is there anything else that should be monitored?

9. Review participant recruitment, sample formation, and the organisation of experimental groups…

10. Arc your methods appropriate? Standardised? Randomised? Will your sample reflect the population of interest?

Even at this stage, just when you think that you are in a 'GO situation', you may find something that is not consistent or not appropriate. It is good that this has been identified now, for all it may cost you is a short delay to make the necessary adjustments to your study before data collection commences. If it had not been identified and you had continued on to data collection, your study might have been flawed and considerable time and expense would therefore have been wasted. A strong element of minimising procedural variation is through *pilot testing* your experimental procedures. This will be discussed in greater detail in the section below with respect to specific measurements, however at this point it is worth considering the inter-relationships arising when all aspects of a study are put together. It is essential that there is a full run through of all aspects of a study's protocol(s) before data collection commences to ensure that there are no unforeseen consequences of, for example, the timing of measurements and the making measurements.

Effect Size

Assuming that we have recruited an appropriately sized sample of participants, we have pilot tested our measures in order to select the most responsive dependent variables and to reduce measurement error, we have standardised our test administration in order to minimise procedural variation, then in a simple two group design study (control group vs. experimental group), a difference in the sample means will provide an estimate of the *effect size*. However, this effect size would not be transferable to other studies or other applications, as it will only relate to the measurement scale of that specific dependent variable. Therefore if you wish to determine a standardised effect size some form of index must be created. If we further consider the design described above of a control group and an experimental group, then a standardised index for effect size can be calculated according to equation (3.1) below:

$$ES = \frac{\overline{X}_1 - \overline{X}_2}{S_{pooled}}$$

Where,   ES   ... Effect size

$\overline{X}_1$ ... Experimental group/condition *mean*[3.8]

$\overline{X}_2$ ... Control group/condition mean

S_{pooled} ... *Standard deviation*[3.9] of the pooled[3.10] sample (i.e. the combined standard deviation for the experimental and control groups/conditions).

[3.8] *Mean* – a statistical measure of central tendency, the average score of the group (refer to chapter 4).
[3.9] *Standard Deviation* – an estimate of the variability of the group scores around the mean (refer to chapter 4).
[3.10] *Pooled* – refers to combined groups or data, in this example the data of the control and experimental groups are combined together, and then the standard deviation of this combined group is determined.

The important question we must ask ourselves at the outset concerns what size of change we would consider to be important from a practical perspective. The easy answer to this question is that it will vary from study to study! For example, a relatively small change in some measure of fitness may be nothing to jump up and down about in a group of sedentary individuals; but in a group of elite athletes – where small changes are hard won – even a modest improvement would be considered important.

One approach to determining an appropriate effect size for your study is to look at the body of published literature in your research field and deduce the average effect size in the dependent variable across a range of studies (this is often achieved by adopting some form of *meta-analysis*[3.11]). Normally effect sizes from this approach are reported in standard deviation units (i.e. multiples of the sample standard deviation), which provide a relative measure in terms of size but may not be readily interpretable in relation to a specific measure. Thus, some researchers prefer to convert effect sizes into a value of percentage variance, where we calculate the variance in the outcome variable that is *accounted for* by the treatment (equation 3.2, below).

$$\%S^2 \quad = \quad \frac{ES^2}{ES^2 + 4}$$

Where, $\%S^2$ ... Percentage Variance *accounted for*

ES ... Sample Effect Size

For some practical guidelines we will again refer you to the work of Cohen (1988), who recommends 0.2 standard deviation units for small effect sizes, 0.5 for medium and 0.8 for large. However, these are relatively arbitrary values with respect to the diversity of research designs

---

[3.11] *Meta-analysis* is a technique of reviewing literature whereby a rule is applied to the quantification of the results of a number of studies to yield a measure that can then be examined and analysed through the application of statistical techniques.

undertaken in the sport and exercise sciences, we will therefore return to the calculation of specific effect sizes in our worked example presented in chapter 10.

Standards of Professional Practice

In chapter 2 we discussed ethics and research and described how research practices are governed by codes of practice that articulate the right and wrong ways of conducting research. The specific detail of these codes will depend upon the affiliations of the researchers, the research participants, the research location and the research agencies involved in the project. Ultimately, the actions of researchers are governed by a duty of care as set down in health and safety legislation (e.g. COSHH regulations for the handling of chemicals). This requires researchers, in common with all other walks of life, to assess the potential risk for the research participants and the research investigators, and to ensure that this is reasonable, appropriate, and of course ethically sound.

In the United Kingdom – outside of the clinical environment where research will be overseen by medical codes of practice – the *British Association of Sport and Exercise Sciences* (BASES) informs practices in the sub-disciplines making up the sport and exercise sciences. BASES prescribe appropriate professional standards for conducting research, as well as for providing sport and exercise services to client groups. These standards are upheld through the BASES *Code of Conduct* (www.bases.org.uk), to which all members agree to adhere. An individual will develop appropriate standards of both practice and behaviour during a period of professional training (i.e. supervised experience), which is overseen by a senior accredited sport and exercise scientist. This process of accreditation is one of continuing professional development, and the professional competency of an accredited sport and exercise scientist is reappraised every five years through a process of re-accreditation. As well as accrediting individuals involved in the sport and exercise sciences, BASES also accredit the research environment such as exercise physiology or sports biomechanics laboratories.

In addition to national and international standards of professional practice, there may be standards that are more locally developed and applied within an institution or an agency. These are referred to as *standard operating procedures* (SOPs), and will take into consideration both national standards of professional practice, and the demands/requirements of a specific task and/or location. Many SOPs are born out of the local application of national standards for safe practice. However, further examples of SOPs include the exercise protocols applied during exercise physiological assessments, the detailed protocols of questionnaire administration in sports and exercise psychology, approaches to force platform data acquisition in sports biomechanics, and perhaps the sequence of injury identification, examination and specific diagnoses in sports therapy.

Summary/Key Points

1. True random sampling is rarely possible, and more often than not in the sport and exercise sciences sample size and composition is constrained by practical considerations; post hoc justification can be applied to demonstrate the quality and appropriateness of your research sample.

2. For most experimental designs we need to identify a control group or condition for comparison, which is not subjected to the experimental intervention or does not experience any change in circumstances that would influence the variable of interest.

3. *Power* refers to the ability to detect true treatment effects, and provides a measure of design sensitivity. *Effect size* refers to the ability to discriminate that two conditions are likely to be different.

4. In making statistical decisions: if we reject the null hypothesis when it is true (i.e. find differences that are not there), then we would have made a type-I error; if we accept the null hypothesis when it is false (i.e. do not identify differences that are there), then we would have made a type-II error.

5. The power of your data analyses will be influenced by: your sample size; the prescribed significance level, where the convention in the sport and exercise sciences is to apply a significance level of 0.05; and the population effect size for the experimental intervention or condition.

6.   Design sensitivity can be maximised by: increasing sample size (though this is normally practically constrained); minimise variation between research participants (i.e. sample homogeneity); maximise measurement sensitivity (i.e. experimental control); and minimise procedural variation (i.e. trial standardisation).

7.   The *independent variable* is the part of the experiment that is manipulated by the researcher.

8.   The *dependent variable(s)* respond to the experimental treatment or condition.

9.   *Standards of Professional Practice*, associational *Codes of Conduct* and locally developed *standard operating procedures* govern the actions of researchers, the experience of research participants, and specific details defining the research location.

10.   The potential risk of the research intervention or experimental conditions must be assessed for both the research participants and the research investigators prior to commencing a study, and you must ensure that this is reasonable, appropriate, and ethically sound.

4

Organising and Illustrating Data

Chapter Objectives

- To explain the purpose of exploring and summarising data
- To explain the uses of pictorial representations and summary statistics
- To identify and construct suitable graphs and diagrams for a given situation
- To identify appropriate summary statistics and how to calculate and interpret them.

Introduction

Before carrying out any complex statistical work with data we have collected, it is essential to thoroughly explore the data and get a 'feel' for what the raw data may be telling us. It is often helpful to summarise data in order to help us make sense of what is happening in the data. Most people can only hold a set of seven numbers in their head at any one time, such that it would be impossible to gain an insight into a data set containing several hundred numbers if the data were left in their raw (as collected) state. A variety of techniques can be employed to explore data in advance of the main analysis, which can broadly be described in terms of either numerical summarisation techniques, or graphical illustration techniques.

Initially the data set needs to be examined to ascertain whether all the values are possible given the variables that have been collected and the scale of measurement. For example, in a data set describing the physiological characteristics of a group of male and female runners, values for maximum oxygen uptake (VO_{2max}) ranged between 37–76 $ml.kg^{-1}min^{-1}$, except for one value of 5.96 $ml.kg^{-1}min^{-1}$. This was clearly an incorrect value, being extreme of the normal 'healthy' physiological range for this particular parameter. Further investigation revealed that the data value had been wrongly transferred from the data collection sheet to the data summary sheet, and the correct value was 59.6 $ml.kg^{-1}min^{-1}$. Had the data set not been subject to initial data exploration this rogue value may not have been identified, and consequently would have had an impact upon the results of the experiment, making the outcome statistics wrong, even if the original experimental design had been good. This type of simple error is easily rectified if you are aware of its existence, but would not have been identified if we had moved directly to the calculation stage of the data analysis at the outset. This is a particular danger now that most analyses are conducted using computer software.

As discussed in chapter 2, the *level of data* is a primary concern as this limits the statistics that we might wish to apply. It is meaningless to use statistical techniques that make calculations on the data if the numbers making up our data set are limited in meaning. For example, if numbers have been assigned to research participants that merely reflect their position in a time trial or running race, they have no real numerical importance in terms of size. Unless 2 truly is half of 4 in the context of the data, then mathematical calculations such as division will have no meaning. This issue will be discussed in more detail later in the chapter.

Apart from manual data entry checks (as in the case of identifying rogue values), and consideration of the scale of measurement of variables, the next step is normally to represent the data in some form of graphical format in order to illustrate characteristics and patterns of the data.

Pictorial Representation of Data

Pictorially representing data through graphical methods is good for gaining an overall impression of what the data may be showing us. A graph should therefore clarify the data and as such a few rules are necessary in order to ensure that this function is fulfilled, this is especially true if you intend to include your graph in a laboratory report, project report, or ultimately in some form of abstract, oral, poster, or paper presentation to the scientific community (refer to chapter 11 for a more comprehensive description of the formats in which you might finally present your research findings). Any graphical method should:

- Provide a clear title so that a reader can make sense of your figure (graph) without needing to read the accompanying text

- Draw the graph to an appropriate size relative to the detail that needs to be included – too small and the data points will lie on top of each other, confusing any patterns in the data; equally too large and the data points become inappropriately spaced apart

- Scale the axes (the vertical y-axis and the horizontal x-axis) appropriately for the magnitude of the data to be presented, and include the origin (point 0,0) if necessary for the reader to understand what the data are doing

- Label axes clearly to show the variables and the units of measure (SI units[4.1])

- Keep it simple and avoid confusion through colour or pattern

- Include a figure legend identifying the items presented on the figure, and maintain a logical progression/order for multiple variables

These points have been considered in the preparation of figures presented in *Using Statistics in Sport and Exercise Science Research*. If a graph or figure does not clarify the data then do not use it – a figure is for clarity and impact, not to provide a break in the text – and needs to be used appropriately for maximum effect. A number of physical characteristics were measured in a group of sixty recreationally trained runners (40 male and 20 female) during laboratory fitness assessments, and these data are reported in appendix: 1, *Physiological Data – Running Study*. The following figures – graphical representations of the data – have been drawn in order to explore part of this data set.

[4.1]   SI units – *Système International (d'Unités)*, the internationally recognised system of units of measure.

Frequency Tables

Using frequency distribution tables (and graphs) is one approach to ordering and presenting data to make interpretation of the raw scores easier. An *ungrouped frequency distribution* contains all possible *scores* (x) in order, and the *frequency* (f) of each score (table 4.1). Often a distribution is more readily appreciated if the data are grouped into classes as in table 4.2. Tables like these are good for identifying outlying values – those values that lie well away from the main body of data. As a guide, reasonable definition can be preserved – while presenting a readily interpreted distribution – with about 10–15 class intervals. These can then be transferred to a frequency graph to allow you to gain an impression of the shape (or pattern) of the data distribution.

For example, the ages of the sample of sixty runners taking part in an experiment could be listed as a frequency table of all observed ages. This table could potentially be sixty lines long, as the chances of two or more runners being born exactly at the same point in time are remote; the problems of adopting very narrow classes are illustrated in table 4.1. However, if the data are grouped, such that each category includes a spread of ages, we are able to gain a clearer view of the shape of the distribution of ages of the study participants (table 4.2).

Age (years)	Frequency
18.7	1
19.9	1
20.0	1
20.1	1
20.5	1
20.9	1
21.0	2
21.2	1
21.3	1
21.4	1
21.7	2
22.0	1
22.3	1
22.4	1
22.6	1
22.8	1
23.1	1
24.0	1
24.2	2
24.6	1
24.7	2
24.8	2
24.9	1
25.2	2
25.3	1
25.4	3
25.6	2
25.8	2
26.0	1
26.3	1
26.9	3
28.3	1
28.4	1
28.9	1
29.1	1
29.6	1
29.8	1
30.4	1
31.8	1
32.1	1
32.8	2
33.0	1
33.4	1
34.3	1
34.5	1
37.7	1
39.3	1
Total	60

Table 4.1   Frequency table of Age (in years) of participants in the *Running Study*.

Age (years)	Frequency
17.0 - 18.9	1
19.0 - 20.9	5
21.0 - 22.9	12
23.0 - 24.9	10
25.0 - 26.9	15
27.0 - 28.9	3
29.0 - 30.9	4
31.0 - 32.9	4
33.0 - 34.9	4
35.0 - 36.9	0
37.0 - 38.9	1
39.0 - 40.9	1
Total	60

Table 4.2   Grouped frequency table of Age (in years) of participants in the *Running Study*.

The steps for producing a grouped frequency table are as follows:

1. Consider the highest and lowest values to find the range of data; in this example the highest value was 39.3 years and the lowest value was 18.7 years such that the age range was 20.6 years

2. Divide this range into a suitable number of groups (or categories) that will allow the shape of the data to be apparent whilst reducing the overall number of data points; in this example each category corresponded to a class width equivalent to 2 years, providing 12 groups into which the sixty participants could be grouped

3. Decide on appropriate labels for each category or group, taking into consideration the measurement accuracy of the data and the need for no gaps or overlaps between groups; in this example the data were reported to one decimal place, and hence the groups are described to one decimal place.

Cumulative frequency distribution tables record the total number of items whose values are up to (but not greater than) the upper limit of each interval. Whilst *cumulative percentage distributions* are essentially the same except the number of counts in each category is expressed as a percentage of the total distribution. Table 4.2 could be amended to include the cumulative frequency and the cumulative percentage frequency as illustrated in table 4.3.

Age (years)	Frequency	Cumulative Frequency	Cumulative Percentage Frequency
17.0-18.9	1	1	1.67
19.0-20.9	5	6	10.00
21.0-22.9	12	18	30.00
23.0-24.9	10	28	46.67
25.0-26.9	15	43	71.67
27.0-28.9	3	46	76.67
29.0-30.9	4	50	83.33
31.0-32.9	4	54	90.00
33.0-34.9	4	58	96.67
35.0-36.9	0	58	96.67
37.0-38.9	1	59	98.33
39.0-40.9	1	60	100.00
Total	60		

Table 4.3   Cumulative frequency and cumulative percentage frequency table of Age (in years) of participants in the *Running Study*.

Various different forms of graphs are used to communicate the shape or pattern of distributions. Tables 4.1, 4.2 and 4.3 can be used, in turn, to draw frequency graphs and polygons. These will be discussed in the following sections.

Bar Charts and Histograms

The most common type of graphs for illustrating frequency distributions, and hence allowing the comparison of the relative frequency of one item with another, are *bar chart* and *histogram*. These forms of graphs allow the shape of a distribution to be more readily appreciated by the reader.

Bar charts may be used for discrete[4.2] (counted) or nominal data, where the height of each bar is proportional to the frequency (i.e. the number of times it occurs) of that item. The x-axis is labelled with discrete names and there are gaps between each of the bars. For example a survey was undertaken to examine the specialist sports of a group of first year undergraduate students enrolled on sport-related degree programmes at a United Kingdom university. The data from this survey is presented in table 4.4; the survey categories are given by the different sports listed in the first column, and the number of students participating in each sport is given by the count or frequency reported in the second column. This frequency data is nominal, as it is not possible to have a fraction of a student participating in a sport such that the data would always be reported as a whole number.

Sport	Frequency
Football	14
Rugby	9
Netball	5
Hockey	15
Sailing	3
Karate	0
Kick boxing	2
Total	48

Table 4.4   Frequency table of specialist sports of a group of first year sports students.

[4.2] *Discrete* (variable) refers to having consecutive values that are not infinitesimally close, the values are distinctly separate. This would necessitate analysis requiring summation.

Data from table 4.4 were used to create a bar chart (figure 4.1); note the gaps between bars – which is consistent with a bar chart format of presentation – also note that it is acceptable to omit karate (with a score of zero), as there are many other possible sports which have not been included on the table and we are only interested in those sports which the students actually *do* pursue. The purpose of this graph is that it enables us to assess the relative popularity of the different sports. This task is easier to perform visually, from the graph, than it is to deduce from the frequency table. Furthermore, it would become increasingly more difficult to deduce from the frequency table if we increased the number of sports included and/or the number of research participants.

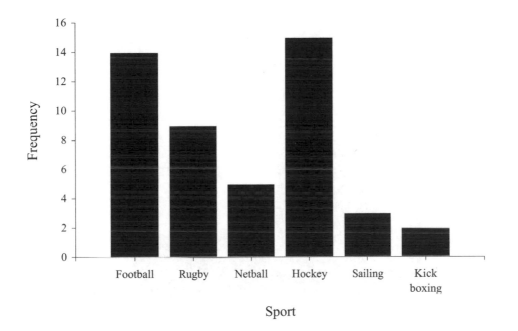

Figure 4.1   Bar chart of specialist sports of a group of first year sports students.

Histograms are used for continuous[4.3] (measured) data, where an area represents the frequency of each of the ranges. As the area is proportional to the frequency of that range, doubling the frequency will result in a doubling of the area. Care is needed in labelling and correctly interpreting histogram axes where the class widths are not all of a uniform size, *as it is the area that is of importance* not simply the height of the bar. Unlike bar charts a histogram does not have gaps between the bars, as the scale is continuous, unless a class is empty. Empty categories on a bar chart may not be included if there is no need to consider those categories, but they will be included on a histogram as the continuous scale needs to be maintained. Figure 4.2 presents a histogram of the age data from table 4.2. Note that the class for the '35.0–36.9 years' category is empty. It appears from this graph that data in the older age categories is more widely spread, with the majority of participants being aged between 21 and 27 years.

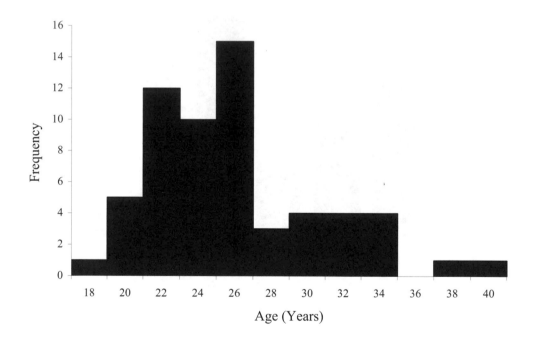

Figure 4.2   Histogram of Age (in years) of participants in the *Running Study.*

[4.3]   The opposite of discrete is *continuous* (variable) referring to having a continuum (not separate) of possible values, such that analysis would involve integration.

Frequency polygons can also illustrate the shape of data. A frequency polygon can be drawn from data that might equally be illustrated with a histogram (i.e. data that has a continuous scale on the x-axis). The frequency polygon is drawn as follows:

1. Plot a point at the middle of the class interval (i.e. the mid-point of each bar) and at a height equivalent to the frequency score for that class
2. The points are then joined by a series of straight lines
3. Each 'end' of the graph should be joined to the x-axis at the mid-class point immediately before the lowest value and after the highest value

This type of graph is useful for examining the pattern of a distribution as it focuses upon the shape depicted by the relative frequencies, and the impact of the comparative heights of the bars is reduced. Returning to the *Running Study*, figure 4.3 presents the frequency polygon for the participants' ages; the *tailing off* in frequency of participants aged over 27 years is clearly evident.

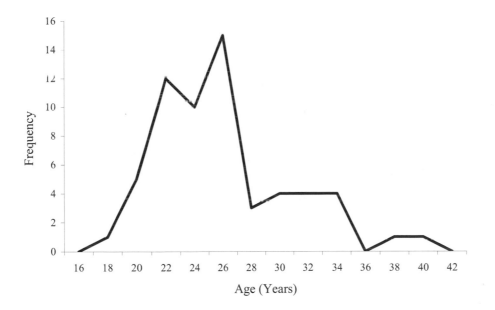

Figure 4.3   Frequency polygon of Age (in years) of participants in the *Running Study*.

Stem and Leaf Plots (or Stemplots)

As discussed previously, pictorial representations of data help us to gain a greater appreciation of the data.   However, transposing raw scores into a graph usually involves some form of simplification of the data. Excessive detail on a graph becomes confusing. Nevertheless, after all the efforts that have gone into collecting our data, it would be highly inappropriate to discard information at the analysis stage of the research process. *Stem and leaf plots* provide a compromise, and whilst these displays rarely see print in a scientific report, they are very useful for exploring data. This is because you retain access to the actual data values while exploring the shape of the distribution, such that a *stem and leaf plot* is like a pictorial way of producing a frequency table.

For example, the following data set represents the number of training days lost through injury over a period of one year for a sample group of athletes:

| 10 | 3 | 12 | 14 | 5 | 2 | 8 | 5 | 9 | 25 |
| 13 | 23 | 32 | 12 | 19 | 33 | 39 | 15 | 16 | 37 |

A five-stage process can be applied to construct the stem and leaf plot:

1.   The 'stems' would be selected by looking at the range of the data set. For this example the range is 3–37 training days, and this would suggest a 'tens' and 'units' approach would best describe the data. So the stems on the left of the diagram – representing the classes – would take the values 0, 1, 2, 3 to indicate no tens, tens, twenties and thirties.

i.e.
```
    0 |  ...
    1 |  ...
    2 |  ...
    3 |  ...
 (Stem)  (Leaves)
```

2. The values would then be transferred to the stems. Thus, the first value '10' is transferred to the '1' stem, and recorded as a zero indicating one 'ten' and no 'units'.

i.e.
```
0 | ...
1 | 0
2 | ...
3 | ...
```

The second value '3' is recorded against the '0' stem, indicating no 'tens' and three 'units'.

i.e.
```
0 | 3
1 | 0
2 | ...
3 | ...
```

3. The process continues until all data have been transferred to the diagram, and results in an *unordered* stem and leaf plot – the plot on the left in figure 4.4.

4. The 'leaves' on the right of the line are then ordered from lowest to highest value, as illustrated in the plot on the right of figure 4.4.

5. Finally, a scale is included to inform the reader of the values assigned to the 'stems' and 'leaves' respectively.

i.e.
```
0 | 3 5 2 8 5 9      Unordered plot     0 | 2 3 5 5 8 9
1 | 0 2 4 3 2 9 5 6      ←             1 | 0 2 2 3 4 5 6 9
2 | 5 3                  →             2 | 3 5
3 | 2 3 9 7          Ordered plot       3 | 2 3 7 9
```

Figure 4.4   Unordered and ordered stem and leaf plots of the number of training days lost through injury (Note: Stem width = 10, such that 1| 4 represents 14 days).

Back-to-back, *stretched* and *squeezed* stem and leaf plots are all an extension of this idea, and are used to compare two different groups for similarity of distribution (back-to-back plots) or to expand or contract the diagram if the original choice of class width for the stem was unsuitable. For example, in the *Running Study* it would have been inappropriate to use a ten-year class width to illustrate age as the majority of participants were between the ages of 20 and 29 years. An expanded stem and leaf plot with class widths of 5 year on the stem may need expanding still further to 3- or 2-year class widths. An example of a back-to-back expanded stem and leaf plot is presented in figure 4.5. The male (left) and female (right) data are presented back-to-back as leaves on a single stem. A 'tens' and 'units' approach has again been chosen to describe the data, however this has been expanded to divide the tens into 0–4 and 5–9. The lowest ages were 19 and 18 for the male and female runners respectively; therefore we need only to record a stem of 1 (ten) for the 5–9 category. For the 'twenty' and 'thirty' categories we must record stems for the 0–4 and 5–9 categories of units, or leaves.

```
                              Male        Female

                                 9 │ 1 │ 8
          4 4 4 4 4 4 4 4 2 2 2 1 1 1 1 1 1 0 0 │ 2 │ 0 0 1 2 2 3 4
                    9 9 8 8 6 6 5 5 5 5 5 5 5 │ 2 │ 5 5 5 6 6 6 8 9
                                  4 4 2 2 2 1 │ 3 │ 0 3 3
                                           9 │ 3 │ 7
```

Figure 4.5   Back-to-back stem and leaf plots of the ages (years) for the male and female participants in the *Running Study* (Note: Stem width = 5, such that 1│ 9 represents 19 years).

Box and Whisker Plots (or Box Plots)

Box and whisker plots (or *box plots*) provide another means of visually examining the shape of a distribution. This approach requires five key pieces of information (which will be discussed in more detail later in this chapter) on the data set:

1. *minimum value* The lowest value in the data set
2. *lower quartile* Corresponds to a value equivalent to one quarter of the data set once it has been sorted into ascending numerical order
3. *median* The middle value when all the data have been sorted into numerical order
4. *upper quartile* Corresponds to a value equivalent to three quarters of the data set once it has been sorted into numerical order
5. *maximum value* The highest value in the data set

Note: These values can be easily counted from an ordered stem and leaf plot.

A diagram is constructed against a scale such that a box is drawn with the ends at the lower and upper quartile values of a data set (refer to figure 4.6). The median is then drawn across the box and equates to the middle of the data set. Thus, the *box* represents the central 50% of the data, with the second and third quarters spread to either side of the median. The *whiskers* are drawn from each end of the box and extend to the minimum and maximum data values respectively, and thus represent the spread of the lowest and highest quarters of the data. The whiskers can be modified to identify the presence of *outliers* (i.e. values that differ considerably from the main body of data). Tukey (1977) suggests that outliers can usually be identified as values that are more than 1.5 times the box length (i.e. distance between lower and upper quartile values) away from the end of the box; extreme outliers are data values that occur more than 3.0 box lengths away from the end of the box. Statistical analysis computer packages, such as SPSS™, follow this rule; the whisker extends to the last value fitting within the criteria, and those beyond 1.5 box lengths from the end of the box are identified by one symbol and those beyond 3.0 box lengths from the end of the box are identified with a different symbol. Some packages also state the value of the outlier, or the participant number that gives rise to the value, facilitating further investigation.

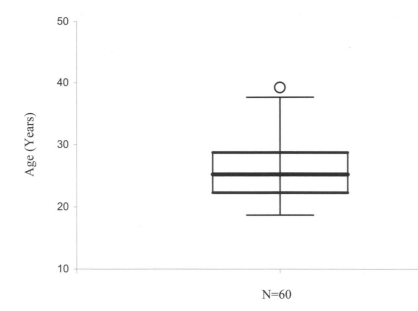

Figure 4.6   Box and whisker plot of Age (in years) of participants in the *Running Study*.

Figure 4.6 presents the age data from the *Running Study* in the form of a box and whisker plot. In this example the lower part of the plot is fairly close together and uniform in spread; that is, the middle 50% of participants are closely clustered around the median age (represented by the box around the thick black line). The area of box above the thick line is almost the same as the area below the line, indicating that the ages of the middle 50% of the study's participants are evenly balanced above and below the middle – median – value. The lower quarter of the data, as represented by the short whisker extending down from the box to the minimum value, also indicates a similar spread of data to the middle 50%. In contrast, the whisker extending from the top of the box to the maximum value is relatively longer, indicating a greater spread of ages in the upper quarter of the data set. We have already identified this from figures 4.2 and 4.3, however the box and whisker plot provides more information by indicating that the oldest participant can be considered as an outlier. This may not be an important point to note at this stage in the data analysis, but if this same participant is observed to behave differently to the majority of the study's participants in other aspects of the investigation, it could be an indication that *age* should be examined as an influencing factor on the aims of the study.

As well as examining the distribution of a single set or group of data, another useful feature of graphing data is the opportunity to compare across data sets or groups of data. Clustered bar charts and grouped box and whisker plots can be used to explore similarities and differences across groups of data. For example, figure 4.7 again presents the age data from the *Running Study*, however in this instance the data is grouped by gender. From this approach to data exploration it is evident that while there is a greater spread of ages in the female runners at the upper end of the age distribution, our outlier comes from the male runner data set.

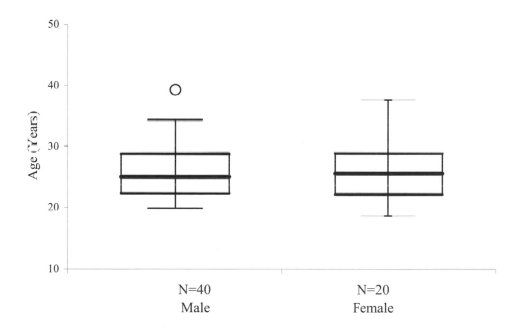

Figure 4.7   Box and whisker plot of Age (in years) of participants in the *Running Study* compared by gender.

Pie Chart

If a sample can be broken down into proportions in relation to responses to a specific variable (e.g. the sports preference survey discussed previously), these proportions of the total data set can be readily presented in the form of a *pie chart*. In this format of graphical data presentation, it is the proportions that are of importance not the actual numbers of respondents in each category. Thus, the circle – or pie – represents the total number of respondents, or the whole sample; the slices represent the distribution of how the sample answered, responded or behaved relative to each category, and the size of each slice can easily be compared. Each respondent can only appear in one category, else the total number of respondents recorded from the pie would be greater than the sample size. Pie charts are often applied to data presented as percentages (e.g. survey data), as percentages are also concerned with relative proportions of the whole or total sample. The calculations for determining the size of each slice are the same whether percentages or raw scores are compared. If we consider the data obtained from the sports preference survey in a sample group of first year sports students (see table 4.4), table 4.5 presents the steps that need to be considered in constructing the corresponding pie chart (figure 4.8).

The diagrams and charts described so far are those most frequently employed during initial data investigations. There are other charts, however, that have specific applications within certain data analysis techniques, and these will be introduced in chapters 5–9 where they constitute a necessary part of the statistical analysis technique.

Numerical Summaries

Numerical summarisation is the next stage of data exploration, and should be conducted following graphical data exploration – but not instead of graphical data exploration. There is a tendency in research to think of statistical work in terms of *mathematics* and *numbers*, and the assumption is then made that anything numeric is 'best'. The problem with numerical data summaries is that they can summarise to such an extent that some of the problems in the data that we considered earlier in this chapter in the graphing section become hidden. As a consequence, if numerical summaries alone are used to explore data they may lead to erroneous conclusions due to false assumptions being made about the data.

Steps	Application to sport preferences data
1. How many people are included in the sample? If the data are presented as percentages this will be a total of 100%	Our data set contains 48 students
2. Divide the total 360° of a circle by the number presented in (1). This will determine the size for each student	$\dfrac{7.5}{48)\overline{360.0}}$ – thus, each student has a slice of angle size 7.5°
3. Multiply the slice size (°), by the number of students indicating a preference for each sport. This will result in a number of different sized slices but the total number of degrees should be 360°	Football1 4 × 7.5 = 105.0° Rugby 9 × 7.5 = 67.5° Netball 5 × 7.5 = 37.5° Hockey 15 × 7.5 = 112.5° Sailing 3 × 7.5 = 22.5° Kickboxing 2 × 7.5 = 15.0° **Total** = **360.0°**
4. The pie chart is then drawn by dividing a circle into slices based on the sizes for each sporting category found in (3)	See figure 4.8

Table 4.5   Approach to constructing a pie chart to illustrate the specialist sports of a sample of first year sports students.

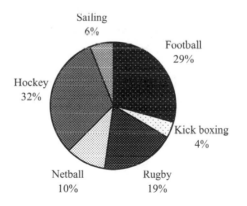

Figure 4.8   Pie chart to illustrate the sports preference proportions of a sample of sports students.

There is a necessity for numerical summarisation in order to make data more readily understandable. Very few of us can remember individual items of a data set, such as the ages of a group of people, but it is quite possible for us to remember the average age of that group of individuals. This *average* can then be used to describe the group as long as we can be confident that it is representative of the group and that there are no extreme outliers.

Measures of Central Tendency

The choice of *measure of central tendency* (i.e. the location of the middle of the data set) depends upon the type, or level, of the data (refer to chapter 2 for a description of the level of data). Other considerations when choosing the preferred measure of central tendency include the nature of the research hypotheses, what you wish to communicate from the data and the shape of the data distribution. The purpose of these statistics is to summarise the data in a *representative* way; you must not select the one that best suits your purpose, as this may be unrepresentative – or biased – with respect to your data set.

The Mode

The *mode* is used with nominal data. It is the most *frequently occurring* data value in a list, and therefore is used as the measure of central tendency for groups or categories of data. It is the measure of central tendency that is the most easily obtained, but it is not widely applicable as it is very sensitive to change. For example, if we look again at the data set relating to student sports preferences (table 4.4), the *modal* sport is hockey (i.e. the sport with the highest frequency, n=15). However, if one hockey player decides that they actually prefer to play football, then a subsequent data collection relating to the same research question in EXACTLY the same sample of participants would reveal a modal sport of football.

The Median

The *median* is concerned with order in data. It is the middle data value determined after all the data have been placed in numerical order. The median divides the ordered data exactly in half. It is not sensitive to the size of the data values and is unaffected by extreme scores, therefore it is often used to summarise data sets that have outliers. For grouped data, the median can be estimated from a cumulative frequency graph. For example, if we consider the distribution of ages for the male participants in our *Running Study*, it appears that there may be outliers at the upper end of the sample distribution. The greater part of the data appear to be grouped around the 22–26 years age range, but several participants are noticeably older and their ages are distributed nearer 40 years of age (figure 4.9). The data level (i.e. ratio level data) would suggest that it is suitable for calculating a mean as the measure of central tendency, however we will determine the median value (refer to calculation box 4.1). In the next section we will also determine the mean and examine which is most representative of the sample.

Figure 4.9   Histogram of Age (in years) of the male participants in the *Running Study*.

Calculation Box 4.1   Median – The Middle Value When Data are Numerically Ordered

1.   Raw age data (as collected):

26.9, 22.3, 21.2, 39.3, 24.9, 24.8, 21.0, 21.4, 25.4, 24.8, 19.9, 24.2, 20.5, 24.0, 31.8, 34.5, 25.8, 29.8, 25.6, 32.8, 21.7, 22.8, 25.3, 21.7, 29.6, 25.6, 21.3, 32.1, 28.9, 20.0, 24.7, 25.2, 26.3, 28.4, 32.8, 24.2, 24.6, 34.3, 22.4, 25.4

2.   When placed in order these data become:

19.9, 20.0, 20.5, 21.0, 21.2, 21.3, 21.4, 21.7, 21.7, 22.3, 22.4, 22.8, 24.0, 24.2, 24.2, 24.6, 24.7, 24.8, 24.8, 24.9, 25.2, 25.3, 25.4, 25.4, 25.6, 25.6, 25.8, 26.3, 26.9, 28.4, 28.9, 29.6, 29.8, 31.8, 32.1, 32.8, 32.8, 34.3, 34.5, 39.3

3.   The middle of the total number of values is found. If this total is odd then the middle will be an actual data value (for example the middle of a data set containing 31 data values will be the 16th data value). If it is even, as in this example, then further calculation is necessary

4.   We have 40 data values. The middle of 40 data values is between the 20th and 21st values. A box has been drawn around those values in the ordered list

$$\text{Median} = \frac{24.9 + 25.2}{2} = \frac{50.1}{2} = 25.05 \text{ years}$$

The Mean

The *mean* is generally the most stable and most widely used measure of central tendency. As will be discussed in chapters 5–9, it is used in many complex statistical analyses as part of the computation. The mean is calculated by summing all the data values, and dividing this figure by the total number of values in the data set. It therefore needs data to be of interval or ratio level, as otherwise these calculations would not make sense. The mean takes into account every data value. As a consequence it can be pulled away from representing the middle of the data set by extremely high or extremely low values. Calculation box 4.2 illustrates the determination of the mean age of the male participants in the *Running Study*.

Calculation Box 4.2   Mean – The Average Value of a Data Set

1.   Raw age data (as collected):

26.9, 22.3, 21.2, 39.3, 24.9, 24.8, 21.0, 21.4, 25.4, 24.8, 19.9, 24.2, 20.5, 24.0, 31.8, 34.5,

25.8, 29.8, 25.6, 32.8, 21.7, 22.8, 25.3, 21.7, 29.6, 25.6, 21.3, 32.1, 28.9, 20.0, 24.7, 25.2,

26.3, 28.4, 32.8, 24.2, 24.6, 34.3, 22.4, 25.4

2.   To calculate the mean of the data set, sum the values and divide by the number of data values. Σ is the Greek symbol used to denote summing, or adding all the data values together.

Thus, $\sum_{i=1}^{n} x_i$ denotes adding all the values (x) together from the first (i.e. $i = 1$) to the last (i.e. $i = n$) in the data set, where n is the total number of values in the data set. In this example $n = 40$.

3.   Using the ages of male participants in the *Running study*, the mean (written $\bar{x}$ and said '*x* bar') is determined as follows:

$$\bar{x} = \frac{\sum_{x=i}^{n} x_i}{n} = \frac{26.9 + 22.3 + \dots + 22.4 + 25.4}{40} = \frac{1038.2}{40} = 25.96 \text{ years}$$

The median age in the male participants from the *Running Study* was 25.05 years and the mean age was 25.96 years. These values are not very different; therefore the outlying oldest participant does not appear to be making the mean unrepresentative of the data set.

If the data for the participants ages had been collected as grouped data (as in table 4.3), the mean would be calculated as described in calculation box 4.3 (applying data derived in table 4.6).

Age (years)	Frequency	Mid-Point of Age Data	Frequency × Mid-Point of Age
17.0-18.9	1	17.95	17.95
19.0-20.9	5	19.95	99.75
21.0-22.9	12	21.95	263.40
23.0-24.9	10	23.95	239.50
25.0-26.9	15	25.95	389.25
27.0-28.9	3	27.95	83.85
29.0-30.9	4	29.95	119.80
31.0-32.9	4	31.95	127.80
33.0-34.9	4	33.95	135.80
35.0-36.9	0	35.95	0.0
37.0-38.9	1	37.95	37.95
39.0-40.9	1	39.95	39.95
Total	60		$\Sigma = 1655$

Table 4.6   Frequency table and product[4.4] of frequency and Age (in years) of participants in the *Running Study*.

Calculation Box 4.3   Mean – Grouped Data Set

1.   For grouped data, the mean can be estimated by treating each set of values in an interval as if they were values at the midpoint of the interval

2.   Find the mid-point of the category (in this example the category is age) by adding the two ends of the category together and dividing by 2

   e.g. Line 1 of table 4.6: Mid-point of age group = (17.0 + 18.9) / 2 = 35.9 / 2 = 17.95

3.   The estimated mean for the grouped data is given by:

   Estimated mean = Σ (frequency × mid-point of age) / n = 1655 / 60 = 27.58 years

---

[4.4] The *product* results from the multiplication of two or more (number) values.

Whilst the measures of central tendency discussed above begin to describe the distributions of numerical data sets, they do not show the whole picture. It is also necessary to measure how the data set varies around its central value (i.e. whether the data set is widely spread or closely packed together). This measure would not be appropriate for nominal level data where numerical labels are only assigned for convenience. Equally it would not be appropriate for ordinal level data based on alphabetic categories, as this only provides information on order and does not provide any indication of the data spread. Measures of variability in the data can therefore only be sensibly applied to interval or ratio level data.

Measures of Variability

Range

The *range* is the simplest measure of variability and represents the difference between the highest and the lowest data values of a data set. It is a single figure representing the *dispersion*[4.5] between two extreme data values, but provides no indication of how the remaining values of the data set are located between these extremes, or indeed where the data set is located within the measurement continuum under consideration. For example, if the range of ages in a group of research participants is given as 31 years, this provides no indication of the actual age of the subjects in the sample. The ages could spread from 0 to 31 years, 40 to 71 years, or any combination within physiological limits. Obviously, common sense would help you locate a 'ball park' within which the ages should range. Unless the research was specifically targeting children it would be likely that the youngest possible age would be 18 years; equally specific characteristics of the research design would dictate the appropriate, or necessary, age range. The range used in conjunction with the median will give a more comprehensive picture. For example, a range of 14 years and a median of 26 years would suggest the ages of the research participants were spread between 19 and 33 years (i.e. 14 [range] / 2 = 7, 26 [median] − 7 = 19 years and 26 + 7 = 33 years).

[4.5] *Dispersion* in this instance refers to how 'widely' data points are distributed. It might also refer to the degree to which values in a data set are scattered around a central point, usually the arithmetic mean or median.

Quartiles and Percentiles

The *quartiles* divide the data into quarters. After the data has been ordered, the *lower quartile* represents one quarter of the way into the data set (i.e. the first quarter), and the *upper quartile* represents three quarters of the way into the data set (i.e. the upper boundary of the third quarter). The Median is used in conjunction with these measures, as it is located half way through the ordered data set. The box and whisker plots presented in figures 4.6 and 4.7 are a pictorial representation of the median and the upper and lower quartiles. The quartiles therefore give the data set a location and provides an indication of the size of measurement. The *inter-quartile range* (i.e. IQR) is the difference between the upper and lower quartiles, and measures the spread of the middle half of the data set. Less widely used is the *semi-inter-quartile range*, which measures half of the range of values in the middle 50% of the distribution (i.e. the theoretical spread of 25% of the data in the middle of ordered data set, 37.5%–62.5%). The quartiles and inter-quartile ranges of a data set are illustrated in figure 4.10. *Percentiles* divide a distribution on a percentage basis starting at the lowest value of a distribution. The median thus corresponds to the 50th percentile, the lower quartile corresponds to the 25th percentile, and the upper quartile corresponds to the 75th percentile.

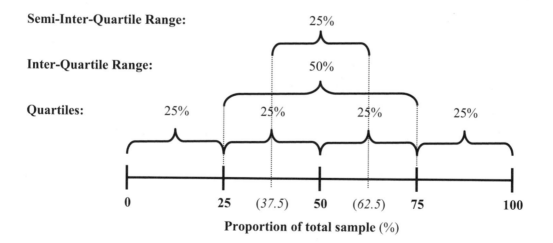

Figure 4.10   Schematic representation of quartiles, the inter-quartile range, the semi-inter-quartile range and percentiles.

The above discussion serves to illustrate how most data sets can be adequately described using the five-value summary (i.e. the minimum, lower quartile, median, upper quartile and the maximum values), discussed with reference to the box and whisker plots earlier in this chapter. However, if you are evaluating central tendency and variability of data prior to performing more powerful forms of statistical analyses (i.e. parametric statistical analyses; refer to chapter 8), then it is important to calculate the *mean* and *standard deviation* (discussed below) of the data set as the summary statistics. These measures form part of the statistical testing procedures in parametric statistics, and are often referred to as part of the decision making process in making judgements about the data.

Variance and Standard Deviation

Variance (S^2) and standard deviation (S) were introduced in chapter 3, where variance was described as a measure of dispersion in data, or the degree to which data are different or divergent, and standard deviation was described as an estimate of the variability of data around the mean. Therefore these summary statistics show how diverse the data are and how representative the mean is of the data set. A large variance and a large standard deviation would indicate a high level of dispersal, or a greater level of spread, in a data set. Statistical software packages readily provide the variance and standard deviation of a data set, as do scientific calculators, however calculation box 4.4 describes the sequence of steps for determining these parameters of a data set.

Calculation Box 4.4   Determining the Variance and the Standard Deviation

1.   Determine the distance of <u>each</u> point from the mean…

2.   Square each of these distances and add the squared values together…

Note: *Due to the way in which the mean is calculated, the distances above the mean will always balance out those below the mean (i.e. taking into consideration + and – values). By squaring the distances this problem is overcome, as all the values will be made positive*

3.   This value is called the <u>sums of squares</u>

4.   Divide the sums of squares by n – 1 (i.e. the number of data values minus one)…

This value is the degrees of freedom (refer to chapter 6; technical box 6.1) for the data set

5.   If data for the entire population has been collected then divide by n (i.e. the total number of data values), rather than n – 1…

…but this does not happen very often as it is very rare to test a whole population

6.   Mathematically, the above stages for determining the variance are summarised by the following formula:

$$s^2 = \frac{\sum_{x=i}^{n}(x_i - \bar{x})^2}{n-1} \qquad \text{or} \qquad s^2 = \frac{\sum_{x=1}^{n} x_i^2 - \frac{\sum_{x=1}^{n}(x)^2}{n}}{n-1}$$

7.   The standard deviation of a data set is the square root of the variance, and is therefore written mathematically as:

$$s = \sqrt{\frac{\sum_{x=1}^{n}(x_i - \bar{x})^2}{n-1}} \qquad \text{or} \qquad s = \sqrt{\frac{\sum_{x=1}^{n} x_i^2 - \frac{(\sum_{x=1}^{n} x_i)^2}{n}}{n-1}}$$

Note: *It is the second of the formulae presented in (6) and (7) that is most commonly presented in books and journals. The formulae are mathematically the same, however the second is quicker to calculate by hand*

We will now work through an example of the calculation presented in calculation box 4.4 with reference to the scoring record of a netball team for five home games. Goals scored were:

$$4 \qquad 6 \qquad 2 \qquad 1 \qquad 9$$

The mean is calculated as follows:

$$\bar{x} \;=\; \frac{4+6+2+1+9}{5} \;=\; \frac{22}{5} \;=\; 4.40 \quad \text{goals} \quad (\ldots\text{this is the sample mean})$$

Applying the second formula from (6) in calculation box 4.4, the variance is calculated as follows:

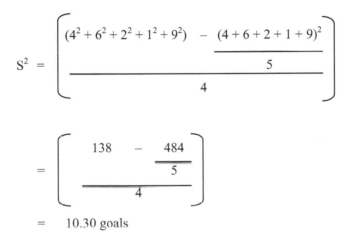

$$S^2 \;=\; \left[\frac{(4^2+6^2+2^2+1^2+9^2) \;-\; \dfrac{(4+6+2+1+9)^2}{5}}{4} \right]$$

$$=\; \left[\frac{138 \;-\; \dfrac{484}{5}}{4} \right]$$

$$=\; 10.30 \text{ goals}$$

From calculation box 4.4, the standard deviation is the square root of the variance, and is calculated as follows:

$$s \;=\; \sqrt{s^2}$$

$$=\; \sqrt{10.3} = 3.21 \text{ goals}$$

The mean of this data set of goals scored during home netball fixtures is 4.40 goals, and the standard deviation is 3.21 goals. The standard deviation is large compared to the mean, and we could therefore conclude that this netball team is not very consistent in terms of scoring goals during home fixtures. Note, actual goals scored will only ever be a whole number – you cannot have a fraction of a goal! Thus, values for the mean and standard deviation of this data set of goals scored should be rounded to 4 and 3 goals respectively.

In reporting data, the mean with either the standard deviation *or* the variance are cited, but not both. It is the standard deviation that is most commonly reported, as the mean and standard deviation in combination are powerful descriptors of a data set. A standard deviation of 'zero' would indicate that all the data points are the same (i.e. equivalent to the mean value). As the standard deviation increases in size, this indicates that the data are more widely spread on either side of the mean value. <u>If the standard deviation is around the same size as the mean value, or even bigger, then it is unlikely that the data set follows a distribution that would be suitable for applying parametric statistical procedures</u> (refer to chapter 5 for further information on data distributions and the applicability of parametric versus non-parametric statistical procedures). If this proves to be the case, then you will need to consider very carefully your next step in analysing your data set.

For small data sets, scientific calculators allow the summary statistics of a data set to be calculated relatively easily. All offer some way for the user to input the data values and their respective frequencies, which are then stored in the memory for subsequent calculations. The specific procedures for data input vary between models of calculators, so it would be appropriate to refer to the calculator handbook. The summary statistics for larger data sets can be calculated using a variety of computer software packages. Nevertheless, the underlying calculations have been presented in this chapter to enable you to understand from where the respective values originate, and consequently how to correctly interpret the data output.

Coefficient of Variation (V)

The *coefficient of variation* provides a measure of the relative variation of a distribution. It does not really sit comfortably with the summary statistics of mean, variance and standard deviation presented in this chapter, but as it provides a further approach to describing the pattern of data distribution it seems appropriate to include it here. Calculation box 4.5 presents the calculation steps for determining the coefficient of variation that, as a ratio measure derived from the sample standard deviation and sample mean, is reported as a percentage (%).

Calculation Box 4.5   Determining the Coefficient of Variation (V)

1. Determine the mean of the data set under consideration, $\overline{x}_s$

2. Determine the standard deviation of the data set under consideration, S_s

3. The coefficient of variation (V) for the sample is given by:

$$V = \left[\frac{100 \times S_s}{\overline{x}_s} \right] \%$$

The coefficient of variation is one approach by which measurement competency might be evaluated. A series of measurements (normally >10) is performed under standardised and controlled conditions. If there were no measurement error or measurement variation, the standard deviation of the resulting data set would be zero, indicating that all readings would be the same and would be equal to the true value. In reality this would not happen, but in practice the lower the coefficient of variation the better the measurement competency or the better the analytical approach. That is unless there is a systematic measurement error or bias; in this case the coefficient of variation may be low, but the measurement would be wrong!

Some Practical Advice…

Before making any decisions about a data set, try to find out as much as possible about it before starting data analysis procedures. This will inform the statistical analysis decision-making process, and will help to ensure that mistakes in data interpretation are not made at the analysis stage of the research study. A worked example of exploratory data analysis is presented in chapter 10.

Measure	Advantages	Disadvantages
Mode	Useful for nominal data that can not be summarised any other way	Very unstable, can be different for each data set drawn from the same research participants, so is only for describing a particular sample – as in survey data
Median	Lacks sensitivity, so good for data where there are outliers	Lack of sensitivity can lead to not seeing differences between two data sets that are in reality quite different
Mean	A good reflection of data set provided there are no outliers	Easily skewed by extremely high or low values, so graphical exploration is essential prior to using means
Range Inter-Quartile Range *…used with the median*	• Easy to compute • Inter-quartile range is less sensitive to extreme data values	• Unstable, a change in a single data item can greatly alter the value
Variance Standard Deviation *…used with the mean* Coefficient of Variation	• Most reliable measure of variability, takes into account the value of every data item • Can be used in further mathematical analyses	• Distorted by extreme values

Table 4.7   Summary of statistics for describing data sets.

Summary/Key Points

1.   Before carrying out any complex statistical work with a data, it is essential to thoroughly explore the data and get a 'feel' for what the raw data may be telling us.

2.   Pictorially representing data through graphical methods is good for gaining an overall impression of the pattern (or distribution) of the data.

3.   Frequency distribution tables (or graphs) are good for identifying values extreme of the main body of the data set (i.e. outliers). Grouping data into appropriately sized classes will improve clarity in discerning the pattern of the data distribution, whilst preserving a reasonable level of definition in terms of the distinguishing features.

4.   Bar charts and histograms are the most common type of graph for illustrating frequency distributions. Bar charts can be used for discrete data sets (where the height of each bar is proportional to the frequency of each item), whilst histograms are appropriate for continuous data (where the area of each bar represents the frequency of each of the ranges).

5.   The shape of a distribution made up of continuous data can also be illustrated by a *frequency polygon*.

6.   *Stem and leaf plots* and *box and whisker plots*, whilst rarely seeing the light of day in scientific publications, are useful approaches for exploring data without the loss of detail associated with other graphical methods. A strength of stem and leaf plots is that, whilst illustrating the shape of the distribution, the actual data values are retained. Box and whisker plots are useful in that we can start to apply objective rules to the data set in the identification of outliers.

7.   Pie charts present data as proportions (or percentages) of the total data set, and are therefore useful for making comparisons between categories (for example in survey data).

8.   Numerical summarisation of data should be conducted once graphical data exploration has been completed. A danger of using numerical summaries alone to explore data is that some of the problems in the data, such as outliers, become hidden and may lead to erroneous conclusions being made.

9.   The choice of measure of central dependency – from *mode*, *median* and *mean* – is dependent upon the level of the data, the nature of the research hypotheses, what you wish to communicate from the data set, and the shape of the data distribution. The purpose of these statistics is to summarise data in a representative way.

10.   Measures of variability describe the spread of the data, the most straightforward of which include *range*, *quartiles*, and *percentiles*. The *variance* and *standard deviation* describe the way data are dispersed around the mean, and therefore give an indication of the data diversity as well as how representative the mean is of the data set.

5

Introducing Inferential Statistics

Chapter Objectives

- To differentiate between descriptive and inferential statistical techniques
- To differentiate between parametric and non parametric tests
- To check data to see if they follow normal distribution parameters.

Introduction

Statistical analysis techniques are research tools that can help you make decisions about the data you have collected. As discussed in chapter 4 they can provide summary information, but they can be further developed using mathematical calculation to provide measures of likelihood that what you have observed will happen again if the experiment or data collection processes were repeated. The *summary* stage uses *descriptive* statistics to describe the data set, where as the second stage uses *inferential* statistics to *measure likelihood* that what is observed in the research sample is happening by chance (i.e. is a fluke!). It is important to note that inferential statistics can only be applied where the sample size is large enough or has been structured so as to be representative of the population from which it was drawn; general statements cannot be made about what might happen in the future if the experiment you have conducted is too limited.

Statistical analyses are only ever as good as the data that have been collected; sophisticated statistics cannot tell you anything worthwhile from poorly collected data. The process of inferential statistics involves formulating hypotheses, and in chapter 2 we discussed the process of formulating the *null* and *alternative (experimental)* hypotheses. Thus, inferential statistics are often discussed in terms of 'hypothesis testing', where possible explanations for the study outcome are mathematically compared and that which achieves greatest support from the data collected is accepted as the more likely explanation.

The statistical test procedure works as follows:

1. A *test statistic* is calculated – this is a mathematical summary of the difference between pre- and post-experiment data, or between two or more groups.
2. This test statistics is compared to a *table of outcomes* – related to the sample size and the type of test used – to assess the likelihood of achieving that value if there was no difference between the pre- and post-data or between the groups (i.e. if the null hypothesis were true).
3. Inferential statistical tests are based on comparing the *means* or *medians* of data sets or groups – which is used will depend on the specifics of the test – to see if the difference between these values is small enough for the groups to be considered as the same, or indeed large enough for the groups to be considered as different (the processes informing whether it is appropriate to compare the means or the medians will be discussed in more detail later in this chapter).
4. This likelihood is measured on a probability scale from zero (impossible) to one (absolutely certain).
5. If the likelihood of the null hypothesis (i.e. there is no real difference between groups) being true is *very small* then it is rejected in favour of the alternative (experimental) hypothesis – this means that we think that it is likely that other samples drawn from the same population, and treated in the same way, would behave in the same way as the experimental sample (i.e. there is a real difference between groups).

6. This likelihood is measured against the *significance level* of the test; it is this that is normally established as 0.05 for most sport and exercise science research that adopts inferential procedures. So the 'very small' reported in step-5 would be anything less than 0.05.

The process of testing considers the result obtained from the test, that is the *test statistic*. The likelihood of the *size* of the test statistic happening by chance is then determined using *distribution tables* for manual calculations, or from the computer printout of test outcomes for computer statistical software packages. This likelihood is expressed as a *probability*, sometimes called the *p-value*. The probability, or p-value, is compared to the significance level of a test, which is commonly 0.05 in sport and exercise science research. If the p-value is *smaller than* 0.05 (i.e. $p < 0.05$), then the likelihood of the result happening by chance is *very small* if the null hypothesis is true. This leads us to *reject* the null hypothesis and *accept* the alternative hypothesis – usually that the intervention has had an effect, or the groups are different, or there is a relationship. While looking at some examples of how the process works in theory, it is important not to lose sight of what is happening in reality. You can obtain 'significant' results from statistical analyses of your data set that are meaningless or nonsensical from a practical perspective. For example, a new starting technique that takes twenty weeks of hard training to master but is shown to improve run time by 1.0 second over the first 100 m of a marathon foot race is, in reality, not likely to be a useful finding despite its 'statistical' significance.

Use of Non-Parametric and Parametric Tests

Before conducting any statistical tests you need to explore your data using some of the descriptive techniques discussed in chapter 4. Do not be tempted to miss this stage out; it may appear too simplistic and not *real* data analysis, but this initial stage provides an opportunity for you to gain a better understanding of your data, and hence, reduce the chances of making mistakes in terms of your analysis decisions. One of the principle decisions that must be made at the outset is whether your data follow a recognised pattern or distribution. If your data set does follow a known distribution then you will be able to apply *parametric* statistical tests to your data set, as the data have known boundaries – or parameters – that may be applied to make sense of the data. In contrast, *non-parametric* tests can be used under less stringent circumstances, where the data do not appear to follow a known pattern. Non-parametric tests are mathematically simpler, and cannot be applied to very complex experimental designs. Parametric tests are regarded as being more powerful than non-parametric tests, that is they are more likely to identify a difference between data sets if one actually exists. However non-parametric tests should not be disregarded; a parametric test applied to data that are of a low numerical level and which do not conform to a recognised distribution pattern may prove meaningless, whilst a non-parametric test applied to the same data could be valuable.

The Normal Curve

The *normal curve* is the most common parametric distribution that sport and exercise science data may follow. Refer to technical box 5.1 for further information, however the essential aspect of the normal distribution is that its shape is symmetric and bell-shaped (figure 5.1). It has a single mode, with mean, median and mode coinciding at the centre (i.e. the highest point of the curve). Approximately 95% of the area lies within two standard deviations of the mean, and almost all (99.7%) of the area lies between –3 and +3 standard deviations. For example, if we consider some data relating to the heights of first year female undergraduate students attending sports related degree programmes at a United Kingdom university, the mean height was measured as 1.64 m with a standard deviation of 0.05 m. Then approximately 95% of the students will be within two standard deviations (either side) of the mean height (i.e. 1.54 m–1.74 m), and nearly all of the students (99.7%) will be within three standard deviations of the mean height (i.e. 1.49 m–1.79 m).

The normal model is particularly good in situations where measurement of people is involved; in the above example, a normal curve fits very well to the heights of female undergraduate sports students. Other examples are mass, distance, speed, and temperature. In many cases where the data collected is discrete rather than continuous (for example questionnaire responses), the normal model is adequate providing the number of respondents is large.

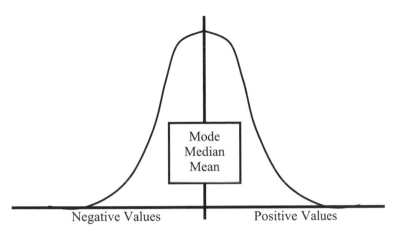

Figure 5.1   Schematic representation of the standard normal distribution.

Technical Box 5.1   The Normal Distributions

There are in fact many normal distributions, all with the same characteristic shape. Each has the same mathematical description expressed in terms of the two parameters μ (mean) and σ (standard deviation)[5.1]. As the same information is known about each normal distribution they can all be transformed into one basic pattern – the **standard** normal distribution – which has $\mu=0$ and $\sigma=1$. To convert from the normal distribution you have observed for your variables (called **X**), to the transformed variables of the standard normal distribution you will need to perform the following operations:

1.   Subtract the mean of your distribution from each of your data points in order to adjust your mean to zero

2.   Divide this value by the standard deviation of your distribution to adjust the spread of the data

(Continued…)

[5.1]   Greek letters are often used to define measurements within a population. Where we use $\bar{x}$ to represent the sample mean, we use μ (pronounced mew) to refer to the population mean. Similarly, s (lower case) is often used to represent the sample standard deviation, while σ (lower case sigma) refers to the population standard deviation.

3.   The mathematical formula to adjust from a non-standard normal random variable $\mathbf{X}$ [5.2] to the standard normal random variable $\mathbf{Z}$ is given by:

$$\mathbf{Z} = \frac{\mathbf{X} - \bar{x}}{s}$$, where $\bar{x}$ is the sample mean and s the sample standard deviation

The areas under the curve between z-values are tabulated in Standard Normal Distribution tables. The tables give probabilities for test statistics if a distribution is normal. Distributions will never be exactly normal, but if they fit between acceptable boundaries of normality (e.g. +2 to –2 on the *skewness* and *kurtosis* ratio checks; refer to calculation boxes 5.1 and 5.2) these probabilities are a good guide. Computer packages compute the probabilities applied in statistical analyses using formulae, which saves you having to look these values up in the tables for yourself

If we now consider the data set from the *Running Study* (appendix: 1), an interesting question to ask is whether the female runners have a lower VO_{2max} than their male counterparts. In determining whether to use a parametric or a non-parametric test to address this question we must first examine the separate distributions of the female and male data; for us to apply parametric test statistics with confidence both groups of data must follow the normal distribution. There are two main approaches to evaluating normality in data sets – visual check and by calculation.

Visual Checks for Normality

Drawing a Histogram

If the data set is drawn as a histogram, as discussed in chapter 4, then this should show a reasonable fit to the characteristic symmetrical bell shape of the normal curve with the majority of the data lying near to the centre. Figure 5.2 presents the VO_{2max} data for the female runners from the *Running Study*. The perfect normal curve for these data has been superimposed (i.e. with the same mean and standard deviation as the sample data). The difficulty is now trying to make sense of the graph; it is helpful to be able to visualise the pattern of data distribution, but it is not clear

---

[5.2]   Upper case X and Z are used to denote the whole variable, while lower case x and z are used to represent each individual observation of the variable.

how close the sample data must be to the ideal curve in order to be considered 'normally distributed'. As you gain research experience it will become easier to identify which distributions are likely to be normal and which are not; whilst this histogram alone will not make that decision, it is an important preliminary check.

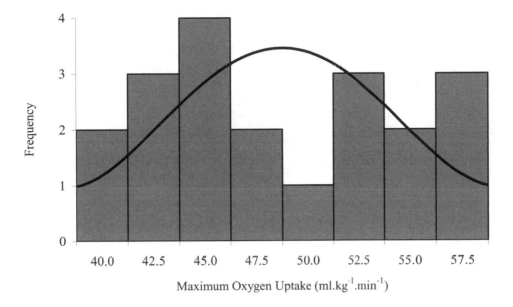

Figure 5.2   Histogram illustrating the VO_{2max} data for the female runners from the *Running Study* with the 'ideal' normal curve superimposed.

Normal Q-Q and P-P Plots

To construct a normal Q-Q plot the grouped frequencies of observed (actual) data values are plotted on Normal Probability paper (i.e. grouped frequencies on the *y*-axis vs. raw scores on the *x*-axis)[5.3]. The data points are evaluated against a line drawn at 45° through the origin (i.e.

[5.3]   The *y-axis* is the vertical axis, and the *x-axis* is the horizontal axis.

through point 0,0), referred to as the line of unity. If the plotted observed values lie along the line of unity, this would indicate that the data were perfectly normally distributed.

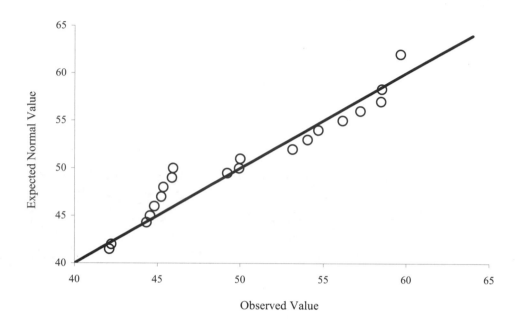

Figure 5.3   Q-Q plot for the female VO_{2max} data from the *Running Study*.

Figure 5.3 presents the Q-Q plot for the female VO_{2max} data from the *Running Study*. In this graph, following the stage of plotting the data on Normal Probability paper, the axes have been re-scaled to reflect the actual units of measure (i.e. millilitres of oxygen per kilogram body mass per minute, $ml.kg^{-1}min^{-1}$). A P-P plot would look very similar but the axes would be scaled to probabilities (i.e. the observed cumulative probability values against the expected cumulative probability values). This graph is read by examining how closely the points are scattered to the line of unity, and that there is no pattern within the scatter (i.e. the scatter is random). The data would not be considered normally distributed if the points were scattered a long way from the line of unity. Equally, if the points snake around the line, or all the points are below or above the line, this would suggest that there is a pattern to the way the data behave in relation to the normal curve and therefore the data are not normally distributed. The points plotted in figure 5.3 do not look too bad, however some calculations can be made to confirm whether the data are normally distributed.

Calculated Checks for Normality

The simplest calculated checks for normality are based on *skewness* and *kurtosis* (figure 5.4). Skewness reflects the amount the data distribution curve deviates from the symmetrical bell shape of the normal distribution. Kurtosis is a measure of the curvature of the model of the distribution, that is whether the graph is too flat or too peaked to be considered bell-shaped. The measures of skewness and kurtosis themselves are fairly complicated to calculate, but statistical computer packages will calculate these for you. The problem with the actual values of skewness and kurtosis is that they are related to the data measurement scales, and so are not easy to directly interpret. However, they too can be standardised similar to the standardisation of the many normal distributions as discussed in technical box 5.1. The way to do this is to divide the skewness by the standard error (SE)[5.4] of the skewness, where the standard error of the skewness is also provided by the computer packages (calculation box 5.1). This gives a standardised value that should fall between –2 and +2 if the data are to be considered normally distributed.

Calculation Box 5.1   Standardised Value of Skewness

The standardised value of skewness is the ratio of skewness to the standard error of skewness, as given by:

$$\frac{\text{Skewness}}{\text{Standard Error of Skewness}}$$

– *value should lie within the range –2 to +2...*

– *values <u>outside</u> this range would lead us to reject the assumption of normality*

[5.4]   The issue of standard error will be revisited later in this chapter with reference to the standard error of the mean.

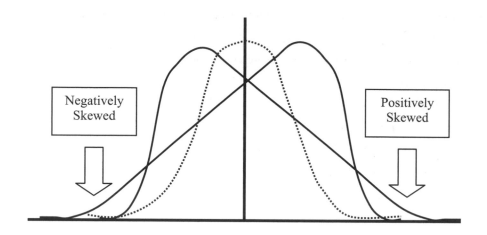

(a)

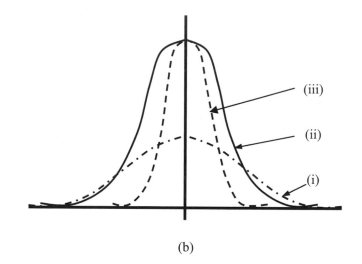

(b)

Figure 5.4   Schematic representation of (a) '*Skewness*' (Note: it is the 'tail' of the distribution
that determines the direction of skew) and (b) '*Kurtosis*' in distribution shapes,
where (i) *Platykurtic* (i.e. flat), (ii) *Mesokurtic* (i.e. average or normal), and (iii)
Leptokurtic (i.e. peaked).

To examine kurtosis in the data, we can treat the kurtosis data in the same way as we did for skewness, that is divide the kurtosis value by the standard error of kurtosis (calculation box 5.2). Similarly, this standardised value of kurtosis should lie between –2 and +2 if the data are to be considered normally distributed.

Calculation Box 5.2   Standardised Value of Kurtosis

The standardised value of kurtosis is the ratio of kurtosis to the standard error of kurtosis, as given by:

$$\frac{\text{Kurtosis}}{\text{Standard Error of Kurtosis}}$$

–   *value should lie within the range –2 to +2...*

–   *values <u>outside</u> this range would lead us to reject the assumption of normality*

As a case example, we will now examine skewness and kurtosis in the VO_{2max} data of the female runners in the *Running Study*. The statistics presented in table 5.1 can be obtained from inputting the data into a statistical analysis computer package (e.g. SPSS™).

Number of participants, n	20
Mean, $\overline{X}$	50.0735
Standard deviation, s	5.90969
Skewness statistic	0.282
Standard error of skewness	0.512
Kurtosis statistic	-1.447
Standard error of kurtosis	0.992

Table 5.1   Descriptive statistics for VO_{2max} of the female runners in the *Running Study*.

Applying the data presented in table 5.1, the standardised values for skewness and kurtosis can be calculated as follows:

1. $$\frac{\text{Skewness}}{\text{Standard Error of Skewness}} = \frac{0.282}{0.512} = 0.551$$

2. $$\frac{\text{Kurtosis}}{\text{Standard Error of Kurtosis}} = \frac{-1.447}{0.992} = -1.459$$

Both the standardised values for skewness and kurtosis fall between –2 and +2, so the female VO_{2max} data appears to be both balanced and to fit within the tolerance values for normal parameters. This data therefore appears to be normally distributed; this is despite the histogram in figure 5.1 not appearing to follow the normal curve very closely. It is important to note that both skewness and kurtosis ratios need to be evaluated as both parameters contribute to defining the shape of a data distribution and evaluating its compliance with the normal distribution. Thus, problems with satisfying either or both parameters could lead you to reject the assumption that the research data follow a normal distribution.

If we consider the male data in the same way, figure 5.5 presents the histogram for the VO_{2max} data of the male runners from the *Running Study* with the 'ideal' normal curve superimposed. The shape of this histogram is about the best you could ever hope to see! It looks certain that the data collected for the male runners will be judged to follow a normal distribution. This view is supported by the data presented in the Q-Q plot (figure 5.6), which shows the data to be tightly clustered around the line of unity. The middle section shows a slight 'snaking' pattern, but this is not very marked.

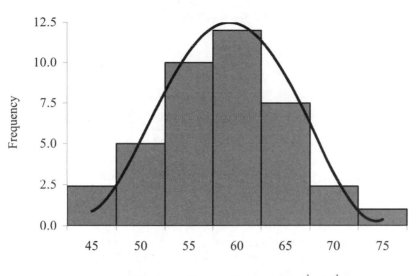

Figure 5.5   Histogram illustrating the VO_{2max} data for the male runners from the *Running Study* with the 'ideal' normal curve superimposed.

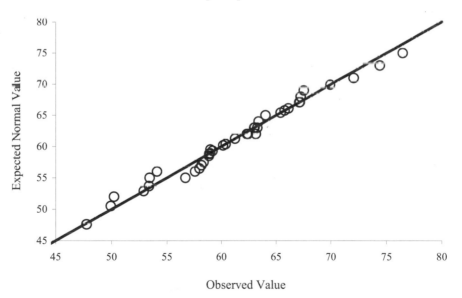

Figure 5.6   Q-Q plot for the male VO_{2max} data from the *Running Study*.

A statistical summary obtained from a statistical software computer package is presented in table 5.2.

Number of participants, n	40
Mean, $\overline{X}$	61.3465
Standard deviation, s	6.40400
Skewness statistic	0.101
Standard error of skewness	0.374
Kurtosis statistic	0.123
Standard error of kurtosis	0.733

Table 5.2   Descriptive statistics for VO_{2max} of the male runners in the *Running Study*.

Applying the data presented in table 5.2, the standardised values for skewness and kurtosis can be calculated as follows:

1.
$$\frac{\text{Skewness}}{\text{Standard Error of Skewness}} = \frac{0.101}{0.374} = 0.270$$

2.
$$\frac{\text{Kurtosis}}{\text{Standard Error of Kurtosis}} = \frac{0.123}{0.733} = 0.168$$

As was the case with the female data, both the skewness and kurtosis ratios for the male runners lie between −2 and +2, so the data can be considered to be symmetrical and follow a normal distribution. Notably, the standardised values calculated for skewness and kurtosis are very small, indicating that these data are very close to the perfect normal distribution. The perfect normal distribution would generate standardised skewness and kurtosis values of zero.

As we are now in a position to be confident that both the female and male data for VO_{2max} in the *Running Study* follow normal distributions, we can return to the question posed earlier in this chapter and to apply a parametric test to examine whether the female runners have a lower VO_{2max} than their male counterparts.

If the data had not followed a normal distribution, further considerations would be needed. As data relating to VO_{2max} are ratio level measurements, the data are of a high enough level to be examined using a parametric test. If the data had not followed normal parameters, but had been fairly close, it is still possible to use a parametric test as it will tolerate some violations of the underpinning assumptions. Parametric tests are known to be *robust*, that is they still function in the required way even if all the assumptions are not met. However, if the two sets of data you are working with are very different in distribution, and one is well outside the normal distribution parameters, then a non-parametric test is the reliable choice. Further difficulties arise when making decisions about parametric and non-parametric testing in more complex experimental designs. Some of these will be addressed in the worked example of a research study presented in chapter 10.

Postscript: Standard Error of the Mean (SEM)

If large, random samples of equal size are repeatedly drawn from any population, the Central Limit Theorem states that the means of each of these samples will be approximately normally distributed, following the same bell-shaped pattern as illustrated in figure 5.1. Furthermore, the mean of this distribution of means will be approximately equal to the population mean. The standard deviation of the theoretical distribution of sample means is called the *standard error of the mean* (calculation box 5.3). As it provides an indication of the distribution of sample means about the population mean, the standard error of the mean provides a measure of sampling error. When reporting mean data it is essential to provide an indication of the potential variation in that data, and as such researchers in the sport and exercise science will report either the standard deviation or the standard error of the mean. The choice of preferred parameter will vary between the sport and exercise science sub-disciplines, and indeed between authors and research groups, such that there is no readily applied rule of thumb. The best advice is to focus upon the information that needs to be conveyed: when describing your research participants it is probably most relevant to report the standard deviation of their mean characteristics (providing an indication of the possible diversity of the research sample); whilst in reporting outcomes we may be more concerned with providing an indication of the sampling error alongside the actual values and therefore should report the standard error of the mean. Alternatively, if our research sample is small we may take the decision that sampling error will consequentially have arisen and that it would be more meaningful to present all the means with a corresponding value for data spread (i.e. the standard deviation).

Calculation Box 5.3   Standard Error of the Mean (SEM)

The standard error of the mean is derived as follows:

$$\text{SEM} = \frac{s}{\sqrt{n}}$$

where,   s is the sample standard deviation

n is the sample size

Summary/Key Points

1.   Statistical analysis techniques are research tools that can help you to make decisions about your data.

2.   The summary stage uses *descriptive statistics* to describe the data set, where as the second stage of data analysis uses *inferential statistics* to measure likelihood that what is observed in the research sample is happening by chance.

3.   Always explore your data using descriptive techniques before conducting any statistical tests.

4.   The statistical test procedures require a *test statistic* to be calculated, which is compared to a *table of outcomes*. Inferential statistics compare the means or medians of data sets to see if the difference between these values is small enough for the groups to be considered the same.

5.   This likelihood – of whether the groups can be considered the same – is measured on a probability scale from 0.0 (impossible) to 1.0 (absolutely certain), and is evaluated against the *significance level* of the test (conventionally 0.05 in the sport and exercise sciences).

6.   One of the principle decisions that must be made about your data is whether it follows a recognised pattern or distribution. If it does, then *parametric statistical tests* can be applied, as your data has known boundaries or parameters. *Non-parametric tests* can be applied under less stringent circumstances.

7.   The normal curve is the most common parametric distribution that sport and exercise science data may follow. The pattern is symmetrical about the mode, median and mean (which are coincidental at the centre – highest point – of the curve), and bell-shaped.

8.   Visual checks of normality include drawing a histogram of the data (which should follow the bell shape of the normal curve with the majority of the data lying near the centre), a normal Q-Q plot where the frequencies of observed values are plotted on normal probability paper (where normally distributed data points should lie along the line of unity), and P-P plots (similar to Q-Q plot excepted the axes are scaled to probabilities – the observed values are plotted against the probability of the expected value).

9.   Calculated checks of normality include skewness (the amount the data distribution deviates from the normal distribution), and kurtosis (a measure of curvature – whether the curve is too flat, *platykurtic* , or too peaked, *leptokurtic*).

10.   The standardised ratios for skewness and kurtosis should fall between –2 and +2 for the data to be normally distributed. The perfect normal distribution would generate standardised skewness and kurtosis ratios of zero.

6

Looking at Relationship and Association:
The Relationship Between Variables

Chapter Objectives

- To identify levels of data suitable for a variety of measures of association or correlation

- To conduct and interpret statistical tests for these relationships

- To identify which measurement of correlation or association is appropriate for particular data.

Introduction

When looking at the data collected during your investigation, one issue of relevance is to examine whether there are any relationships between the different variables measured. For example, in a sporting context it might be useful to determine if the volume of training undertaken by an athlete is associated with improvements in performance and possibly with their finishing positions in races. Alternatively in an occupational context where different forms of physical or psychometric selection tests may be implemented, it is important to be able to determine whether more people are likely to pass one kind of test than another. If the data are of a *high enough level* (i.e. ordinal, interval or ratio levels; refer to chapter 4), we can give a measure of *strength* to the relationship.

Furthermore, we can also evaluate whether a relationship observed in data collected from a sample of research participants is *likely* to occur more generally in the population from which the sample was drawn.

The important point mentioned above is that the *level* of the data collected governs the extent to which a relationship can be investigated. You will recall that *nominal data* are simply data that have been coded into categories. As the numbers assigned have no value-based meaning, they cannot be used for any calculations and therefore no strength of relationship can be ascertained. Consequently, nominal data can only be investigated for association between categories. For example, if we consider the data presented in chapter 4 concerning the specialist sports of a group of first year sports students, we might be interested in ascertaining whether there is association between the gender of students and their choice of sport. One question we may wish to challenge the data with is, are male students more likely to take part in contact sports? *Chi-squared tests* (denoted by the Greek symbol χ^2 and pronounced 'K-eye' squared – as in tie or fly) are used to evaluate association in categorised data. That is, data where participants can only be in one category or group; in the specialist sport survey the categories of interest may be male or female, alternatively in the example above contact sport or non-contact sport. In situations where a participant may be placed in more than one group a *Cochran Q test* or a *Mc Nemar's test* can be used, however this will be discussed in greater detail later.

In contrast to nominal level data, calculations can be made on ordinal, interval or ratio level data to determine the direction and the strength of relationship. We can see whether the relationship between variables is such that as one increases so does the other (i.e. a positive relationship), or as one variable increases the other decreases (i.e. a negative, or inverse, relationship).

There are two correlation coefficients[6.1] that can be used to evaluate the *strength* of relationship: *Spearman's rank correlation coefficient* is applied when one or both of the variables contain ordinal level data (i.e. data that have been placed into a rank order on the basis of some identifiable characteristic, where numbers identify the rank of a data point but do not represent equal differences in the attributes being measured); and, *Pearson's product moment correlation coefficient* is used with interval level data (i.e. data, where the values also allow an assessment of the size of difference between observations) or ratio level data (i.e. measurement scales that have both equal intervals and an absolute zero).

Chi-Squared (χ^2) Tests for Nominal Data

There are two different types of chi-squared test – *the χ^2 goodness of fit test* and the *χ^2 test of association* based on the analysis of contingency tables; both examine the association between variables. The simpler test, the goodness of fit test, looks at several categories and determines whether they are all equally likely to occur. The test is also able to examine if the incidence of observations, or the pattern of data, can be predicted or predetermined from previous experience. For example, it may be of interest for a leisure centre to evaluate the popularity of scheduling specific exercise classes at different times in the day; are all the class times *equally* popular with the leisure centre clients? In contrast, it would not be sensible to examine if the incidence of heart attacks *were the same* for men in their twenties, thirties, forties or fifties. In the latter example, intuitively, or based on previous research, you might suggest that there would be an increase in the incidence of heart attacks in the older age groups. Thus, our research hypothesis would reflect an age related pattern, and a χ^2 *goodness of fit test* statistical test would be conducted to see whether the actual data collected *fit* the hypothesised pattern.

[6.1]   Coefficients can generally be thought of as numerical (i.e. numbers) values that represent some form of measurement. In this particular example they will reflect the relationship between the variables being examined.

χ^2 *Goodness of Fit Test*

A χ^2 goodness of fit test is applicable in a situation which gives rise to a series of observations based on one factor. If we return to our heart attack example, unfortunately heart attacks will continue to occur in individuals in society, and each incidence of a heart attack will be recorded as an observation. A χ^2 *goodness of fit test* might be applied to this series of observations to assess if it fits a *predicted pattern*, as defined by our research hypothesis. Data are collected from our research sample – which in this example may be a geographical locality or health authority district – and the number of observations in each age group is entered into a frequency table (refer to chapter 4), where each age group will represent a discrete category in the table. From this discussion we can summarise that the χ^2 *goodness of fit test*:

- Is applied to nominal data in a single sample that can be classified into categories, where each individual can only fit into one category

- Is used to test whether the number, or proportions, of observations in each category in a defined sample corresponds to the expected, or predicted, numbers or proportions

- It is therefore often applied to test whether category numbers or proportions are the same, but this does not have to be the case

The steps to follow for applying a χ^2 *goodness of fit test* are presented in calculation box 6.1.

Calculation Box 6.1 χ^2 Goodness of Fit Test

1. Determine categories for the research data that are mutually exclusive and exhaustive. That is, a research participant or research observation cannot be in more than one group, and every participant/observation must fit into a group

2. We determine a research hypothesis about the distribution (or pattern) of observations, and apply this hypothesis to calculate the corresponding expected (or predicted) frequencies or number of incidents in each category:

   i.e. E_i $(i = 1, ..., n)$ where i is the number of categories

                                             n is the number of observations

   These *expected* frequencies will often be equal (denoting that each observation has an equal chance of occurring), but this is not always the case

3. A research sample is selected (refer to chapter 3), and observations are made giving rise to a series of *observed* frequencies (i.e. the actual number of incidents in each category) category:

   i.e. O_i $(i = 1, ..., n)$ where n is the total number of categories

                                             i is the number of observations

4. The expected value (i.e. E_i) is subtracted from the observed value (i.e. O_i) for each category:

   i.e. $(O_i - E_i)$

5. Each of the values from *step 4* are squared:

   i.e. $(O_i - E_i)^2$

6. Each value from *step 5* is divided by the *expected* value for that category:

   i.e. $\dfrac{(O_i - E_i)^2}{E_i}$

   (Continued…)

7. You will recall that the total number of categories was given by n, thus the test statistic χ^2 is calculated by adding together (i.e. summing, Σ) the values determined in *step 6* for all the categories. Mathematically this is given by:

i.e. $$\chi^2 = \sum_{i=1}^{n} \frac{(O_i - E_i)^2}{E_i}$$

If the *fit* to the data is *poor* then the calculated χ^2 value will be *high*; the worse the fit the higher the χ^2 value

To understand what would be regarded as a "*high*" value, we need to use 'look up' tables related to the distribution of the χ^2 statistic. Look up tables are, normally, books of tables reporting the values contained within a mathematical distribution or pattern. As well as the χ^2 distribution, other common distributions include the normal distribution described in chapter 5, the *t* distribution that will be introduced later in this chapter, and the binomial distribution. To use these tables we need to determine the *degrees of freedom* (i.e. d.f. or ν) for a particular situation. The concept of degrees of freedom is difficult to define; very simplistically we might consider the degrees of freedom in terms of rules governing our selection of numbers – the more rules present the fewer degrees of freedom we can exercise in our number choice. The degrees of freedom will vary with different inferential statistical techniques, however in the χ^2 goodness of fit test the degrees of freedom is always given by the number of categories minus one.

i.e. d.f. = $n - 1$ where *n* is the number of categories

This calculation of the degrees of freedom reflects the simple one factor structure of this series of observations. Refer to technical box 6.1 for a more complete discussion of degrees of freedom. Reported with each distribution in the look up tables are instructions of how the tables should be used in the course of your statistical analyses. If the value from the calculation given in step 7 above is *greater than* the *probability value* given in the χ^2 tables, then the data *do not fit* the hypothesised pattern. If a computer software package is used to conduct the χ^2 goodness of fit statistical test, then the value computed and provided as part of the output analysis is the probability of the test statistic, and a book of 'look up' tables will not be required.

Technical Box 6.1   Degrees of Freedom (d.f. or v)

Degrees of freedom are described in a number of research methods texts to be equal to the number of observations or scores minus the number of parameters that are being estimated. Thus, if N observations were being used to estimate a population mean, where the mean is one parameter, the d.f. would be $N-1$. This is further explained in that if a prescribed number of observations or scores are being used to estimate a parameter about which we might draw conclusions, then as soon as we establish this score or estimate (and prescribe a parameter) the original observations lose a certain amount of freedom – they become located, or tied, relative to that parameter.

This is perhaps better described in terms of an example. If you were asked to select four numbers, you would have total freedom of choice in which numbers you chose for each of the four observations. Therefore you would have 4 d.f.. If you were then instructed that the sum of your four numbers must equal 20, you would still have complete freedom in the selection of the first three numbers but the choice of your fourth number will be dependent upon your previous three choices in order to achieve the final total of 20. If we assume that our first three numbers were 4, 11, and 21, our fourth number would therefore have to be –16:

i.e. $4 + 11 + 21 + (-16) = 20$

Our number choice was restricted on one of the observations – three choices were free, the fourth had *lost* its freedom. Thus, d.f. in this example is given by $N-1 = 4-1 = 3$. If we introduce more restrictions, this will reduce the d.f.. Degrees of freedom will be specifically discussed relative to the different inferential statistical techniques discussed in chapters 6–9.

As a case example, we will now examine the application of the χ^2 goodness of fit test to data obtained during the evaluation of a lifestyle fitness programme. A random sample of forty-eight (i.e. N = 48) smokers participated in a lifestyle fitness programme. The research participants were asked whether they thought an exercise programme would help ease the withdrawal side effects associated with giving up smoking, and were required to respond either 'AGREE', 'DISAGREE', or 'DO NOT KNOW'. The results of the survey were: AGREE (n = 27), DISAGREE (n = 9), and DO NOT KNOW (n = 12).

The χ^2 goodness of fit test was used to test the null hypothesis that opinion is equally divided between the three viewpoints of agree, disagree and do not know. If this null hypothesis was correct and opinion was equally divided, then the number of responses in each category would be 16 (i.e. 48 ÷ 3 = 16). Calculation of the test statistic is best organised using a table, and is described in table 6.1:

	AGREE	DISAGREE	DO NOT KNOW
Observed (O_i)	27	9	12
Expected (E_i)	16	16	16
$O_i - E_i$	11	-7	-4
$(O_i - E_i)^2$	121	49	16
$(O_i - E_i)^2 / E_i$	7.5625	3.0625	1

Table 6.1   Calculation of the χ^2 goodness of fit statistical test from the lifestyle fitness programme.

The sum of the expression $(O_i - E_i)^2 / E_i$ for the three categories (i.e. 'AGREE', 'DISAGREE', or 'DO NOT KNOW') is given by:

$$\chi^2 \;=\; \sum_{i=1}^{3} \frac{(O_i - E_i)^2}{E_i} \;=\; 7.5625 \;+\; 3.0625 \;+\; 1.0000 \;=\; 11.625$$

There are three groups, therefore the degrees of freedom is given by:

d.f. $= 3 - 1 = 2$

If we now refer to look up tables for the χ^2 distribution (refer to appendix: 2), by looking along the row for 2 degrees of freedom (d.f.) and down the 0.05-column (i.e. the 5% level of significance, where the likelihood of the statistic happening by chance is $p < 0.05$), the critical value is given as 5.99. As our calculated χ^2 test statistic of 11.625 <u>is greater than</u> 5.99 the null hypothesis is rejected. The evidence from our data collection does not support the belief that opinion is equally divided, however the type of data collected does not allow any further analysis to be conducted. Nevertheless, if we examine our raw scores this might lead us to suggest that the 'AGREE' and 'DISAGREE' are the source of the difference as these columns show the greatest disparity between the expected (i.e. n−16) and observed values.

One restriction is always present in this statistical test, which is that the sum of the observed values must always equal the sum of the expected values:

i.e. $\displaystyle\sum_{i=1}^{n} O_i = \sum_{i=1}^{n} E_i$

Any other restrictions will depend upon the null hypothesis. However, it should be noted that if any of the expected values is < 5, then two or more adjacent classes or groups (categories) should be merged until the values are all 5 or more. This is because the test will not make reliable decisions based on the behaviour of less than 5 individuals. By combining groups we will reduce the number of degrees of freedom on the one hand, but on the other hand we will ensure that our decisions made on the data are reliable.

The χ^2 Test of Association Based on Contingency Tables[6.2]

The χ^2 goodness of fit test is applicable when data are grouped relative to one factor; in the previous health-related exercise example data were grouped relative to the research participants' opinions concerning exercise and easing the withdrawal side effects associated with giving up smoking. The three groups were mutually exclusive, and exhaustive in that every participant was located within one of the three categories but did not appear in more than one category. However, more complex situations often arise where individuals may be classified according to two, or more, exhaustive sets of attributes. This means that all (i.e. exhaustive) research participants making up the sample must fit into one (i.e. exclusive) category in relation to two, or more, variables. It is of interest to determine whether there is evidence that the classifications of category are independent, or whether there is evidence of association between them. From this discussion we can summarise that the χ^2 *test of contingency table*:

- Is used with *independent* groups or samples each with nominal or ordinal level data in two or more categories
- Is used to examine whether there is association between the variables (each of which contain two or more categories) or whether they are independent

The steps to calculate a χ^2 test of association are presented in calculation box 6.2.

[6.2] A *contingency table* can be described as a sequence of numbers describing the frequency of occurrence of events in each of a number of samples.

Returning to our health-related exercise example addressing forty-eight smokers, we may wish to further categorise our research participants according to their smoking habits; that is, we may differentiate our sample of smokers into 'heavy' smokers and 'light' smokers according to the average number of cigarettes they smoke in one day. Thus, each participant will be either a 'heavy' or 'light' smoker, and will respond with either 'AGREE', 'DISAGREE', or 'DO NOT KNOW' to the research question. In such situations it is of interest to determine whether there is evidence that the classifications or categories are independent or whether there is association. In the present example, we might hypothesise that the response to the research question might be influenced by whether the research participant was a 'heavy' or 'light' smoker; if smoking habits did influence opinion then we would say that there is *association* between the categories. This is where the *contingency table* comes in to play. As each individual is classified based on more than one factor, the contingency table has to have one factor described by the *rows* and the other factor described by the *columns*. This is presented in table 6.2. If there were a third factor, this would be added as a layer over this first table, making a three dimensional construction.

		Variable – 2: *Opinion*		
		Agree	**Disagree**	**Do not know**
Variable – 1: *Extent of smoking habit*	**Heavy Smoker**			
	Light Smoker			

Table 6.2   Contingency data describing the research participants' responses grouped relative to smoking habits.

Calculation Box 6.2 χ^2 Test of Association

1. Set up two classifications (variables) for the data. The classifications must be mutually exclusive and exhaustive (i.e. every research participant/observation must fit into one group for each of the variables)

2. Collect appropriate data from a research sample and classify appropriately into the groups or categories that are relevant for the investigation

3. Set up a two-way table (i.e. a *contingency table*) with the categories within the variables entered in the rows and columns of the table

4. Enter the *observed frequencies* in the table, and determine the totals for each row and each column. These are known as *marginal totals*. The data concerning forty-eight smokers in our health-related exercise example entered into a contingency table would look like this:

	AGREE	DISAGREE	DO NOT KNOW	TOTAL
Heavy Smoker	17	2	4	23
Light Smoker	10	7	8	25
TOTAL	27	9	12	48

5. The null hypothesis is that there is *no association* between the variables. Calculate the *expected frequencies* (their sum must be the same as the sum of the observed frequencies) based on the null hypothesis. If the null hypothesis were true, the marginal totals will all be the same for each expected values, and the frequencies for each group will be equal to reflect that there is not expected to be an association between the categories

6. Choose an appropriate level of significance. You will recall from chapter 3 that this is known as the alpha level and is denoted by the Greek letter α

    (Continued…)

7. Calculate the degrees of freedom, d.f., by applying the following:

    i.e. d.f. = (number of rows − 1) × (number of columns − 1)

8. Refer to 'look up' tables for the χ^2 distribution and identify the critical value for the degrees of freedom (denoted by d.f. in the table) at the level α – that is look <u>along the d.f. row</u> for the degrees of freedom and <u>down the 0.05-column</u> for the significance level of the test

9. Calculate the test statistic using:

$$\chi^2 = \sum_{i=1}^{n} \frac{(O_i - E_i)^2}{E_i}$$

   If the test statistic, χ^2, *is greater than* the tabled value then we must reject the null hypothesis – that is, there is evidence of association between the variables.

   A further correction will need to be made at this point if the degrees of freedom are 1. This will occur in a *two row* by *two column* contingency table, and in this case you would need to apply a correction called *Yates' continuity correction* and the calculation for 2 × 2 contingency tables is modified to:

    i.e. $$\chi^2 = \sum_{i=1}^{n} \frac{(|O_i - E_i| - 0.5)^2}{E_i}$$

   The two vertical lines $|\ |$ denote an *absolute value*. That is the difference between the observed and expected values expressed as a positive number.

The χ^2 test of association examines how closely the data collected or the *observed* values fit with the theoretically *expected* values. It is therefore regarded as an approximation based test, and as discussed previously can give unreliable results if the values in combinations of groups have an expected value of less than 5. This is because the approximation is then based on a theoretical behaviour that has insufficient numbers to generate a reliable comparison. If the expected value is less than 5, the observed value will not have the ability to fluctuate by many making any conclusions questionable. It is not advisable to proceed if more than 20–25% of the group combinations are in this situation of attaining values of less than 5 unless a number of categories can be meaningfully combined. For the same reason it is not advisable to use this test if more than 10% of the group combinations have an expected value of one or less (Cochran and Cox, 1957).

As a case example, we will now examine how the χ^2 test works in a real exercise science situation. A civil engineering company recruited contract engineers to undertake work on oilrigs in the North Sea. As part of a battery of physical, psychometric and professional selection tests, the company also implemented a survival swim test. With changes in health and safety guidelines, specifically in relation to fitness level and cold water survival times, it was felt that it was appropriate to change the format of the swim test. The aim of the swim test was to ensure that all employees working on the oilrigs had an *appropriate level* of swimming ability for their personal safety, therefore the test operated on a pass-fail basis. The company needed to determine whether there was association between the number of passes or fails and the format (old vs. new) of the swim test, as the standard of swimming skill for each group of new employees needed to be the same. Data were collected identifying the swim test undertaken by each candidate and whether they passed or failed the test. The null hypothesis was that the pass-fail rates would be the same for the *old* and the *new* test. The outcome data was: old swim test – pass n=81, fail n=31; new swim test – pass n=69, fail n=43. Table 6.3 presents the contingency table of the observed values and the expected values.

		Pass	Fail	Total
Old Test	**Observed**	81	31	112
	Expected	*75*	*37*	*112*
New Test	**Observed**	69	43	112
	Expected	*75*	*37*	*112*
Total		150	74	224

Table 6.3   Contingency table of the observed values and the expected values for the old and new swim tests.

The expected value for each box (or *cell*) is calculated by multiplying the row total by the column (observed) total, and then dividing by the over all total (i.e. in this example the overall total would be 224):

i.e.   Expected frequency   = $\dfrac{\text{(row total)} \times \text{(column total)}}{\text{over all total}}$

In the present example:

Expected pass frequency   = $\dfrac{(112) \times (150)}{(224)}$ =   75

Expected fail frequency   = $\dfrac{(112) \times (74)}{(224)}$ =   37

It would now be helpful to organise the data in another table to aid calculation of the χ^2 test statistic (table 6.4). The *Yates' continuity correction*[6.3] is included in the end column. Degrees of freedom (d.f.) are calculated as follows.

d.f.   =   (number of rows – 1) × (number of columns – 1)

    = $(2 – 1) \times (2 – 1)$

    =   1

[6.3]   As discussed previously, if the number of categories or cells is only two, such that d.f. = 1, then the calculated χ^2 is likely to be an overestimation, necessitating an adjustment to avoid possible erroneous conclusions. *Yates' correction* for lack of continuity can effect such an adjustment, and involves subtracting 0.5 from the numerator of each category of χ^2 (refer to the end column of table 6.4).

Referring to the look up tables for the χ^2 distribution (appendix: 2), the critical value for 1 degree of freedom (look along the row for 1 degree of freedom) at the 5% level of significance (look down the 0.05-column) is given as 3.84.

Observed (O_i)	Expected (E_i)	$\lvert O_i - E_i \rvert$	$\chi^2 = \sum\limits_{i=1}^{n} \dfrac{(\lvert O_i - E_i \rvert - 0.5)^2}{E_i}$
81	75	6	$(6-0.5)^2 / 75 = 0.403$
31	37	6	$(6-0.5)^2 / 37 = 0.818$
69	75	6	$(6-0.5)^2 / 75 = 0.403$
43	37	6	$(6-0.5)^2 / 37 = 0.818$
Thus…			$\chi^2 \qquad = \qquad \mathbf{2.442}$

Table 6.4   The χ^2 calculation table for the old and new swim tests.

From table 6.4 we can see that the calculated χ^2 test statistic ($\chi^2_{(1)}$ = 2.442) *is less than* the tabulated value of 3.84 (d.f. = 1; α = 0.05). This means that the null hypothesis is accepted – there is no evidence of association between pass-fail rates and the type of swim test undertaken. This would suggest that, from a statistical analysis perspective, the two swim tests are comparable in standard. The reporting convention for the results of this test statistic is given by ($\chi^2_{(d.f.)}$ = … , p= …); for the present example, the test result would be reported as ($\chi^2_{(1)}$ = 2.442, p > 0.05).

Importantly, the χ^2 test of association assumes that different people or different observations comprise each group; the groups are *mutually exclusive* with research participants or research observations only appearing in one group or category. In the previous example evaluating two occupational swim tests, observations were made on 224 different new employees. This has inherent problems; there is every chance that some of the employees are better swimmers than others. As the employees were randomly assigned to either the *old* or the *new* swim test, there is always the possibility that all the better, or poorer, swimmers are, by chance, assigned to the same swim test. If this occurred the outcome to the swim test evaluation would be biased which, in turn, could hide the fact that in reality there are differences between the two tests.

A better, more robust, experimental design would be to have all employees in the research sample complete both swim tests in a randomised order of *old* and *new* swim test. The outcome data from such an experiment would still be nominal level data – the pass-fail and old-new swim test representing data categories. However, these groups of data present in the categories will no longer be mutually exclusive, as each employee participating in the study will appear in two groups and there will therefore be some level of association between the groups. This inherent association means that the χ^2 test discussed above cannot be applied in this situation. If the experimental design is a comparison of 2 groups, then the alternative method of statistical analysis is the *M°Nemar test*; for designs involving more than two groups a *Cochran Q* test is applied. The *Cochran Q* test will be considered in *Using Statistics in Sport and Exercise Science Research – Book 2*.

If the occupational swim test study was repeated in a sub-sample of 49 recruits who all completed both the old and the new swim test, there would only be two possible outcomes – pass or fail – for both tests and therefore the *M°Nemar test* could be applied to the outcome data. Table 6.5 presents all the possible combinations of outcome for a single employee across the two tests, giving four different combinations of outcomes to compare. The end column, number of pairs, provides a count of the number of employees who demonstrated this particular outcome after completing the two swim tests. For example, 21 employees passed both the old and the new swim tests, where as 11 employees passed the old swim test but failed the new swim test, and so on.

Result of Test		
Old Test	**New Test**	**Number of Pairs**
Pass	Pass	21 (a)
Pass	Fail	11 (b)
Fail	Pass	8 (c)
Fail	Fail	9 (d)
Total		**49**

Table 6.5   Outcome combinations for the old and new occupational swim tests.

The *McNemar test* applies the binomial distribution[6.4] to examine the pattern of outcome data. The test uses the idea of equally likely splits between the pass/fail and the fail/pass categories ((b) and (c)), that is the locations where the outcomes are not the same. It computes a test statistic that is an approximation to the χ^2 statistic and then the χ^2 'look-up' table is used to determine whether there is association between the outcome and the test. In the present example, the outcomes of greatest interest are those of the employees who perform differently across the two swim tests as this might highlight potential differences between the tests, thus the middle rows, b and c, are of most interest.

[6.4]   The *binomial distribution* is a distribution that has exactly two possible outcomes for every trial (or test) that takes place. The probability of each of the two outcomes does not have to be equal, although this is assumed to be the case for the McNemar test.

The calculation of the test statistic, χ^2, involves subtracting the smaller of the two values (in this example c) from the larger (in this example b) in order to determine the absolute difference. This absolute difference is then divided by the square root of the two values added together.

i.e. $\chi^2 \quad = \quad \dfrac{|b-c|}{\sqrt{(b+c)}}$

$$\chi^2 \quad = \dfrac{|8-11|}{\sqrt{11+8}} = \dfrac{3}{\sqrt{19}} = \dfrac{3}{4.359} = 0.688$$

As the calculated χ^2 test statistic ($\chi^2 = 0.688$) *is less than* the tabulated χ^2 value of 3.84 (d.f. = 1; α = 0.05), the null hypothesis is accepted – there is no evidence of association between pass-fail rates and the type of swim test undertaken and it appears that the two swim tests are comparable in standard.

If the number of observations is small, the above formula is adjusted as detailed below. Remember that the subtraction of c from b is to determine the absolute size of the difference between these data values. This adjustment is the equivalent of using the Yates' continuity correction in the χ^2 test for a 2 × 2 table. 'Small' is not determined by an actual value, it is a subjective decision based upon the specific details of the study being undertaken.

i.e. $\chi^2 \quad = \quad \dfrac{|b-c|-1}{\sqrt{(b+c)}}$

Correlation

The statistical procedure of *correlation* can be applied to numeric data that can undergo calculation (i.e. data above nominal level). It is another means of evaluating association between two variables (normally denoted by X and Y). As the data have numeric meaning the notion of association can be extended to give a measure of *the extent* to which changes in one factor are *associated* with changes in another. A correlation therefore refers to a quantifiable relationship – in terms of its strength and direction – between two variables, a *bivariate relationship*. It also allows us to evaluate the likelihood of a relationship observed in the experimental sample also being present in the population from which the sample was drawn.

As part of your initial data exploration it is essential to draw a *scatter diagram*, or *scatter plot*, of your raw data. The scatter diagram will allow you to examine the pattern of your data and provide an early indication of whether there is likely to be a linear relationship between the two variables. If the relationship were deemed to be non-linear, then correlations would not be useful in describing the strength of relationship in this situation. There are separate procedures available for evaluating non-linear relationships, but these are beyond the scope of the present text and will be addressed in *Using Statistics in Sport and Exercise Science Research – Book 2*.

In chapter 2 we posed the hypothetical sport biomechanics research question concerning the relationship between lower limb length and performance of the 110 m high hurdle track and field event. We can develop this example here to illustrate some aspects of statistical correlation. If we assume that we have a sample of male high hurdlers drawn from a population of county league standard athletes. Statistical convention is to use X and Y to denote the variables, but x_1 and y_1 to x_i and y_i for the observations within the variable, where 'i' is the number of athletes (or observations). The variables X and Y in this example would be the lower limb length (X) of each athlete and their respective personal best race time for the 110 m high hurdle event (Y). The values of the variables X and Y for each athlete (observation) are plotted as points [(x_1, y_1), … (x_i, y_i)]. Inspection of the *scatter diagram* provides a guide to the direction and extent of the relationship between the variables X and Y, as well as demonstrating whether there is a linear pattern. Figure 6.1 provides schematic examples of scatter diagrams to illustrate the types of patterns we might observe. If high values in one variable are associated with high values in the other variable, and conversely low values are associated with low values, then the correlation is said to be *positive*. The *scatter diagram* points will run from lower left of the diagram to upper right (figure 6.1a). However, if high values on the first variable are associated with low values on the second and *vice versa*, then the *scatter diagram* points will run from upper left to lower right in the diagram, and the correlation is said to be *negative* (figure 6.1b). When the points of a scatter diagram are distributed randomly all over the diagram, with no obvious pattern or directional tendency, this will indicate that there is no correlation between the two variables (figure 6.1c).

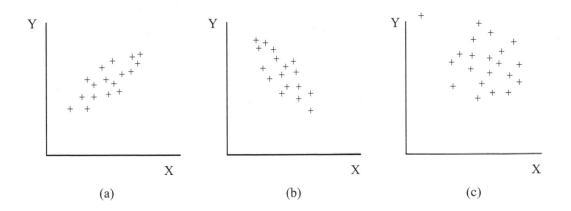

Figure 6.1   Schematic representations of scatter diagrams illustrating (a) positive, (b) negative and (c) no correlations.

The statistic that provides an index of this relationship is termed a *correlation coefficient*; this is a measure of the closeness of the points of a scatter diagram to a straight line. A perfect linear relationship is one in which the points lie exactly on a straight line (sloping either upwards – positive, or downwards – negative). As discussed in chapter 5, if this line passes through the origin [i.e. point (0, 0)], and extends at a 45° angle to both the *x* and the *y*-axes, this line is termed the line of unity. If the line is a perfectly horizontal or perfectly vertical, then the data are not suitable for correlation analysis as there is a specific relationship between the variables that causes this pattern. Rarely in the sport and exercise sciences will data cluster around a straight line, more commonly data points will form a looser cigar or lozenge shape; the wider the lozenge – the greater the spread in the data and the lower the strength of relationship between the two variables. The strength of relationship is denoted by '*r*', which always lies between (−1) and (+1). If the data pairs lie on a straight line where *r* = −1, a *perfect* negative slope is indicated, if *r* = +1 a perfect positive slope is indicated, where as *r* = 0 would indicate a random scatter with no linear relationship.

Correlation coefficients must only be used as an indicator of relationship if the relationship could be described as *linear* (i.e. tending towards a straight line). Figure 6.2 presents a number of scatter diagrams that represent patterns of data distribution that would not suggest the use of linear correlations. Figure 6.2 (a) and figure 6.2 (b) illustrate data sets where there *is* a relationship, but a straight line would not describe these particular relationships satisfactorily. In mathematical terminology these patterns are described by a *quadratic*[6.5] relationship and are pictorially represented by a curve. A measure of linear relationship would not be appropriate to describe this data, and would not reflect the perfect curved relationships of the data. Figure 6.2 (c) shows one data point that is very different from the rest (i.e. an outlier). If we calculated a linear correlation value for this data set, it would be much reduced by the fact that this point is so far removed from the others. Any line that was applied to the data set would therefore not describe anything very well.

[6.5]   Quadratic [equations] are those where one or more terms in the equation are raised to the power of 2, but no more than the power of two.

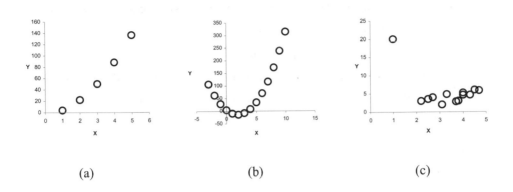

Figure 6.2   Examples of non-linear relationships: (a) and (b) represent quadratic relationships, and (c) represents a data set with an outlier.

It is important to note that computer software packages will perform correlation analyses on any appropriately entered data sets, whether it is statistically correct to do so or not. Consequently, an *r* value will be generated for data sets that may well yield relationships such as those presented in figure 6.2. Therefore it is very important to draw a scatter diagram of your data before undertaking correlation analysis, for only by looking at your plot would you be able to determine if the data were appropriate for linear analyses.

The degree of correlation observed between two variables in one population, may be different in another population. Possibly the relationship itself differs, or its pattern of variability may differ, or the two variables may be influenced by a third variable. This points to two important points to remember about correlations:

1.   When reporting a correlation coefficient, the population should be specified
2.   The correlation between two variables does not mean that change in one variable CAUSES change in the other …only that the changes in the two variables are related to each other. There is often something else that is causing the changes in both variables.

For example, a positive relationship was observed between basketball shooting accuracy and shoe size in primary school children (i.e. aged 4 to 11 years), but foot size does not affect shooting accuracy. Maturational age will affect shoe size through normal growth across this age span, and will also affect shooting accuracy through strength and coordination development as well as greater opportunity to learn and practice this skill.

The precise terms by which numerical correlation values are described in texts varies between authors, between books and between different journal publications. Figure 6.3 provides some of the common words applied to anchor numerical correlation strengths.

Pearson's Product Moment Correlation Coefficient (r_P)

The best-known correlation coefficient is *Pearson's product moment correlation coefficient*, which can be applied to interval or ratio level data. Data do not have to be normally distributed if we are only interested in calculating correlation coefficients. This is an important point to note as many texts infer that this test should be performed on data from distributions with known parameters. Such texts also suggest that if the parameters of the data distribution were not known, then the equivalent non-parametric test would be *Spearman's rank correlation coefficient*, which is described later in this chapter. Evaluating the normality of variable distributions only becomes important if further analyses are required, for example if we need to determine the *confidence interval* for the correlation coefficient. Confidence intervals and their application in statistical analyses will be discussed in greater detail in *Using Statistics in Sport and Exercise Science Research – Book 2*, but suffice to say here that confidence intervals (or levels of confidence) provide a measure of certainty that a value is representative of the population.

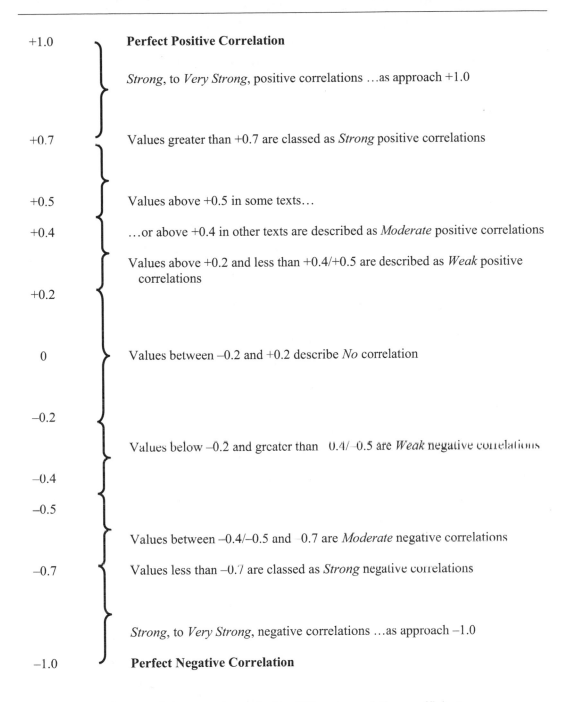

+1.0   **Perfect Positive Correlation**

Strong, to *Very Strong*, positive correlations …as approach +1.0

+0.7   Values greater than +0.7 are classed as *Strong* positive correlations

+0.5   Values above +0.5 in some texts…

+0.4   …or above +0.4 in other texts are described as *Moderate* positive correlations

Values above +0.2 and less than +0.4/+0.5 are described as *Weak* positive correlations

+0.2

0   Values between –0.2 and +0.2 describe *No* correlation

–0.2

Values below –0.2 and greater than   0.4/ 0.5 are *Weak* negative correlations

–0.4

–0.5

Values between –0.4/–0.5 and 0.7 are *Moderate* negative correlations

–0.7   Values less than –0.7 are classed as *Strong* negative correlations

Strong, to *Very Strong*, negative correlations …as approach –1.0

–1.0   **Perfect Negative Correlation**

Figure 6.3   Indicators of the strength attached to different correlation coefficients.

Pearson's product moment correlation coefficient is calculated as follows:

$$r_p = \frac{\sum\limits_{i=1}^{n}(x_i - \bar{x})(y_i - \bar{y})}{\sqrt{\sum\limits_{i=1}^{n}(x_i - \bar{x})^2 \sum\limits_{i=1}^{n}(y_i - \bar{y})^2}}$$

You will find many variations of this formula in the many statistical and research methods textbooks. However this is one of the simplest forms if you need to perform the calculation by hand[6.6], and will aid understanding of the underlying principles in the context of the present discussion.

As a case example, we will now examine data from the 20 female runners who participated in the *Running Study* (table 6.6). Pearson's product moment correlation coefficient will be calculated from this data set to determine if there is a relationship between their maximum minute ventilation (i.e. V_E) in units of litres per minute (i.e. $l.min^{-1}$) and their maximum oxygen uptake (i.e. VO_{2max}) in units of millilitres per kilogram body mass per minute (i.e. $ml.kg^{-1}min^{-1}$). First, we must draw a scatter diagram of the data to evaluate whether it is a sensible relationship to explore, in that there is a definite linear tendency apparent in the data. Figure 6.4 presents a scatter diagram of maximum minute ventilation (*x*-axis) against maximum oxygen uptake (*y*-axis) for the 20 female runners.

[6.6] Small differences may arise between values derived through calculations undertaken by hand (i.e. manual) and computer software derived values, as a computer retains a high number of decimal places in data during long calculations. For manual calculations it is customary, depending upon your measurement sensitivity, to report data in tables to 2 decimal places and to report up to 3 decimal places in outcome data. This will necessitate the 'rounding' of decimal numbers part-way through calculations, where the convention for rounding is to round up if the next number is ≥ 5 (e.g. rounding to 2 decimal places: 23.4_53_451 would be reported as 23.4_5_; and 23.4_57_453 would be rounded up and reported as 23.4_6_). Thus, small differences between computer derived and manually derived outcome data may simply be due to such *rounding errors*.

V_E (l.min^{-1}) (X)	VO_{2max} (ml.kg^{-1}min^{-1}) (Y)
84.90	54.68
107.50	59.65
91.40	57.21
105.40	58.46
92.38	49.93
93.85	45.23
94.20	45.88
86.45	44.35
96.44	54.03
83.53	42.12
78.71	44.82
76.60	45.36
92.64	56.14
83.03	42.24
79.29	49.22
99.59	53.13
82.51	45.95
103.10	58.51
84.00	44.56
94.50	50.00

Table 6.6   Maximum minute ventilation (V_E) and maximum oxygen uptake (VO_{2max}) data for the 20 female runners who participated in the *Running Study*.

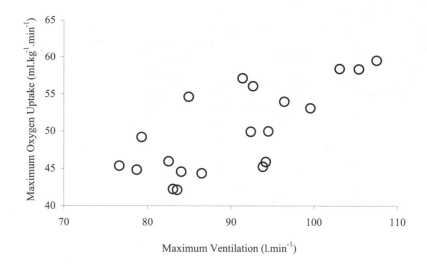

Figure 6.4   Scatter diagram of V_E (l.min^{-1}) against VO_{2max} (ml.kg^{-1}min^{-1}) in female runners in the *Running Study* (n=20).

From figure 6.4 it is evident that there is a linear tendency in the data and it would therefore be appropriate to calculate Pearson's product moment correlation coefficient. Similar to determining χ^2, where mathematical calculations were made on each variable in the data set, determination of Pearson's product moment correlation coefficient also requires calculations to be made on every variable and is therefore best completed by recording each step in a table (table 6.7). Referring to the equation for calculating Pearson's product moment correlation coefficient, we must first determine the mean values for the two variables, maximum minute ventilation and maximum oxygen uptake X and Y (i.e. $\bar{x}$ and $\bar{y}$ respectively). The next step is to subtract these mean values from each of the respective data values of X and Y; these calculations are presented in columns 3 and 4 of table 6.7. The product of the values derived in columns 3 and 4 is given in column 5, and the squares of the values in columns 3 and 4 are given in columns 6 and 7 respectively.

V_E (X)	VO_{2max} (Y)	$(x_i - \bar{x})$	$(y_i - \bar{y})$	$(x_i - \bar{x})$ $\times (y_i - \bar{y})$	$(x_i - \bar{x})^2$	$(y_i - \bar{y})^2$
84.90	54.68	-5.60	4.61	-25.82	31.36	21.25
107.50	59.65	17.00	9.58	162.86	289.00	91.78
91.40	57.21	0.90	7.14	6.43	0.81	50.98
105.40	58.46	14.90	8.39	125.01	222.01	70.39
92.38	49.93	1.88	-0.14	-0.26	3.53	0.02
93.85	45.23	3.35	-4.84	-16.21	11.22	23.43
94.20	45.88	3.70	-4.19	-15.50	13.69	17.56
86.45	44.35	-4.05	-5.72	23.17	16.40	32.72
96.44	54.03	5.94	3.96	23.52	35.28	15.68
83.53	42.12	-6.97	-7.95	55.41	48.58	63.20
78.71	44.82	-11.79	-5.25	61.90	139.00	27.56
76.60	45.36	-13.90	-4.71	65.47	193.21	22.18
92.64	56.14	2.14	6.07	12.99	4.58	36.85
83.03	42.24	-7.47	-7.83	58.49	55.80	61.31
79.29	49.22	-11.21	-0.85	9.53	125.66	0.72
99.59	53.13	9.09	3.06	27.82	82.63	9.36
82.51	45.95	-7.99	-4.12	32.92	63.84	16.97
103.10	58.51	12.60	8.44	106.34	158.76	71.23
84.00	44.56	-6.50	-5.51	35.82	42.25	30.36
94.50	50.00	4.00	-0.07	-0.28	16.00	0.01

$\bar{x} = 90.50$ $\bar{y} = 50.07$

$\Sigma = 749.61$ $\Sigma = 1553.61$ $\Sigma = 663.52$

Table 6.7   Calculation table for Pearson's product moment correlation coefficient for maximum minute ventilation (V_E) and maximum oxygen uptake (VO_{2max}) data of the 20 female runners who participated in the *Running Study*.

From table 6.7 we can fill in the formula to calculate the Pearson's product moment correlation coefficient:

$$r_p = \frac{\sum_{i=1}^{n}(x_i - \bar{x})(y_i - \bar{y})}{\sqrt{\sum_{i=1}^{n}(x_i - \bar{x})^2 \sum_{i=1}^{n}(y_i - \bar{y})^2}}$$

$$r_p = \frac{749.61}{\sqrt{1553.61 \times 663.52}}$$

$$r_p = \frac{749.61}{1015.31} = 0.738$$

If we refer back to figure 6.3, $r_p = 0.738$ suggests that there is a strong, positive correlation between V_E and VO_{2max} for this particular sample of 20 female recreational runners. Interesting though this finding may be, and whilst there is a logic to this observation for the population as a whole, it does not provide any indication of whether we can have any confidence in there being a relationship in the population of female recreational runners as a whole. In order to evaluate whether a correlation is indicative of a population relationship we need to conduct a further test on the data, which applies the standard error of the estimated correlation. As discussed in chapter 5, *standard error* (SE) refers to the estimated standard deviation of a parameter, the value of which is not known exactly. For example an estimate of the population mean will be obtained from a sample, but we accept that it will change slightly with each different sample we look at and will only ever be representative of where the population mean might be (i.e. standard error of the mean, SEM). The standard error is a way of evaluating the potential extent of fluctuation of the population parameter. In this instance we are referring to the error in our estimated correlation, and the formula for calculating standard error of the estimated correlation, *SE (r_p)*, is given by:

The formula used is $SE(r_p) = \sqrt{\dfrac{1-(r_p^2)}{n-2}}$ and, $t = \dfrac{r_p}{SE(r_p)}$

The formula for *SE (r_p)* uses the strength of relationship that has been calculated (i.e. r_p), and the size of the sample (i.e. number of observations, n) used in the calculation of that value. In practice we are evaluating the *magnitude* of the *potential error* given the *strength of the relationship* determined in that particular *size of sample*. The next stage, the determination of *t*, normally requires the assumptions of normality to have been satisfied. The *errors* for the correlations are assumed to follow a normal distribution, and are used to calculate a test statistic that follows a *t-*distribution[6.7]. The look up table for the *t* distribution is given in appendix: 3. If the *t* statistic we obtain from the previous calculation is *greater than* the *t* statistic in the look up table for the appropriate degrees of freedom, then we can determine the level of probability that the relationship seen in the sample is likely to be representative of the relationship in the population. In using the look up table we must first determine the degrees of freedom for this statistical comparison. In this example, two variables (V_E and VO_{2max}) are being compared and n = 20. Therefore the degrees of freedom are given by:

d.f. $-$ n   2   where,   n is the number of observations

d.f. $-$ 20   2 = 18

[6.7]   The non-normal *t-distribution* follows a similar pattern to the normal distribution but is influenced by sample size. As samples become smaller, their distributions become flatter and more spread out. Thus there are different t-distributions for each sample size.

So for our correlation of $r_p = 0.738$ ($r_p^2 = 0.545$), calculated from a sample of 20 female recreational runners, the t statistic is given by:

$$SE(r_p) = \sqrt{\frac{1 - 0.738^2}{20 - 2}} = \sqrt{\frac{1 - 0.545}{18}} = \sqrt{0.025} = 0.158$$

$$t_{(18)} = \frac{0.738}{0.158} = 4.671$$

Looking up $t_{(18)}$ in the table (appendix: 3), at the 5% level of significance (i.e. $\alpha = 0.05$) the t-statistic is 2.101. Our t statistic (i.e. 4.671) is *greater than* the tabulated value (i.e. 2.101), therefore the correlation between V_E and VO_{2max} is said to be significant and it is likely that this result is indicative of a relationship in the population (the reasons behind being able to say this will be explained more fully in chapter 8). The reporting convention for the results of this test statistic is given by ($r_p = \dots$, p = ...). Thus, for the present example, we might conclude that there was a linear relationship between V_E and VO_{2max} in female runners ($r_p = 0.738$, p < 0.05). Calculation box 6.3 summarises the steps in the determination of Pearson's product moment correlation coefficient.

You will note that for both the χ^2 test statistic and Pearson's product moment correlation coefficient, we have suggested that the reporting convention takes the form of ([*test statistic*] = ..., p = ...). Computer software packages are considered to be more sensitive than traditional manual methods of calculation that involve look up tables. With look up tables you are only able to make decisions in terms of the distribution values reported in the tables for significance levels of 0.05 or 0.01, where these levels have been arrived at through research conventions. In contrast, computers are able to generate exact values from mathematical functions describing the distribution of interest (e.g. normal, χ^2, t or binomial distributions). Consequently, computer derived outcome data will generally report the actual p-value as 'p = ...' rather than 'p < 0.05 or 0.01' or 'p > 0.05'. The strength of reporting the actual p-value is that it is then left to the reader to decide how important this observation is, given the specific details of the experimental design. For example, if we refer back to the occupational swim test study, the actual p-value was p = 0.08 and we accepted the null hypothesis based on the test significance level being set at p < 0.05. However, in certain situations (e.g. small sample size, participant heterogeneity, small population effect size of intervention, high procedural variation, and poor measurement sensitivity), a p-value of 0.08 would suggest a good chance of a difference (i.e. [1.00 – 0.08] is 92% confident).

Calculation Box 6.3   Determination of Pearson's Product Moment Correlation Coefficient

1.   Table the data for the two variables, X and Y, being compared

2.   Calculate the mean values, $\bar{x}$ and $\bar{y}$, for the variables X and Y respectively

3.   Calculate and table the respective values for $(x_i - \bar{x})$, $(y_i - \bar{y})$, $(x_i - \bar{x}) \times (y_i - \bar{y})$,

   $(x_i - \bar{x})^2$ and $(y_i - \bar{y})^2$

4.   Determine the sum for each column $(x_i - \bar{x})$, $(y_i - \bar{y})$, $(x_i - \bar{x}) \times (y_i - \bar{y})$, $(x_i - \bar{x})^2$ and

   $(y_i - \bar{y})^2$

5.   Calculate the test statistic using:

$$r_p = \frac{\sum_{i=1}^{n} (x_i - \bar{x})(y_i - \bar{y})}{\sqrt{\sum_{i=1}^{n} (x_i - \bar{x})^2 \sum_{i=1}^{n} (y_i - \bar{y})^2}}$$

6.   To determine the significance of this correlation coefficient for these variables we must then calculate the standard error of the estimated correlation, and the test statistic t, which are given by:

$$SE(r_p) = \sqrt{\frac{1 - (r_p^2)}{n - 2}} \quad \text{and} \quad t = \frac{r_p}{SE(r_p)}$$

(Continued…)

---

7. Calculate the degrees of freedom, d.f., by applying the following:

   i.e.   d.f. $= n - 2$ where n is the number of observations

8. Refer to 'look up' tables for the t distribution (appendix: 3) and identify the critical value for d.f. degrees of freedom at the level α – that is look <u>along the d.f. row</u> for the degrees of freedom and <u>down the α column</u> for the significance level of the test

9. If the test statistic, *t*, *is greater than* the tabled value then the correlation is said to be significant at the α-level.

Spearman's Rank Correlation Coefficient (r_s)

Spearman's rank correlation coefficient is used in the same way as Pearson's product moment correlation coefficient. In contrast, however, when either one or both of the variables contain ranked (ordinal level) data, Spearman's rank correlation coefficient should be applied. Remember, Pearson's product moment correlation coefficient can only be used to calculate the strength of relationship between variables that are interval or ratio level data. To illustrate this point, let us now reconsider the data collected on the twenty female runners in the *Running Study*; suppose our data for V_E and VO_{2max} was only collected in terms of rank order – that is we would know which was the highest value, which was the lowest value, and the relative order of values in between. Thus, the data presented in table 6.6 are now presented in rank order in table 6.8a.

Spearman's rank correlation coefficient is calculated by looking at the difference in rank (*d*) between the variables for each individual. The formula used for the calculation of Spearman's rank correlation coefficient is:

$$r_s = 1 - \frac{6\sum_{i=1}^{n} d_i^{\,2}}{n(n^2 - 1)}$$ where d_i is the difference in ranks for each participant

Rank of V_E	Rank of VO_{2max}	Rank difference (*d*)	Rank difference Squared (*d²*)
8	15	-7	49
20	20	0	0
10	17	-7	49
19	18	1	1
11	11	0	0
13	6	7	49
14	8	6	36
9	3	6	36
16	14	2	4
6	1	5	25
2	5	-3	9
1	7	-6	36
12	16	-4	16
5	2	3	9
3	10	-7	49
17	13	4	16
4	9	-5	25
18	19	-1	1
7	4	3	9
15	12	3	9
			$\Sigma=428$

(a)   (b)

Table 6.8   Maximum minute ventilation (V_E) and maximum oxygen uptake (VO_{2max}) data for the 20 female runners who participated in the *Running Study* expressed in rank order (a). Spearman's rank correlation coefficient calculations (b).

As with Pearson's product moment correlation coefficient, Spearman's rank correlation coefficient is best calculated by using a table to record each calculation step in the equation (table 6.8b).

Using the information determined in table 6.8b, we can calculate the Spearman's rank correlation coefficient, r_s:

$$r_s = 1 - \frac{6\sum_{i=1}^{n} 428}{20(20^2 - 1)} \quad = 1 - \frac{2568}{7980} \quad = 1 - 0.322 \quad = 0.678$$

To check whether this moderate correlation is significant (or statistically generalisable, or not due to chance) the same calculation as for the significance of Pearson's product moment correlation coefficient can be applied together with look up tables for the t distribution (appendix: 3). You may also find look up tables for Spearman's rank correlation coefficient, these are published in many statistical texts and may be used alongside this calculation.

It is important to note that whilst both correlation coefficients were calculated from the same sample of research participants (i.e. the sample of female runners), the value determined for Pearson's product moment correlation coefficient was *stronger* than that determined for Spearman's rank correlation coefficient (i.e. $r_p = 0.738$ vs. $r_s = 0.678$). In real terms this difference is not that great, but this point serves to illustrate that as the data used for Pearson's product moment correlation coefficient is of a *higher level*, this measure can be more sensitive to the presence, or not, of actual relationships between variables.

Misapplications of Correlations

In conducting research in the sport and exercise sciences, generally we are concerned with examining whether there is a relationship (i.e. association), or a difference, between variables. In terms of the former, correlation coefficients are occasionally determined in situations that are not consistent with the principles underlying these statistical analyses. In the sections below we will discuss a number of considerations and common errors in the application of correlation coefficients.

Sample Considerations

First, it is important to consider the sample, drawn from the population of interest, in which we wish to examine association. It should go without saying at this point that our research sample must reflect the characteristics and behaviour of the wider population; as you will recall from chapter 3, this can usually be confirmed by various approaches to post hoc justification. Furthermore, the selection of the sample should be randomised (though we have discussed previously the difficulties of selecting a truly random sample); if the sample is non-random then any calculation of correlation may not be reflective of the relationship between variables. Equally, we should consider our sample size; it is essential that our sample is large enough to ensure that a single research participant or data point does not exert a disproportionately large influence over the calculation of relationship. Correlations performed on small data sets (e.g. n < 15 to 20) should be viewed with a healthy dose of scepticism! Conversely, very large sample sizes will always yield a statistically significant correlation, but the actual strength of this correlation may not necessarily be meaningful in practice.

Finally, it is important to check that your research sample does not contain different sub-groups. Obvious sub-groups in the sport and exercise sciences would be to differentiate research participants in terms of male and female. To understand the influence of these sub-groups on the determination of relationship, we will consider a case example based upon the relationship between time spent per week performing volitional physical activity (i.e. recreational sport and exercise) and percentage body fat. Intuitively we would suggest that those individuals who are physically active for longer each week would have a lower percentage body fat. Indeed, a correlation performed on a sample of males, or a sample of female, would provide evidence to support a strong relationship between these two variables.   However, if a correlation was performed on a mixed sample of male and female research participants, this comparison would not be appropriate as body composition is known to vary between males and females. This example of the influence of sub-groups on the determination of relationship is somewhat contrived, perhaps less obvious examples might include markers of fitness where the sub-groups may reflect sporting preference, some mode of skilled performance where sub-groups may arise due to right or left hand dominance, or measurements of range of motion about a joint where sub-groups may arise from injury history, or evaluation of attitudes to exercise where sub-groups may arise due to socio-economical groups.

Time Factor

Conducting research where variables are recorded over time is likely to yield larger correlation values than might be rationally expected. Such values may be referred to as *spurious correlations*, in that an enhanced impression of a relationship is presented. Almost all variables measured repeatedly over time will correlate. Thus, if you really wish to determine correlation values on variables that have been collected over time, any time related trends must first be removed. If our research design is such that we wish to make a baseline (i.e. initial or time zero) measurement, and then monitor the change in that measure over time, a correlation of this data will again yield a falsely high reading. This is because our initial measurement at time zero will partly define or underpin, all subsequent measurements. As a consequence, the baseline measure will always have a relationship with any subsequent measures.

As a case example from the exercise sciences, consider how a healthy living programme – designed to reduce blood pressure – might be evaluated. Specifically, we might be interested in evaluating whether the effectiveness of the programme is related to an individual's blood pressure at the start of the programme. The baseline measure would therefore be the initial blood pressure reading (BP_1). The second measure would be the change in blood pressure from this initial value to a measure taken at some future point in time, say for example after four weeks of participating in the programme (BP$_4$). Thus the difference (i.e. ΔBP) between the initial blood pressure and the 4-week blood pressure readings is given by:

$$\Delta BP = BP_1 - BP_4$$

The variables we would be correlating would be the initial blood pressure (i.e. BP$_1$) and the difference in blood pressure from the baseline measure to the measure taken in week-4 (i.e. the change in blood pressure over 4 weeks, ΔBP). As the initial blood pressure measure is constituent of both measures in this correlation, there will always be a strong correlation between the variables. This would happen even if the healthy living programme did not actually reduce blood pressure.

Alternatively, if you take the average of the initial reading (BP$_1$) and the week-4 reading (BP$_4$), that is:

$$\overline{BP}_{1-4} = \frac{BP_1 + BP_4}{2}$$

A correlation of the change in blood pressure (i.e. ΔBP) and the mean blood pressure over the 4-week programme (i.e. BP$_{1-4}$) will be more indicative of the actual relationship you wished to explore. This is an important issue in the sport and exercise sciences, as frequently you will encounter research designs where the relationship between a baseline measure and the same measure at some future point in time is examined. The problem being that the baseline measure, by its very nature, will always be related to the same measure taken at some point in the future. For example, a talent identification programme might chose to evaluate sprinting performance in young children as an indicator of future sprinting potential, and hence identify those young athletes who might best benefit from early exposure to appropriate coaching and scientific support. Whilst we accept that there are many factors that will ultimately contribute to elite performance in any sport, it is logical to suggest that having the right physical and physiological make-up from the start has to be a fairly strong component. Consequently, being able to sprint fast as a child, though not necessarily technically well, should be an indicator of future potential. A correlation between initial (i.e. youth) sprinting speed and senior sprinting speed would always yield a value indicative of a strong relationship, and therefore this needs to be taken into account when making such a comparison, such that the *real* strength of relationship is determined.

Looking for Agreement Between Measures

In the sport and exercise science literature, a number of researchers have chosen to apply correlation analyses to evaluate the agreement between different methods of measurement. For example, you may wish to evaluate the agreement between two different approaches to estimating percentage body fat in a specified population. Our chosen approaches may be an estimation based upon the measurement of skin-folds using instrumented anthropometric callipers, and an estimation based upon the measurement of electrical impedance (i.e. bio-electric impedance analysis or BIA). Both approaches are relatively easy and quick to undertake by trained personnel, and are therefore extensively used in applied sport and exercise science research. A correlation between data obtained from these two methods is likely to be high – after all they are attempting to estimate the same physiological parameter. However, a strong correlation in this context only serves to show that the values are related, not that the two methods are the same. If, for example, one method always resulted in values that were twice the values obtained from the other method, a correlation on this data would yield a perfect positive correlation (i.e. $r = +1$).

e.g.   Percentage body fat (%) determined from sum of skinfolds, X: 5, 6, 7

Mean percentage body fat (%) from sum of skinfolds, $\bar{x}$:   6

Percentage body fat (%) determined from BIA, Y: 10, 12, 14

Mean percentage body fat (%) from BIA, $\bar{y}$:   12

But quite evidently these two sets of data would not be the same, and therefore the two methods are not in agreement. There are a number of approaches that will allow us to more satisfactorily evaluate agreement between data sets, and these will be discussed in greater detail in *Using Statistics in Sport and Exercise Science Research – Book 2*.

Chapter Decision Tree

Figure 6.5 presents an overview of the questions you should ask prior to examining relationships and association, and the resulting decision processes as described in this chapter.

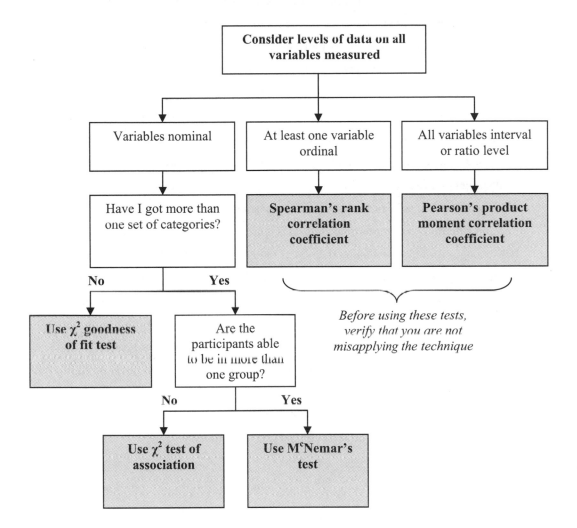

Figure 6.5   Decision tree for looking at relationship and association.

Summary/Key Points

1.   The extent to which relationship can be measured is dependent on the level of data; if the data are ordinal, interval or ratio we are able to give a measure of strength to the measure.

2.   Association in nominal level data can be evaluated by the χ^2 *goodness of fit test* (where observations are based on one factor divided across a number of exclusive categories), the χ^2 *test of association* (where observations are based on two or more factors each divided across a number of exclusive categories), and *M'Nemar's test* for cases where each individual can be in two groups.

3.   A correlation refers to a quantifiable linear relationship – in terms of its strength and direction –between two variables. A scatter diagram or scatter plot should be drawn from the data to evaluate linearity prior to any calculations; separate procedures are available for evaluating non-linear relationships.

4.   Correlation is a measure of association, not causation.

5.   Pearson's product moment correlation coefficient measures the strength of relationship between two variables containing interval or ratio level data. Data do not have to be normally distributed if we are only interested in calculating correlation coefficients; evaluating normality only becomes important if further analyses – such as determination of confidence intervals – are required.

6.   The standard error of the estimated correlation must be applied to your Pearson's product moment correlation coefficient in order to evaluate whether a correlation observed in a sample is indicative of a population relationship.

7.   Spearman's rank correlation coefficient measures the strength of relationship between two variables when one or both variables contain (ranked) ordinal level data.

8. The defining characteristics and size of a sample will influence any measures of association. The sample must be representative of the research population in terms of the principle characteristics of interest. If the sample is too small, single data points or research participants will exert a disproportionately large influence over the calculation of relationship. Equally, excessively large samples will always yield a significant correlation, but this may not be of any real practical importance. Finally, it is important to check that your research sample does not contain different sub-groups that would influence measures of association.

9. Conducting research where variables are collected over time is likely to yield larger correlation values than might be expected. Such values are referred to as spurious correlations. All values collected over time will correlate (e.g. in reliability studies), thus an initial step prior to conducting any form of association calculations is to remove any time related trends.

10. A correlation to evaluate agreement between to methods of measurement will generally be quite high, as the methods will be attempting – to varying degrees of success – to measure the same attribute. A strong correlation in this context will only serve to show that the values are related, not that the two methods are the same. There are a number of more approaches that are more appropriate than correlation for evaluating agreement between data sets.

7

Using Relationship for Prediction:

Regression Analysis

Chapter Objectives

- To recognise situations in which linear prediction is appropriate
- To find the regression equation for bivariate (two variables) data, and to use this information to make predictions
- To consider how well a regression line fits the data
- To extend these concepts to multivariate situations.

Introduction

In situations where earlier work has shown strong correlations between variables it is possible to produce a *line of best fit* – known as a regression line – to describe the relationship between variables and which in turn will allow us to make predictions from the data. This line is not positioned subjectively 'by eye', but is calculated. This means that any two researchers determining a regression line for the same sample of data should produce *exactly* the same regression line, as long as the same method of determining that line is adopted (i.e. objectivity, refer to chapter 2). This line can then be used to describe the nature of the relationship between the variables, and it is this specific knowledge of the relationship that will allow predictions to be made on further samples drawn from the *same population* as the original data.

Simple Linear Regression

Simple linear regression is the most basic of the regression techniques. It uses a single independent (or *predictor*) variable to predict another single dependent (or *response*) variable. The process requires there to be a *strong relationship* between the two variables, if this is not the case then any predictions made from the independent variable will be of limited value. Determining the *correlation coefficient* is therefore a necessary first step in the analysis process; it indicates whether the *variation in the dependent variable* can be explained by the *variation of the independent variable*.

If we consider the steps explained in chapter 6 relating to correlation:

1.   From a *scatter diagram* we will be able to examine whether the data appear to have a linear pattern and gain an indication of the strength of correlation from the shape the scatter diagram presents.

2.   A *correlation coefficient* will provide a value to describe the strength of the relationship between the two variables. As simple regression relies upon one variable being used to predict the other, the relationship between these two variables has to be strong, showing a correlation value greater than 0.7 [7.1]. If this is not the case, any equation determined defining this relationship would not be useful for the purposes of prediction.

3.   Finally, the data need to be further analysed to ensure that the correlation coefficient determined from the sample data is indicative of the relationship between these two variables in the population.

[7.1]   In sport and exercise psychology regressions will often be conducted on data with lower correlation strength in order to describe a precise relationship between a particular response variable and other (several) predictor variables. But a strong correlation is still required for prediction.

These three stages need to be completed before simple linear regression techniques are applied to your data. The first step is necessary for if the data do not seem to follow a straight-line pattern, trying to fit a straight line through the data will not give a satisfactory result. The second step provides an indication of how well this line is likely to fit the data; the higher the correlation coefficient, the better the line will fit the data, and the better will be any future predictions based upon this relationship. The third step is equally as important; if in evaluating the correlation coefficient it is found that the correlation is not applicable to the population (i.e. the probability or p-value is greater than 0.05, $p > 0.05$), it will not be possible to make future predictions from this relationship. A strong relationship (i.e. $r > 0.7$, $p < 0.05$) is necessary for regression analysis to be undertaken, and there needs to be an indication that the relationship can be generalised to the population. An approach based upon the determination of confidence intervals might also be used in this case rather than p-values. This approach will be discussed in greater detail in *Using Statistics in Sport and Exercise Science Research – Book 2*.

The *least squares method* is one of the most straightforward approaches to regression analysis. The aim of this approach is to draw a straight line through the data such that the distance of each data point from this line is as small as possible. This distance between the line and the data point represents the *error of a prediction* for that particular point (i.e. how far a prediction would be away from the actual value, where the prediction is given by the straight line), as illustrated in figure 7.1. Whilst it is of no real use to predict the values of data points we already know, these points can be used as a guide to the behaviour of the population as a whole. However, this assumes that the sample is of an appropriate size and is representative of the population.

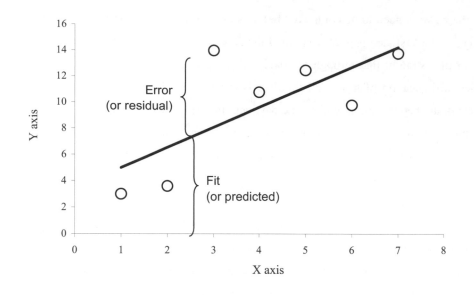

Figure 7.1   Application of the least squares method to regression analysis.

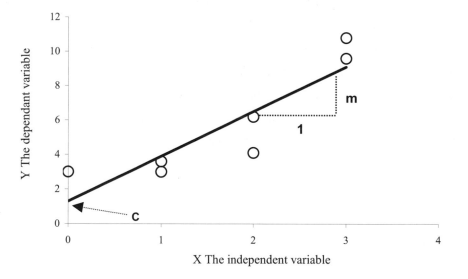

Figure 7.2   Illustration of the standard equation of the straight line.

Figure 7.2 illustrates the standard formula for a straight line, as given by the equation:

$y = mx + c.$ where, y is the dependent variable

m is the gradient

x is the independent variable

c is the y-axis intercept[7.2]

Values for m and c can be calculated (as described in calculation box 7.1) to achieve the *best fit* line describing the relationship between variables x and y.   The *best fit* line is that where the (distances) errors – sometimes referred to as residuals – between the line and the actual data points is as small as possible.

Calculation Box 7.1   Determination of m and c

The parameters m and c are calculated (using mathematical, calculus techniques) in order to minimise the sum of the squares of the errors.   Hence the technique is known as "least squares".

1. m is given by:

$$m = \frac{\sum_{i=1}^{n} [(x_i - \bar{x})(y_i - \bar{y})]}{\sum_{i=1}^{n} (x_i - \bar{x})^2}$$

An alternative form of this equation that may be easier to apply is given by:

$$m = \frac{\sum_{i=1}^{n} x_i y_i - n\bar{x}\bar{y}}{\sum_{i=1}^{n} x_i^2 - n\bar{x}^2}$$ where n is the number of observations

2. c is given by: $c = \bar{y} - m\bar{x}$

[7.2]   The intercept is where the line describing the relationship between the variables x and y crosses the y-axis; in figure 7.1 the intercept is 3.

We will now examine the least squares method to regression analysis in a worked example, and consider how good the regression process is for particular data through exploring how useful the derived regression equation is for further prediction. A study was conducted examining the influence of sports beverages on recovery from prolonged, constant pace running. Research participants, in this case endurance trained runners, were required to attend an exercise physiology laboratory for the experimental trials on two occasions separated by at least 7 days. Each trial consisted of a 90-minute treadmill run at a running speed that would elicit 70% VO_{2max}, followed by a 4-h controlled recovery period, and then a further treadmill run at 70% VO_{2max} to volitional fatigue (where volitional fatigue was defined as the point at which the runners could not sustain the required running speed). During the 4-h recovery period, the runners were prescribed either a dilute (6.9%) carbohydrate beverage (low-CHO) or a concentrated (19.3%) carbohydrate beverage (high-CHO) in a randomised, counter-balanced cross-over design (refer to chapter 3). The efficacy of the recovery sports beverage was evaluated in terms of run time to fatigue in the second exercise bout of each trial. The study also examined the effect of the recovery sports beverage (i.e. low-CHO vs. high-CHO) on mood states at the end of the 4-h recovery period using a mood states questionnaire. In this worked example we shall focus upon the mood states data, and specifically the *confidence* and *composure* mood states, to evaluate whether the runners' *confidence* following the 4-h recovery with the low-CHO beverage could predict the runners' *composure* following the 4-h recovery with the high-CHO beverage.

In this relatively artificial example, the number of research participants is small for the form of analysis we are performing; nevertheless it will serve to illustrate a number of important analytical points that we wish to highlight in developing your understanding of this approach. With the larger data sets that would normally be analysed by this approach it would be appropriate to conduct the regression analysis on a computer, as this reduces the potential for incurring any calculation errors. However, understanding the process of regression analysis – whether you or the computer undertakes the process – is essential for interpreting the outcomes of the analysis appropriately.

Runner	Confidence Score Low-CHO X	Composure Score High-CHO Y	$x - \bar{x}$	$(x - \bar{x})^2$	$y - \bar{y}$	$(y - \bar{y})^2$	$(x - \bar{x})(y - \bar{y})$
1	26	17	1.21	1.47	-2.93	8.58	-3.56
2	30	19	5.21	27.19	-0.93	0.86	-4.84
3	23	13	-1.79	3.19	-6.93	48.01	12.37
4	26	26	1.21	1.47	6.07	36.86	7.37
5	36	34	11.21	125.76	14.07	198.01	157.80
6	20	12	-4.79	22.90	-7.93	62.86	37.94
7	19	19	-5.79	33.47	-0.93	0.86	5.37
8	32	28	7.21	52.05	8.07	65.15	58.23
9	26	24	1.21	1.47	4.07	16.58	4.94
10	16	12	-8.79	77.19	-7.93	62.86	69.66
11	17	13	-7.79	60.62	-6.93	48.01	53.94
12	27	27	2.21	4.90	7.07	50.01	15.66
13	16	11	-8.79	77.19	-8.93	79.72	78.44
14	33	24	8.21	67.47	4.07	16.58	33.44
	$\bar{x} = 24.79$ $\bar{y} = 19.93$			$\Sigma = 556.36$		$\Sigma = 694.93$	$\Sigma = 526.79$

(a)	(b)

Table 7.1   The runners' *confidence* and *composure* mood state scores for the low- and high-CHO recovery sports beverages (a). Regression analysis calculations (b).

Moods states data were collected, coded for the sub-scales of questions for each of six mood states, summarised for the positive and negative scores, and the relevant *confidence* and *composure* mood state scores for each of the fourteen runners are presented in table 7.1a. Referring back to the three stages preceding simple linear regression presented earlier in this chapter, we must first draw a scatter diagram of the data points to inspect whether it is sensible to model the data using linear techniques. Figure 7.3 presents a scatter diagram of the confidence scores from the low-CHO and composure scores from the high-CHO recovery sports beverage experimental trials; the low-CHO confidence scores are plotted on the *x*-axis and the high-CHO composure scores are plotted on the *y*-axis.

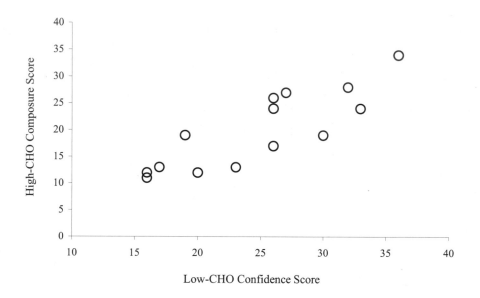

Figure 7.3   Scatter diagram of the runners *confidence* mood state scores for the low-CHO and *composure* mood state scores for the high-CHO recovery sports beverages.

From figure 7.3 we can see that the data follow a straight line, therefore it would be appropriate to apply the processes of linear correlation and regression on this data set.

Stage two requires that we calculate the *Pearson product moment correlation coefficient*, which has been completed below using the method presented in chapter 6. The use of computer spreadsheet programmes, such as *Excel*™, would be particularly appropriate for this multiple calculation, reducing the risk of incurring calculation errors. *Pearson's product moment correlation coefficient*, r_p, is given by the equation:

$$r_p = \frac{\sum_{i=1}^{n}(x_i - \bar{x})(y_i - \bar{y})}{\sqrt{\sum_{i=1}^{n}(x_i - \bar{x})^2 \sum_{i=1}^{n}(y_i - \bar{y})^2}}$$

Substituting the appropriate derived values from table 7.1 (b), will yield:

$$r_p = \frac{526.79}{\sqrt{556.36 \times 694.93}}$$

Thus,

$$r_p = \frac{526.79}{621.80} = 0.847$$

The data in this example of *confidence* mood state scores in endurance runners following a low-CHO prescribed recovery period, and *composure* mood state scores following a high-CHO prescribed recovery period, have a strong linear correlation ($r_p = 0.847$). The final stage preceding regression analysis is verification that this correlation observed in our sample of data is indicative of a relationship in the population. This is achieved by calculating the *standard error statistic*, as described in chapter 6, and determining the corresponding *t*-distribution value.

The standard error statistic (SE (r_p)) is given by:

$$SE(r_p) = \sqrt{\frac{1-(r_p{}^2)}{n-2}}$$

In our worked example examining 14 endurance runners, $r_p = 0.847$. Thus:

$$SE(r_p) = \sqrt{\frac{1-0.847^2}{14-2}} = \sqrt{\frac{1-0.717}{12}} = \sqrt{0.0236} = 0.154$$

The degrees of freedom (d.f.) are given by:

$$
\begin{aligned}
\text{d.f.} \;&=\; n-2 \\
&=\; 14-2 \\
&=\; 12
\end{aligned}
$$

The *t* statistic is given by:

$$t = \frac{r_p}{SE(r_p)}$$

Thus, substituting the values for $r_p{}^2 = 0.717$ and SE $(r_p) = 0.154$, with 12 degrees of freedom:

$$t_{(12)} = \frac{0.847}{0.154} = 5.500$$

The final step is to look up the value from the *t*-distribution (appendix: 3), at the 5% significance level (i.e. $\alpha = 0.05$) corresponding to 12 d.f.. In this example the *t*-statistic is 2.179. As our *t*-

statistic (i.e. 5.500) is *greater than* the tabulated value (i.e. 2.179), the correlation can be said to be indicative of a relationship between these two variables in the population.

Having completed the necessary preliminary checks, we are now in a position to continue with the simple linear regression analysis to predict the runners' *composure* scores following the 4-h recovery with the high-CHO beverage from the runners' *confidence* scores following the 4-h recovery with the low-CHO beverage. Again, the regression analysis calculations can be completed on a computer, which would be especially appropriate for large data sets. However, to illustrate the process we will articulate the manual steps in this calculation, and these are more easily completed by constructing a calculation table as described in chapter 6. Table 7.1b contains all the necessary calculation columns required for determining m and c in the regression formulae presented in calculation box 7.1.

Applying the formulae from calculation box 7.1 and the values derived in table 7.1b, m and c are calculated as follows:

$$m = \frac{\sum_{i=1}^{n}[(x_i - \bar{x})(y_i - \bar{y})]}{\sum_{i=1}^{n}(x_i - \bar{x})^2} = \frac{526.79}{556.36} = 0.95$$

and:

$$c - \bar{y} - m\bar{x}$$
$$c = 19.93 - (0.95 \times 24.79) = 19.93 - 23.47 = -3.62$$

The regression equation resulting from this analysis is:

$$y = 0.95x + -3.62$$

Taking into consideration the negative sign of the constant, this is more appropriately written as:

$$y = 0.95x - 3.62$$

When using a spreadsheet computer programme to perform the regression you may generate an equation in this format, or alternatively some software packages present output tables of unstandardised coefficients from which we can read off the values of m and c. The unstandardised coefficient corresponding to m can usually be found next to the variable name of your independent variable, and the coefficient for c will usually be labelled as a *constant*. At this point it is worth mentioning that the way in which you conduct the analysis will have an effect on the final equation derived. In this example we used a spreadsheet to complete the repetitive calculations, rounding the totals to two decimal places before providing hand calculated equations. If you undertook the whole calculation by hand you are likely to round values earlier in the calculation, and therefore your final outcome values will differ slightly from the part-computer derived values presented in this text (refer to chapter 6). The same would be true if you used a computer to complete all the calculations, where rounding would not occur until the final derivation of the equation.

Figure 7.4 presents the runners' *confidence* scores following the 4-h recovery with the low-CHO beverage plotted against the runners' *composure* scores following the 4-h recovery with the high-CHO beverage, with the corresponding regression line superimposed. From visually inspecting the pattern of the data, the predictions look as though they would be fairly good. However, the final stage of any regression analysis is to investigate how good these predictions are by evaluating how well the line fits the data. This operation is called *assessing the fit of the model*.

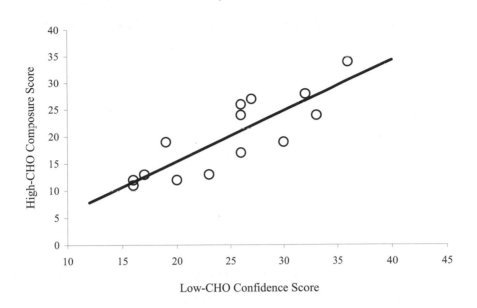

Figure 7.4   The runners *confidence* mood state scores for the low-CHO and *composure* mood
state scores for the high-CHO recovery sports beverages.

Assessing the Fit of the Model

From a statistical analysis perspective, a *model* usually refers to a mathematical description of the pattern of the data. The accuracy of a model to predict the dependent variable is related to the linear correlation between the independent and dependent variables being examined. That is, the higher – or stronger – the correlation the greater the accuracy of prediction; a perfect correlation would yield a perfect prediction. However, in reality the correlation will be less than perfect, and the error that this will introduce into your prediction must be evaluated. In drawing the line of best fit the aim is to minimise this error. The error – or deviation of the point away from the line of best fit – can be calculated by predicting a corresponding *dependent* variable value for each observation of the *independent* variable. The standard deviation of the resulting set of errors of prediction is known as the *standard error of the estimate (SEE)*. The *standard error of the estimate* provides an index of the accuracy of prediction; it provides a measure of the *unexplained* or *background variability*. The standard error of the estimate is not easy to interpret, as it needs to be considered in relation to the scale of predictions that are being made from the data. If the standard error is large in relation to the predictions, then the equation you have developed will probably not be acceptable as a model of the data.

In the case of our worked example examining the influence of sports beverages on recovery from prolonged, constant pace running, to determine the standard error of the estimate we would need to:

1.   Use our regression equation to predict a value for the high-CHO *composure* state from each low-CHO *confidence* state score.

2.   The predicted value is then subtracted from the actual value that was collected for the high-CHO *composure* mood state; this gives the error for each point.

3.   The standard deviations of these errors are then determined using the method for calculating standard deviations described in chapter 4 (calculation box 4.3). As you can see, we never stop applying the simplest statistical techniques to help us continue to organise and evaluate our findings.

4.   This standard deviation value is the value of the *standard error of the estimate*[7.3].

[7.3]   SPSS™ computer software reports the standard error of the estimate as the mean error of the estimate. It is therefore important to understand the statistical processes to avoid being misled by differences in terminology.

Confidence Low-CHO	*Composure* High-CHO	Predicted *Composure* High-CHO	**Error** (Predicted vs. Actual) *Composure* High-CHO
26	17	21.08	4.92
30	19	24.88	5.12
23	13	18.23	4.77
26	26	21.08	4.92
36	34	30.58	5.42
20	12	15.38	4.62
19	19	14.43	4.57
32	28	26.78	5.22
26	24	21.08	4.92
16	12	11.58	4.42
17	13	12.53	4.47
27	27	22.03	4.97
16	11	11.58	4.42
33	24	27.73	5.27

Table 7.2   The runners *confidence* mood state scores for the low-CHO and *composure* mood state scores for the high-CHO recovery sports beverages, the predicted high-CHO *composure* scores determined from the corresponding regression line, and the errors between the predicted and actual scores.

Table 7.2 presents the actual values for the *confidence* mood state in the low-CHO and the *composure* mood state scores in the high-CHO experimental conditions. Also reported are the predictions of the high-CHO confidence mood state scores derived from the regression equation. For example, working along the first data line in table 7.3:

1.   Actual low-CHO confidence mood state score was 26. Substituting 26 into the regression equation determined from the pairs of observed low-CHO and high-CHO mood state scores:

       y $= 0.95x - 3.62$
       Prediction $= (0.95 \times 26) - 3.62 = 21.08$

2.   Subtracting the predicted high-CHO *composure* mood state score from the actual score:

       Error: $26 - 21.08 = 4.92$

3.   The mean of this set of errors is calculated by adding all the errors together (i.e. sum of errors) and dividing by the number of observations. Thus, the mean value of the errors for this worked example is 4.86. Applying calculation box 4.3, the standard deviation of this set of errors is calculated as 0.33.

4.   Thus, the *standard error of the estimate* for this set of data is 0.33. Therefore we can express the behaviour of the errors in terms of mean error $\pm$ standard error of the mean error. In this example, $\bar{x} \pm SEE.$ is 4.86 ± 0.33.

The standard error of estimate for this set of data (i.e. 0.33) is small in relation to the size of the measurements, which range from 11 to 34 on the *composure* variable. Therefore, the regression equation determined for the example data is said to yield reasonable predictions of the dependent variable from the independent variable.

Another measure by which we can evaluate the fit of the model is the *sum of squared deviations*, r^2. This is a measure of the proportion of the original variability of the data that is explained by the straight-line model (i.e. the regression equation). As the choice of letter implies, (r^2) this measure is derived from the square of the Pearson product moment correlation coefficient. It is important to note that many statistical computer packages often denote r and r^2 by the upper case letters R and R^2 respectively, but these refer to the same derived statistic. If $r = 0.7$, this is considered to be a strong correlation, however $r^2 = 0.49$ suggesting that a 'strong' correlation does not necessarily make a very good predictor as the percentage of variation explained would be $0.49 \times 100 = 49\%$. The closer r^2 is to 1.0, the better the prediction and the more confidence we can have in our predicted data. There is a link between the threshold correlation value of $r = 0.7$ and the resulting quality of our predictive model; if $r < 0.7$, $r^2 < 0.5$, and the regression equation would be regarded as not acceptable. Nevertheless, ultimately it is up to the reader to decide what is acceptable under the specific circumstances of the research study being reported.

It is good practice to plot the errors on a graph in order to check that there is not a systematic pattern to their distribution. It is possible for the standard error of the estimate to be small and for the coefficient of variation to be large suggesting a good model, and for there to be a systematic over-prediction or under-prediction at certain points of the data model. A graph of the errors – or residuals – should follow a normal distribution (refer to chapter 5) if there is no systematic pattern. Figure 7.5 illustrates the normal probability graph of the errors for our worked example. The points lie relatively close to the line and do not indicate any obvious pattern. Again, we can take this as an indication that the model is acceptable. An observation that would further strengthen the case for the appropriateness of our model and the confidence we might have in predictions based upon this model is to look at *standardised residuals*. This is an option available in most statistical software packages. The errors – or residuals – are adjusted (standardised) to fit a particular normal distribution. It is this *standard normal distribution* that forms the basis of many of the calculations we will use in chapters 8 and 9, and which form the base of the look up tables. It is no longer appropriate to transform the residuals by hand; this would be undertaken as part of a computerised analysis. If these standardised residuals fit between −3 and +3 we can have confidence in our model as none of the predictors are deemed to be too dissimilar to the actual values.

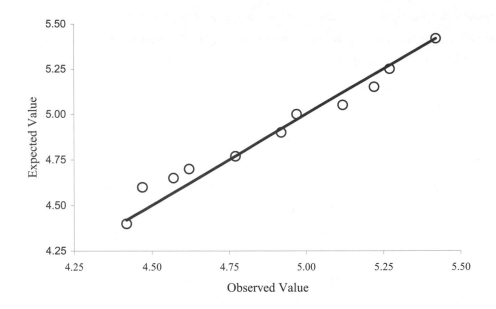

Figure 7.5   A Q-Q plot for the residuals (errors) of the regression model in the worked example.

Now that we are satisfied that the model we have developed for our data is appropriate, we can examine what the regression equation is actually telling us about the data. The equation $y = 0.95x - 3.62$ indicates that the value for the *composure* mood state after the high-CHO treatment (y), is very closely related to the *confidence* mood state after the low-CHO treatment (x). This is indicated by the coefficient 0.95 multiplying the low-CHO (x) value. The constant value of 3.62, that is subtracted from every variable value of ($0.95 \times x$) to give the prediction, indicates that the *composure* mood state does not score so highly after the high-CHO treatment as the *confidence* after the low-CHO treatment. We are now in a position to predict the *composure* mood state following the high-CHO treatment for an individual who had only completed the low-CHO treatment. Following this process of evaluation we can have confidence that our prediction is reasonable, though it will contain some errors.

For example, inputting a confidence mood state score of 21 for the low-CHO treatment will allow us to calculate a *composure* mood state score for the high-CHO treatment for the same research participant as follows:

$$y = 0.95x - 3.62$$
$$\text{Prediction} = (0.95 \times 21) - 3.62 = 16.33$$

Thus, the predicted *composure* mood state score for the high-CHO treatment for this research participant would be 16. Using our knowledge for the potential error of this prediction (or standard error of estimate of 0.33), we can consider that our prediction is likely to be between 16.00 and 16.66 (i.e. 16.33 ± 0.33)

Multiple Regression

The worked example exploring the influence of different sports beverages on recovery from prolonged, constant pace running involves using one variable to predict the behaviour of another variable. In reality, it is rarely the case that the behaviour of one variable will provide adequate insight to the behaviour of another. Often the variable we wish to predict is influenced by a complex combination of several other factors. An analytical technique known as *multiple regression* allows us to predict one dependent or response variable from a combination of several other independent (or predictor) variables. The mathematics underpinning this process is fairly complex, being an extension of that described for simple regression, and is beyond the scope of this text.

The resulting regression equation will be in the form:

$$y = m_1 x_1 + m_2 x_2 + m_3 x_3 + \ldots + m_i x_i + c$$

where, y is the dependent variable

$m_{1\text{-}i}$ are the gradient(s)[7.4]

$x_{1\text{-}i}$ are the independent variable(s)[7.5]

c is the y-axis intercept

Many statistical textbooks will write this equation with the Greek letter β being applied instead of m, but the structure is essentially the same. Statistical computer packages will conduct the multiple regression process for you using a variety of methods for including the independent – predictor – variables. These methods will be briefly outlined in the following sections.

Hierarchical Methods

All the selected independent – predictor – variables can be included in the equation, regardless of how important they actually are, by using the initial correlation with the dependent – response – variable to determine the size of the coefficient (m_i) in the final equation. This means that each variable is considered as if it is the most important variable for the prediction. This process is useful if you want to make sure that every variable you have collected (i.e. every measurement taken) should be included in the final equation.

If your research aim is to replicate studies that have already been completed, possibly to explore further applications, then you may wish to *force* some variables into an equation before others. Remember, the intention here is to examine how closely your findings mirror, or not, the earlier findings. *Hierarchical methods*[7.6] enable you to do this by setting your own order of entry of each variable into the equation. This method effectively allows you to override the computerised analysis of variables that will establish criteria for entry of variables into the equation. Not all

---

[7.4] This is an extension of the single variable case (i.e. $y = mx + c$) to include more than one predictor variable.
[7.5] *Ditto*
[7.6] Hierarchical methods arrange each grouping (i.e. $m_{1\text{-}i} x_{1\text{-}i}$) of the equation in a graded order of importance.

computer packages will allow you to do this, as it should not be undertaken without considerable prior experience of regression modelling.

Stepwise Methods

Stepwise methods of multiple regression analysis are available within most software packages. These approaches develop a mathematical model, starting with a simple regression equation using one independent – predictor – variable. This variable is identified as that which correlates most highly with the dependent – response – variable. Subsequent variables are identified in an order of importance by adjusting the correlations of all the remaining variables to *partition out* the effect of the variable(s) that have already been included in the equation. The size of the resulting *partial correlations* is used to select the next variable to be included in the equation; that variable should be the one with the highest partial correlation with the response variable of all the remaining variables. Unlike simple regression analysis, the correlation values in multiple regression do not have to be greater than 0.7 as it is the combination of independent – predictor – variables that is important, not any one variable. Nevertheless, it should be a significant partial correlation, indicating that the correlation would be present in the population and that the variable is useful for predictions within that population. Partial correlations will be considered in greater detail in *Using Statistics in Sport and Exercise Science Research – Book 2*. The stepwise method evaluates the appropriateness of each model as a new variable is added, in this way the effect of each variable can in turn be evaluated. These methods are widely used in sport and exercise science research, though some authors of statistical texts advise against their use as the criteria for including a variable in the equation are based solely on statistical measures. Moreover, these statistical measures have only been observed in the one sample. The final equation is therefore totally dependent on the chance behaviour of that single sample and the variations and relationships (possibly very small ones) between the observations recorded.

Assessing the Fit of a Multiple Regression Model

Checks for the fit of multiple regression models are the same as those discussed for simple regression models. However, there is the added requirement that not only should the residuals – errors – be normally distributed, but also the variance for each set of residuals should be similar;

this property of having equal variance is called *homoscedasticity*. A visual check for homoscedasticity can be made by looking at the scatter diagrams of the residuals. You should be able to draw a *lozenge* shape around the residuals that is more or less the same width across all values. If the pattern of residuals is fan shaped, then the variation of the residuals is not similar, and we have *heteroscedasticity*, which weakens the applicability of the model. A mathematical check for *homoscedasticity* can normally be performed within the computer software used for the regression analysis.

To illustrate some of the above concepts we will now describe a worked example of multiple regression. A sports psychology study was undertaken to investigate the intensity and direction of *competitive state anxiety* and *self-confidence* in a female soccer team. Measures of *anxiety* and *self-confidence* were taken immediately before the start of matchplay using a mental readiness form that contains three *Likert scale*[7.7] response items. The respondent also records a directional value so that the anxiety can be evaluated to see if it is facilitative (i.e. enabling) or debilitative (i.e.disabling). Two independent judges gave measures of performance using a technique developed by McMorris (1986). The data collection protocol was carried out over several games for both the first- and second-half of play. Data were analysed to see if the intensity and direction of anxiety, and the intensity of self-confidence, could be used to predict performance.

During one particular game, none of the variables were seen to correlate strongly with the performance measure (i.e. $\mathbf{r} < 0.7$ for every variable). An equation was generated for performance using statistical software. The equation produced was as follows:

$$Performance = 0.289\ C_I + 0.035\ C_D - 0.481\ S_I + 0.623\ S_D + 0.155\ SC_I - 0.146\ SC_D + 3.728$$

where,	C_I...	cognitive anxiety intensity	S_D...	somatic anxiety direction
	C_D...	cognitive anxiety direction	SC_I...	self-confidence intensity
	S_I...	somatic anxiety intensity	SC_D...	self-confidence direction

---

[7.7] A *Likert scale* is a type of closed question that requires the research participant to respond by choosing one of an odd number of scaled items.

This equation returned an $\mathbf{R}^2$ (note, upper case R is used in multiple regression) value of 0.894 indicating that the predictive ability of this equation was very high, even though no one variable indicated strong correlation with the dependent variable. The equation produced can be used to predict performance from the *anxiety* and *self-confidence* responses in the same way as in simple regression, although the calculation is somewhat longer. Values for each of the separate variables need to be multiplied by the required coefficient, and then added or subtracted as indicated, in order to provide a predicted *performance* score. The predictions can be assessed to see how good the *fit of the model* is in exactly the same way as before, and the additional check of *homosedasticity* employed. Further discussion and worked examples of multiple regression can be found in *Using Statistics in Sport and Exercise Science Research – Book 2*.

Problems with Regression Techniques

Non-Linearity

Sometimes an initial inspection of a scatter diagram might indicate that the data are non-linear. Trying to fit straight lines to such data will not be successful, and using non-linear regression techniques is a complex alternative. It may be preferable to transform the data in the first instance (for example, through the application of natural logarithms – data transformations will be discussed in greater detail in *Using Statistics in Sport and Exercise Science Research – Book 2*), such that a straight line can be fitted to the transformed data. This has the additional advantage of yielding residuals that are more likely to satisfy the assumptions needed for later work.

Number of Research Participants

The number of research participants in relation to the independent – predictor – variables in multiple regression analysis is also important. Too few and you will get an apparently good result that is, in reality, meaningless. Some statistical texts suggest a baseline figure such as five research participants for each independent variable as a minimum number of cases (Ntoumanis 2001, Vincent 1995). Other texts suggest that a formula should be applied to determine the necessary minimum number of research participants.

One such formula reported by Tabachnik and Fidell (1996) is given by:

Number of Research Participants = 8 × (Number of Independent Variables) + 50

For *stepwise multiple regression* methods there is a general consensus that a ratio of 40 research participants to each independent – predictor – variable is required. If you have very few research participants with several independent variables, you can have little confidence that any resulting equation will be useful for prediction outside of the sample used to generate the equation (e.g. predicting back to the research population). If this were the case, then application of multiple regression analyses would be a waste of time for prediction purposes. As discussed previously with reference to simple linear regression, sport and exercise psychologists may carry out such procedures because they are interested in how the different variables relate *together* when acting on the dependent variable for the particular sample group. Importantly, they are not necessarily looking to develop beyond the sample group.

Outliers in Data

Outliers in a data set will cause problems with predictions, as they will affect the position of the regression line. The smaller the number of cases used to develop the model describing the pattern of the data, the greater the effect of an outlier. This means that it is important to explore data thoroughly before undertaking any form of regression analyses, such that outliers can be identified early and their potential influence on the model considered during the analysis.

Multicolinearity and Singularity

As well as the possible presence of outliers, *multicolinearity* and *singularity* need to be explored by examining scatter diagrams and correlations prior to multiple regression analysis. *Multicolinearity* is where two variables have a very strong correlation, and *singularity* is present when two variables correlate exactly (i.e. $r = \pm 1.0$). This situation often occurs when one variable is a mathematical computation of the other. For example, in a sample of cardiac patients enrolled on an exercise rehabilitation programme, we may be interested in modelling a number of physiological parameters to predict exercise tolerance. Obvious parameters to include in this model would be measures of cardiac function, such as heart rate and cardiac output. However, cardiac output is a mathematical computation of heart rate, being the product of heart rate (number of beats per minute) and stroke volume (volume of blood pumped by the heart per contraction or per heart beat). Thus, it is highly likely that cardiac output and heart rate will show *multicolinearity*. The problem with *multicolinearity* and *singularity* is that they give rise to redundant variables; that is, only one of these highly correlating pairs will add anything of further value to a regression equation.

And Finally …A Few Things to Remember

Simply because we can use one or more predictor variables to predict a response variable, it does not mean that there is a *causal* relationship between the variables – it may be that such a relationship has happened by chance and/or does not have any meaningful significance in a practical context. Furthermore, any regression model produced has come from *one* set of observed data. If the equation is to have credence and reliability as a predictor for new cases, then the equation needs to be validated through repetition of the procedures on a new, different sample, and adjusted where necessary, over several sets of data drawn from the same population.

Chapter Decision Tree

Figure 7.6 presents an overview of the questions you should ask prior to undertaking regression analysis, and the resulting decision processes as described in this chapter.

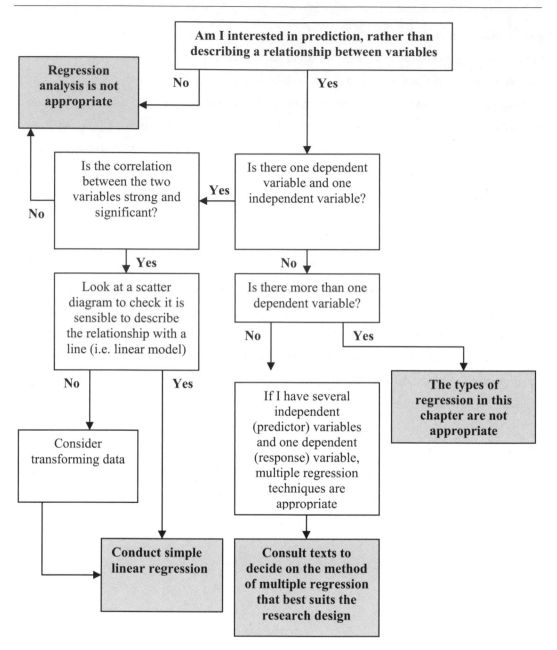

Figure 7.6   Decision tree for regression analysis.

Summary/Key Points

1. In situations where earlier work has shown strong correlations between variables it is possible to produce a *line of best fit* – known as a regression line – to describe the relationship between variables and which in turn will allow us to make predictions from the data.

2. Simple linear regression uses a single independent (or predictor) variable to predict another single dependent (or response) variable. The process requires there to be a strong correlation (i.e. $r > 0.7$) between the two variables, and this can be visually verified from a scatter diagram.

3. The least squares method is one of the most straightforward approaches to regression analysis, where a straight line is drawn through the data such that the distances (errors) of each data point from the line (i.e. sometimes referred to as the residuals) is as small as possible.

4. Once a strong correlation has been observed in the sample we must then verify that this is indicative of a relationship in the population. This is achieved by calculating the standard error statistic and determining the corresponding *t*-distribution value.

5. From a statistical analysis perspective a model refers to a mathematical description of the pattern of the data.

6. The accuracy of a model to predict the dependent variable is related to the linear correlation between the independent and dependent variables. The standard deviation of the resulting set of errors (or deviations of the points away from the line of best fit) of prediction is known as the standard error of the estimate, which provides an index of the accuracy of prediction.

7. The sum of squared deviations, r^2, is another method of evaluating the fit of a model. Derived from the Pearson product moment correlation coefficient, this is a measure of the proportion (often expressed as a percentage) of the original variability of the data that is explained by the regression equation.

8. Multiple regression analysis allows the behaviour of one dependent response variable to be predicted from a complex combination of several independent predictor variables. Checks for the fit of multiple regression – models – equations are the same as discussed for simple regression models. However, there is the added requirement that the residuals – errors – should be normally distributed, and that the variance of each set of errors should be similar (i.e. demonstrate homoscedasticity).

9. Problems of regression techniques arise from non-linearity, inappropriate number of research participants, outliers in the data, and multicolinearity and singularity.

10. A causal relationship between the variables cannot be assumed because we can use one or more predictor variables to predict a response variable. It may be that such a relationship has happened by chance and/or does not have any meaningful significance in a practical context.

8

Testing Differences Between Two Groups

Chapter Objectives

- To make decisions about when to use a non-parametric test and when a parametric test would be more appropriate
- To identify difference tests applicable to related and independent group designs
- To use two group tests of difference to make decisions about population differences.

Introduction

In chapter 3 we discussed the importance of considering the form of statistical analyses to be undertaken on the research data as part of the planning stage. Experimental research design and the resulting data analyses should be viewed as part of the same process, and both activities will inform the methods of data collection. To this end, a number of assumptions can be made on the data before the first number has been collected and recorded. For example, it may be reasonable to assume that the samples drawn from a parent population will be normally distributed as long as sound sampling techniques have been applied. For this to be verified, data would need to be of an interval or ratio level of measurement and would then need exploration to check the assumption.

Alternatively, if data are reported as a set of ranks, the values that participants can achieve are limited and therefore will not follow a normal distribution.

Depending upon the type of data we are collecting there are a variety of analysis procedures available to explore research hypotheses addressing possible differences between two groups (or sets) of data. Interval or ratio level data can be evaluated to test for normal distribution of the parent population. If such tests confirm that the data conforms to the assumptions of normality, then we are in a position to apply *parametric tests* in our statistical analyses. The importance of this is that in performing parametric tests we will be in a position to make decisions on the data with greater sensitivity than if the assumptions of normality were not met. In the event of the latter, that is we cannot confirm that our data conforms to the assumptions of normality, then we should apply a set of distribution free, or *non-parametric*, tests that do not make *a priori*[8.1] assumptions about the data. As non-parametric statistical tests make no assumptions, and fewer demands on the data, they can be applied to a wider range of situations than parametric tests. Non-parametric tests are less sensitive than parametric tests, and are less likely to identify real differences in data. Parametric statistical techniques are probably more widely used in the sport and exercise sciences, as evident in published studies in the scientific literature despite, not always checking or conforming to the assumptions of normality.

In chapter 8 we will describe approaches to examining differences between groups. It is important to remember that in evaluating possible differences in groups you must be measuring and comparing the same variable. If we consider the worked example reported in chapter 7, which examined the influence of different sports beverages on recovery from prolonged, constant pace running. It would be appropriate to explore for differences between the low- and high-CHO treatments within any of the mood states assessed by the mood states questionnaire, as long as you are comparing like with like (e.g. confidence in the low-CHO condition vs. confidence in the high-CHO condition). It would not be appropriate, nor would it have practical relevance, to look for

---

[8.1]   *A priori* refers to knowing something to be true independently or in advance of experience.

differences between different mood states across the two experimental conditions (e.g. confidence in the low-CHO condition vs. composure in the high-CHO condition).

With reference to statistical sensitivity, the more sensitive parametric tests are able to detect *smaller* differences between observations made on two populations in comparison with less sensitive non-parametric tests. This is because parametric tests are able to apply known population parameters (i.e. boundaries or constraints) to assist in identifying real differences in data sets, while non-parametric tests can only rely on the observed behaviour of two sample groups to provide an indication of the behaviour of the population. If there were no inherent differences between the abilities of the parametric and non-parametric tests to discriminate between data sets, non-parametric tests would be the approach of choice as they are easier to compute by hand and their output from statistical software packages is usually easier to understand and interpret. However, assuming that the distribution criteria for parametric tests are satisfied, parametric tests have more *power* by virtue of their greater *sensitivity*. You will recall from chapter 3 that the power of a statistical test is its probability of rejecting the null hypothesis when it is false (i.e. less chance of making a type-II error), or alternatively the probability of retaining the null hypothesis when it is true. That is, statistical power refers to the ability of a test to make a correct decision. For any given sample of data, a parametric test will have a greater chance of reaching *the right decision* than the corresponding non-parametric test. This is partly due to the fact that parametric tests are applied to interval or ratio level data, which provide the maximum amount of information to the researcher. For example, suppose we collected a raw data set comprising of a series of distances measured in kilometres:

    i.e.   45, 35, 15, 11 and 10

If we convert these ratio level data points to their corresponding ordinal level data points, we will be left with the following data set:

    i.e.   1, 2, 3, 4 and 5.

In ranking the data in this way, we now only know the order of the data and we lose information concerning the comparative size of the distances. For example, we now no longer know that the first distance is three times the size of the third distance. Equally, we must not try to insert information that is not present in the data, such as suggesting that the gap between 1 and 2 is the same size as the gap between 4 and 5. As a non-parametric test uses the data rankings it has less information, and as a result is less useful as a discriminator between the null and experimental hypotheses – it is less powerful. Thus, providing the data satisfy the underlying assumptions a parametric test is to be preferred to a non-parametric test. If we select a parametric test where its use is not justified, false conclusions could be drawn from the results of your analyses (i.e. usually the incorrect rejection of H_0 incurring a type-I error). However, parametric tests function well even if there is some violation of the assumptions of normality, and so may well be employed anyway where data are interval or ratio level. Though this does need to be considered carefully. If numbers of participants are very small *and* there is a possibility that data are not from a normally distributed parent population, then there is no advantage to using parametric tests as any value in increased sensitivity will be lost. This is a very grey area and one that promotes must discussion among researchers. The important thing to remember is that you are not alone in having to make decisions about which test to use, so do not be afraid to discuss the merits of different approaches with others.

Inspecting the Data

We addressed methods of evaluating whether data conform to parameters defining a normal distribution in chapter 5. It is important to note at this stage that *data* are not parametric or non-parametric. The data simply report the outcome of a measurement taken at a certain level – nominal, ordinal, interval or ratio. As discussed above, if data are measured at the interval or ratio level there is the possibility that they might follow normal distribution parameters, and therefore the data should be evaluated to verify if this is the case. If the sample size of our data is less than 10–15 research participants, it will not form a distribution that can adequately be checked for normality. As sample sizes in the sport and exercise sciences are often small, the assumption of normality is often made without verification. This omission allows for potential misapplication of statistical tests, and subsequent discussion of results needs to reflect this possibility. Whilst checks for normality may not be able to identify *for certain* that data conform to normal distribution parameters, they will be able to assess if data definitely *do not* conform to the parameters (e.g. SE for skewness and SE for kurtosis fall between -2 and $+2$).

As well as checking that the data for each group follow a normal distribution, we must also carefully consider the design of the data collection. We must determine whether the data have been collected from the same individuals across different time points, or after different treatments or different activities. If this is the case we have a *within groups repeated measurements design*, and consequently the statistical test needs to be one for related groups. This is the strongest form of experimental design as the individual variation for each research participant is controlled for, as far as possible, by requiring each participant to complete every time point, every treatment, or every activity. Sometimes this is not possible, as the first treatment or intervention cannot be reversed.

For example, from a sports psychology perspective if we were evaluating the efficacy of two different coaching programmes in developing a skill, it would be impossible to return a sports performer to their starting skill level after one programme in order to evaluate the efficacy of another programme. The preferred approach under these circumstances would be to carefully match research participants into pairs[8.2]. This *matching* would be based upon initial performance level, relevant experience, age, and any other factors that may be considered important in the execution and development of the specific skill. One participant from each pair would then be assigned to each coaching programme. As research participants have been matched in this example, we should similarly apply a test appropriate for *related samples*[8.3]. Alternatively, if research participants are randomly assigned to treatment/intervention groups, and no attempt is made to make the groups the same (except possibly in terms of the size of each group), a test for

---

[8.2]   *Matched groups/samples* are where research participants are linked relative to one or more matching variables that are specific to the research question (refer to chapter 3 for further information).
[8.3]   *Related samples* are where two or more research samples are connected or associated in some way (e.g. the same research participants or matched research participants). Consequently, if one participant fails to complete a research trial, then all the data for that pair should be removed.

independent samples[8.4] should be applied; we are looking for differences *between* different *groups*. Refer to chapter 3 for a more comprehensive discussion of experimental design and data collection.

We will examine four tests of difference, two parametric tests and two non-parametric tests, where each test is appropriate for either a related or an independent sample design (figure 8.1).

	Non-parametric test	**Parametric test**
Two related samples	Wilcoxon test	Paired samples *t*-test
Two independent samples	Mann-Whitney U test	Independent samples *t*-test

Figure 8.1   Parametric and non-parametric tests of differences for related and independent samples.

Non-parametric Tests of Differences

The *Wilcoxon test* and the *Mann-Whitney U test* are non-parametric tests of differences that compare the medians of two sample groups. The *Wilcoxon test* is applied to data collected from related groups, where each research participant in one group is matched with, or is identical to (i.e. the same person), a research participant in the other group. In contrast, the *Mann-Whitney U test* is applied to data collected from independent groups, where *different* subjects are assigned to either a control or an experimental condition.

[8.4] *Independent samples* are where two or more research samples are not connected or associated in any way.

Calculation Box 8.1   The Wilcoxon Test

The Wilcoxon test is used when evaluating differences between medians of two related samples (i.e. the null hypothesis is that the medians are equal). Therefore the data must at least be at the ordinal level of measurement. The procedure for *the Wilcoxon test* is as follows:

1.   Calculate the differences between group 1 and group 2.

2.   Rank the differences from the smallest (rank-1) to the largest (rank-i) ignoring signs.

3.   The respective sign is placed before each rank – zero ranks are discounted and tied ranks shared (refer to example below).

4.   Two tests statistics are then calculated, T^+ (the sum of the positive ranks) and T^- (the sum of the negative ranks). A check of these calculations is that their sum is given by:

$$\frac{n(n + 1)}{2} \qquad \text{where n is the sample size.}$$

5.   The smaller of T^+ and T^- is simply labelled as T and, for small n, is compared to tabled values (Appendix: 4); the null hypothesis, H_0, is rejected if T *is less than or equal to* the tabled value.

6.   For n > 15 (approximately) the distribution of T is approximately normal, where its mean and variance are given by:

$$\mu = \frac{n(n + 1)}{4} \qquad \text{and} \qquad \sigma^2 = \frac{n(n + 1)(2n + 1)}{24}$$

7.   Thus, for large samples the data are transformed by using the equations in step 6, and a Z-score is determined as described in technical box 5.1 (chapter 5)

8.   The result is then evaluated using a normal distribution look up table (appendix: 5).

Calculation Box 8.2   The Mann-Whitney U Test

The Mann-Whitney U test is used when evaluating differences between medians of two independent samples (i.e. the null hypothesis is that there is no difference between the population medians of the two groups). The data must be at least at the ordinal level of measurement. Assuming the number of subjects in group A is n_A, and the number of subjects in group B is n_B; the procedure for *the Mann-Whitney U test* is as follows:

1.   The data is ranked treating the two groups as if they were one, but retaining the group identification of each data point. Identical data values are dealt with by sharing ranks in the same way as for *the Wilcoxon test*.

2.   The ranks for group-A are added together to produce rank total ΣR_A and the ranks for group-B are added to produce ΣR_B.

3.   Calculate
$$U_A = n_A n_B + \frac{n_A(n_A + 1)}{2} - \sum R_A$$

and,
$$U_B = n_A n_B + \frac{n_B(n_B + 1)}{2} - \sum R_B$$

4.   The test statistic U is then the smaller of U_A and U_B.

5.   For small samples, the U is compared with the tabled critical value (appendix: 6) at the chosen significance level for the group sizes used (i.e. n_A and n_B). The null hypothesis is rejected if U *is equal to or less* than the critical value. Note: different tables have to be used for different significance levels.

6.   For large samples, the distribution of U is approximately normal, where μ and σ^2 are given by:

$$\mu = \frac{1}{2} n_A n_B \qquad \text{and} \qquad \sigma^2 = \frac{1}{12} n_A n_B (n_A + n_B + 1)$$

(Continued…)

7.   As in *the Wilcoxon test*, for large samples the data are transformed by using the equations in step 6 and a Z-score is determined. The result is then evaluated using a normal distribution look up table (appendix: 5).

To consider situations where the *Wilcoxon* and *Mann-Whitney U* tests might appropriately be applied, we shall consider the data presented in chapter 7 which was collected during a study examining the influence of sports beverages on recovery from prolonged, constant pace running. The mood states questionnaire adopted a *Likert scale* and therefore the data collected from fourteen research participants (i.e. n = 14), are at the ordinal level of measurement. Therefore the data are not of a level where we might consider applying parametric approaches to data analysis, although certain conditions where parametric testing of ordinal data is used will be considered at the end of this chapter. In this small sample of 14 research participants, each participant was measured on two occasions relative to six mood state sub-scales following a 4-h recovery with a low-CHO beverage and following a 4-h recovery with a high-CHO beverage. If the reason for the study was to examine hypothesised differences in particular mood states between the two recovery treatments, *the Wilcoxon test* would be appropriate as data for the low- and high-CHO treatments were collected from each research participant. However, if we were interested in hypothesised differences between the male and female research participants with respect to each recovery intervention separately, then *the Mann-Whitney U test* would be appropriate to examine the male and female groups for each sub-scale under each experimental condition.

The Wilcoxon Test

In the worked example for *the Wilcoxon test* we will examine if the *energetic* mood state is influenced differently by the low- and high-CHO recovery interventions. You will recall that the purpose of applying a statistical test is to examine the likelihood of potential differences observed in the experimental sample, being observed in further participants drawn from the same population. It is therefore important to word the research hypotheses in terms of population differences, not in terms of the particular sample being observed. The hypotheses for the present example could be articulated in terms of difference alone, for example:

Null hypothesis

H_o: The amount of carbohydrate administered during the recovery period will have no effect on perceived energy

Alternative hypothesis

H_1:   The amount of carbohydrate administered during the recovery period will have an effect on perceived energy

The alternative hypothesis suggests that one recovery intervention will result in a higher level of perceived energy than the other, but does not specify which treatment (low-CHO or high-CHO) we would expect to elicit the higher energy levels. These are two-tailed hypotheses and would require us to adopt a *two-tailed* test procedure. The procedure is two-tailed because we are looking for differences between the perceived energy based on two different carbohydrate doses. Difference could occur by the low-CHO dose giving lower perceived energy scores, or higher perceived energy scores, than the high-CHO treatment. As the difference can occur through two alternatives, the required test is known as a two-tailed (2-tailed) test. Before progressing, we need also to establish our level of significance at which we will acknowledge that there is a *real* difference. As discussed previously, the convention in the sport and exercise sciences is for the level of significance to be set at 5% (i.e. $p < 0.05$).

Table 8.1(a) presents the runners *energetic* mood state scores for the low- and high-CHO recovery sports beverages. Taking the data from table 8.1(a), the *Wilcoxon test* statistic is determined by first calculating the difference between the low- and high-CHO recovery treatments; these differences are reported in column-1 of table 8.1(b). The differences in column-1 are then ranked – ignoring whether the sign is positive or negative – as in column-2. The signs from the difference column (column-1) are then reassigned to their corresponding rank (column-3).

Runner	*Energetic* **Mood State Score** Low-CHO	*Energetic* **Mood State Score** High-CHO	Column-1 **Low-high**	Column-2 **Rank**	Column-3 **Signed Rank**
1	30	5	+25	13	+13
2	14	9	+5	4	+4
3	9	8	+1	1.5	+1.5
4	30	15	+15	12	+12
5	30	25	+5	4	+4
6	13	2	+11	8	+8
7	8	15	-7	6.5	-6.5
8	29	15	+14	10.5	+10.5
9	7	20	-13	9	-9
10	7	2	+5	4	+4
11	7	0	+7	6.5	+6.5
12	13	13	0	-	-
13	15	14	+1	1.5	+1.5
14	34	20	+14	10.5	+10.5
Group Medians	**13.5**	**13.5**			

        (a)   (b)

Table 8.1   (a) The runners' *energetic* mood state scores for the low- and high-CHO recovery sports beverages. (b) Calculation of signed ranks for *the Wilcoxon test* for the runners' *energetic* mood state scores for the low- and high-CHO recovery sports beverages.

The next step is to calculate the T values, (for T^+ and T^-), as follows:

$$T^+ = 13 + 4 + 1.5 + 12 + 4 + 8 + 10.5 + 4 + 6.5 + 1.5 + 10.5 = 75.5$$

$$T^- = 6.5 + 9 = 15.5$$

To verify these calculations you will recall from calculation box 8.1:

$$[T^+ + T^-] = \frac{n(n+1)}{2}$$

where, $[T^+ + T^-] = 75.5 + 15.5 = 91$

$$\frac{n(n+1)}{2} = \frac{13(13+1)}{2} = \frac{13 \times 14}{2} = \frac{182}{2} = 91$$

From the above calculations we can verify the accuracy of the values obtained for the sums of positive and negative ranks. The smaller value of T, (i.e. 15.5), is taken as the test statistic, and this is compared to the values provided in the two-tailed *Wilcoxon* table for n = 13 (appendix: 4). Note – one data point is disregarded because the difference in ranks was zero. If the calculated test statistic, T = 15.5, is less than or equal to the tabulated value we can reject the null hypothesis. The tabulated value at the 5% significance level is 17; as 15.5 is less than 17, we can reject the two-tailed hypothesis H_o at the 5% significance level.

However, if prior reading of the scientific literature, or practice-based experienced, provides evidence to suggest that one treatment should result in greater perceived energy in comparison with the other, then *one-tailed* (1-tailed) hypotheses – which look for directional patterns in the data – could be tested. In the study examining low- and high-CHO recovery interventions on subsequent running performance, it was observed during a pilot study that the high-CHO dose was associated with feelings of lethargy, drowsiness, and nausea. Such a profile would not be consistent with the higher perceived energy scores that we would have anticipated for this 'high energy' intervention; the high-CHO dose appeared to be too high, giving rise to an adverse recovery response in the runners. Thus, to test whether this pilot study observation was evident in the research population, our one-tailed hypotheses might be written as:

Null hypothesis

H_o: A low carbohydrate treatment administered during the recovery period will not result in greater perceived energy than a high carbohydrate treatment

Alternative hypothesis

H_1:   A low carbohydrate treatment administered during the recovery period will result in greater perceived energy than a high carbohydrate treatment

In this example the difference of interest is identified as being in one direction only – we are not interested in the high carbohydrate treatment giving higher perceived energy – so the required test would be one-tailed. The test procedure is the same in terms of the calculation as in the 2-tailed test, except the one-tailed *Wilcoxon* table is used to check for statistical significance as reported previously. Though notably care must be taken when evaluating one-tailed hypotheses; H_0 can only be rejected if the sum of the ranks in *the Wilcoxon test*, or the medians of the groups, indicates that it is definitely the low-CHO treatment that gives the greater values for the *energetic* mood state. Examining the medians alone would not allow this decision to be made as, from table 8.1(a), the medians are the same. If the ranks are now examined, the positive ranks result from the high-CHO treatment giving rise to lower energy scores in comparison with the low-CHO scores. The sum of positive ranks yielded a much higher T value than the negative ranks, indicating that it was the low-CHO treatment that elicited the greater perceived energy. This point is very important; it is possible to obtain a one-tailed result that is statistically significant but for it to be due to the exact opposite of the research hypothesis being examined.

If statistical software packages are used to undertake these tests, they will compare exact probabilities with the pre-set significance level of $p < 0.05$ (i.e. the 5% level). If you are performing a 2-tailed test to evaluate a two-tailed hypothesis, then the comparison is straightforward in that the p-value provided in the computer output is directly compared with 0.05. However, if the test is 1-tailed, evaluating a one-tailed hypothesis, then the probability (i.e. p-value) provided in the computer output should be halved before comparison with 0.05. It is still important to check the direction of the difference to ensure that the significant difference we have identified is the one that we were expecting (as defined by our one-tailed hypothesis).

At this point it is important to note that the decision whether to apply a 1-tailed or 2-tailed test is addressed at the outset of the research project, during the planning stage, when you construct your research hypotheses. It is not the case that you can start your project examining two-tailed hypotheses, and switch part way through simply because it looks like the data will tolerate 1-tailed tests. There must always be a clear theoretical rationale or common sense reason underpinning the wording of the hypotheses, and in turn informing the design of your study and the structure of your statistical analyses.

The Mann-Whitney U Test

If we now consider an alternative comparison, it might be of interest to explore whether there were any differences in mood states between the male and female runners. For example, we will consider the *clearheaded* scale for the male and female runners following the low- and high-CHO recovery interventions. It will be assumed that there is no reason to believe that one gender should be more *clearheaded* than the other, and we will therefore test the following two-tailed hypotheses:

Null hypothesis

H_o: How *clearheaded* a runner feels following a high-CHO recovery

           treatment is not affected by the gender of that runner

Alternative hypothesis

H_1: How *clearheaded* a runner feels following a high-CHO recovery treatment is affected by the gender of that runner

Table 8.2 presents the runners *clearheaded* mood state scores for the high-CHO recovery sports beverage.

Clearheaded **Mood State Score** [Male] High-CHO	*Clearheaded* **Mood State Score** [Female] High-CHO
26	17
14	23
17	28
24	14
36	7
14	29
	12
	28

Table 8.2   The male and female runners' *clearheaded* mood state scores for the high-CHO recovery sports beverage.

The first step in *the Mann-Whitney U test* is to rank the data regardless of the group from which the data are drawn (table 8.3). The data have been combined into one ranked list by organising the values in order in the two shaded columns (column-2 and column-3). The ranks can then be assigned across the combined data whilst still being able to see from which group data originated. The original data sets are shown in the un-shaded columns (male data in column-1 and female data in column-4). The next step is to determine the sum of ranks for the male (i.e. $\Sigma R_m = 47.5$) and female (i.e. $\Sigma R_f = 57.5$) runners respectively.

Applying the equations from calculation box 8.2, U_m and U_f can be calculated as follows:

$$U_m = n_m n_f + \frac{n_m(n_m+1)}{2} - \sum R_m = (6 \times 8) + \frac{6(6+1)}{2} - 47.5 = 48 + \frac{42}{2} - 47.5 = 21.5$$

and,

$$U_f = n_m n_f + \frac{n_f(n_f+1)}{2} - \sum R_f = (6 \times 8) + \frac{8(8+1)}{2} - 57.5 = 48 + \frac{72}{2} - 57.5 = 26.5$$

The smaller U_m and U_f value is assigned as the test statistic U, which is then compared with the Mann-Whitney critical values (appendix: 6). If U is *less than* or *equal to* the tabulated critical value then the null hypothesis, H_0, is rejected. Taking the 5% significance level, the tabulated value for unequal groups of $n_m = 6$ and $n_f = 8$, is 8.0. As the calculated value of 21.5 is greater than 8.0 we accept the null hypothesis. The conclusion from this analysis is that a runner's response to the high-CHO recovery treatment, in terms of the clearheaded mood state, is not affected by the gender of that runner.

If this test had been undertaken on a computer, the sums of ranks for both groups would be identified as in this worked example. The software would generate a probability for the test statistic, and if this p-value were less than 0.05 we would reject the null hypothesis at the 5% level.

	Column-1 Clearheaded **Mood State Score** [Male Ranks] *High-CHO*	Column-2 Clearheaded **Mood State Score** [Male] High-CHO	Column-3 Clearheaded **Mood State Score** [Female] High-CHO	Column-4 Clearheaded **Mood State Score** [Female Ranks] *High-CHO*	
			7	1	
M			12	2	F
A	4	14	14	4	E
L	4	14			M
E	6.5	17	17	6.5	A
			23	8	L
R	9	24			E
A	10	26			
N			28	11.5	R
K			28	11.5	A
S			29	13	N
	14	36			K
	$\Sigma R_m = 47.5$			$\Sigma R_f = 57.5$	S
		Combined Data Order			

Table 8.3   Calculation of signed ranks for *the Mann-Whitney U test* for the male and female runners' *clearheaded* mood state scores for the high-CHO recovery sports beverages.

Parametric Tests of Differences

The *Wilcoxon* and *Mann-Whitney U tests* are non-parametric tests of differences, and as discussed previously they do not make specific assumptions about population distributions. In contrast, parametric tests assume that certain parameters are known which constrain the population(s) from which the sample(s) have been derived, and these parameters are used for comparative purposes during the course of the tests. Whilst it is important to be aware that the *normal distribution* is not the only statistical distribution, it is the most common parametric distribution encountered in conducting sport and exercise science research, and is therefore the principle distribution that we have concentrated upon in this text. The integrity of many statistical tests depends upon the data satisfying the assumptions of normality. However, problems arise if:

1.   Outliers are present.

2.   There is a marked skewness.

3.   There is considerable disparity of variances (especially when coupled with samples of markedly different sizes).

Checks for normality have been discussed in chapters 4 and 6, and it is important to ensure that such checks are undertaken before parametric tests are applied to the data. The family of parametric tests we shall investigate for two group tests of difference are called *t*-tests or student *t*-tests. The model underlying a *t*-test assumes the data to have been derived from normal distributions with equal variance, so these assumptions need to be checked during a preliminary exploration of the data. There are three different *t*-test structures for data comparison. Each structure has the same underlying mathematical aim, which is to compare two means to see if they are indicative of the groups having been drawn from different populations. However, the three tests have slightly different functions, and these are described as follows:

1.   *The one sample t-test* – This tests one sample of data against a known population parameter (e.g. a national average) to see if the sample is different from the population with respect to that particular factor. Height and weight (body mass) charts are based on this kind of test.

2.   *A paired samples t-test* – Looks for differences between two sets of related data that follow normal distribution parameters. These related samples could be carefully matched pairs of research participants or repeated measures of a variable (e.g. over time or over condition) taken on the same research participants.

3.   *An independent samples t-test* – This looks for differences between two sets of data that are unrelated and follow normal distribution parameters.

It is important to note that the *t*-test will tolerate some violation of assumptions provided the samples are:

1.   Not too small – if n > 8 the test will usually cope, but if n < 8 sensitivity to identify differences is markedly compromised.

2.   Do not contain outliers.

3.   Are of equal or nearly equal size.

If violations do occur, solutions include using a nonparametric alternative, or (systematically[8.5]) removing the outliers and continuing. The second solution should not be undertaken lightly. Check the source of the outlier(s) for data collection or recording error and consider whether it is necessary to include those data in order to have a representative sample. If the removal of outliers has an important effect on the overall interpretation of the data that appears inappropriate, or if there are several outliers such that they have combined importance, they must not be removed.

The One Sample t-test

This test does not sit comfortably in the subject matter of the present chapter, but is appropriate to include here as the test has applications within sports and exercise science research. There are two different groups of data to test, but only one experimental sample. This sample is tested against a

---

[8.5]   In removing outliers it is appropriate to have a clear rationale or set of rules governing this decision making process. It is not normally appropriate to ignore data points purely for the reason that it makes the data analyses problematic; assuming good experimental procedures have been followed, outliers are often the data points of greatest interest.

known mean, or a hypothesised mean, where this value might be based on earlier studies or on national statistics. Calculation box 8.3 describes how the test statistic *t* is calculated.

Calculation Box 8.3   The One Sample t-test

The One Sample t-test is used with a single sample of normally distributed data to test whether the population mean is, or has agreement with, an expected known value. The null hypothesis is that the population mean is equal to *k*, where *k* is known from the literature or may be from national statistics.

1.   Calculate the mean ($\overline{x}$) and standard deviation (*s*) of the sample

2.   The degrees of freedom, d.f. = n – 1   where,   n is the number of observations

3.   The test statistic *t* is calculated using the formula:

$$t_{(d.f.)} = \frac{\overline{x} - k}{s/\sqrt{n}}$$

where   *s* is the sample standard deviation

k is the hypothesised mean

$\overline{x}$ is the sample mean

4.   The *t* statistic is compared with critical values from the *t*-table with the required degrees of freedom for the test (appendix: 3). If the *t* value is *greater than or equal to* the critical value from the *t*-table the null hypothesis is rejected.

We will now present a worked example of the *one sample t-test* based upon the calculation presented in calculation box 8.3. Whilst the example is relatively contrived, it does serve to illustrate the principle tenants of this approach to statistical analysis. A team of rugby players often had cause to visit the casualty department in their local hospital. In the waiting area a sign indicated, "Average waiting time is 30 minutes". They decided to test whether this was the case, and asked the reception administrator for data on the waiting times (in minutes) for the last 20 patients.

The research hypotheses are:

> *Null hypothesis*
>
> H_o: The average waiting time is 30 minutes (i.e. $\mu = 30$ min)

> *Alternative hypothesis*
>
> H_1:   The average waiting time is not 30 minutes (i.e. $\mu \neq 30$ min)

This is a two-tailed hypothesis test, as the rugby players had no evidence that the waiting time was likely to be longer or shorter than 30 minutes. The data provided by the reception administrator were as follows:

20, 30, 45, 40, 15, 50, 30, 25, 30, 50, 80, 20, 10, 50, 60, 25, 20, 20, 35, 60

The mean ($\bar{x}$) and standard deviation (s) of this small data set are calculated as described in chapter 1, to yield $\bar{x} - 35.75$ and $s - 18.16$. There were 20 observations; therefore the degrees of freedom are given by:

d.f. $= n - 1$

 $= 20 - 1 = 19$

Applying the formula from calculation box 8.3:

$$t_{(d.f.)} = \frac{\bar{x} - k}{s/\sqrt{n}}$$

The calculation for $t_{(19)}$, where 19 is the degrees of freedom, is given by:

$$t = \frac{35.75 - 30}{18.16 / \sqrt{20}} = 1.416$$

The statistic t is therefore a value resulting from a mathematical calculation of the differences between the two means and takes into account the number of individuals whose data were included (i.e. the sample size). It can be thought of as a summary statistic (i.e. mathematically summarising attributes of the sample, $\bar{x}$ and n), which is compared to a tabulated value that represents the size of t at which the means can be said to be different. The critical value of the test is looked up on tables for the t distribution (appendix: 3), and is applied to interpret the calculated value of t. In this case $t_{(19)} = 2.093$ at the 5% significance level. As the calculated t value is less than the critical value from the t-table (i.e. $1.416 < 1.729$), the null hypothesis is accepted and is reported as ($t_{(19)} = 1.416$, p > 0.05). The results of the test, if taken from computer output that provides an exact p-value, should be reported as ($t_{(19)} = 1.416$, p = 0.173).

Paired Samples t-test

The *paired samples t-test* is applied to data similar to that for which you might consider using a *Wilcoxon* non-parametric test, with the added condition that it fulfils the requirement of being normally distributed. If the data appear normally distributed then the *t*-test is more powerful than the *Wilcoxon* test, that is it is more likely to detect a difference in the data if there is one. It is important to remember that the samples will either be *matched pairs* (where matching is relative to a series of population characteristics that are considered to be important or influential with respect to the research question), or it can be the same sample with repeated measures (e.g. over time or across two conditions) taken during the experimental procedure.

Calculation Box 8.4   The Paired Samples *t*-test

The *t*-test is concerned with investigating whether there is a difference in population means based on the observed sample. The *paired samples t-test* is used with two matched samples, or one sample with two repeated measures, of normally distributed data. The null hypothesis is that there is no significant difference between the sample means of two matched samples, and this is tested against an alternative hypothesis that the means of the samples are different.

1.   First calculate the differences, *d*, between the pairs of values (e.g. the before and after scores)

2.   The degrees of freedom, d.f. = n – 1   where,   n is the number of paired observations

3.   The test statistic *t* is calculated using the formula:

$$t = \frac{\overline{d}}{s_d / \sqrt{n}}$$ where s_d is the sample difference standard deviation

$\overline{d}$ is the mean of the differences between the values

n is the number of matched pairs

$\overline{x}$ is the sample mean

4.   The *t* statistic is compared with critical values from the *t*-table with the required degrees of freedom for the test (appendix: 3). If the t value is greater than or equal to the critical value from the *t*-table the null hypothesis is rejected.

We will now present a worked example to illustrate the application of the *paired samples t-test*. A general practitioner initiated a *Healthy Living Clinic* to combat rising levels of obesity within patients on his medical centre's lists. Patients diagnosed as clinically obese undertook a 6-week weight-loss and gentle exercise programme, where the exercise component involved treadmill walking, under careful supervision, with patients stopping exercise when they began to feel out of breath or unduly tired. The length of time the patients were able to sustain the walking exercise was recorded at the start of the programme and 6-weeks later. The general practitioner wished to evaluate the efficacy of the programme in terms of body weight loss and changes in exercise tolerance as reflected in longer walk times. There will be many factors that will influence patient exercise tolerance in this scenario, where medical conditions associated with obesity will further impinge upon exercise capacity and the ability of patients to comply to an exercise regime. Nevertheless, the markers of weight loss and walk time intuitively should provide a general, non-invasive, guide to the efficacy of the programme.

The research hypotheses are:

Null hypothesis

H_o: The weight loss and exercise programme do not increase duration of walking time

Alternative hypothesis

H_1:   The weight loss and exercise programme increases duration of walking time

The research hypotheses are one-tailed, in that the practitioner was investigating whether walk time increased as a result of the healthy living programme. The data from this study are presented in table 8.4. The column of differences (pre- vs. post-walk times) assists in the calculation of the *t*-test statistic. The formula takes into consideration that the measures are related – in this example the measures are taken from the same research participant – and the data are compared to assess the effect of the intervention on each individual. Thus, the analysis is performed on the *difference* data.

There are 40 research participants in this study; therefore the degrees of freedom are given by:

d.f. $= n - 1 = 40 - 1 = 39$

Pre-Walk Time (min)	Post-Walk Time (min)	Difference (Post – Pre) (min)
7.17	9.95	2.78
14.42	17.20	2.78
10.37	14.00	3.63
12.03	14.81	2.78
14.31	17.09	2.78
12.48	15.26	2.78
15.28	18.06	2.78
6.06	9.00	2.94
12.11	14.89	2.78
15.16	17.94	2.78
3.40	6.18	2.78
13.04	18.00	4.96
15.32	18.10	2.78
13.24	16.02	2.78
13.04	15.82	2.78
4.34	7.50	3.16
13.00	15.78	2.78
17.29	20.07	2.78
7.48	10.26	2.78
9.09	11.87	2.78
12.23	15.50	3.27
11.43	14.21	2.78
15.37	18.15	2.78
13.16	15.94	2.78
12.07	14.85	2.78
15.35	19.00	3.65
10.22	13.00	2.78
15.09	17.87	2.78
12.20	15.00	2.80
16.00	18.78	2.78
13.51	16.29	2.78
9.48	12.26	2.78
11.55	15.00	3.45
9.48	12.26	2.78
12.00	14.78	2.78
9.19	11.97	2.78
10.42	13.20	2.78
9.00	11.78	2.78
9.00	12.00	3.00
11.18	13.96	2.78
$\bar{x}_B = 11.66$	$\bar{x}_A = 14.59$	$\bar{d} = 2.93$

Table 8.4   Pre- vs. post-walk times for the general practitioner's *Healthy Living* Programme.

From table 8.4, the mean of the differences is calculated to be 2.93 and the standard deviation of the differences is 0.40 (to 2 decimal places). Applying the formula from calculation box 8.4:

$$t_{(39)} = \frac{\bar{d}}{s_d / \sqrt{n}}$$

Thus,

$$T_{(39)} = \frac{\bar{d}}{s_d / \sqrt{n}} = \frac{2.93}{0.40 / \sqrt{40}} = 46.33$$

From the *t*-tables, the critical value for d.f. = 39 at the 5% level for a 1-tailed test is 1.685. As the *t* value (i.e. 46.33) is *greater than* the *t*-table critical value (i.e. 1.685) we can reject the null hypothesis ($t_{(39)}$ = 46.33, p < 0.05). This is a one-tailed test as we are evaluating whether the walk times of the patients are increasing, we must therefore confirm that the walk duration times are indeed longer before we can accept the alternative hypothesis. Looking at the means for the two walk tests, the mean of the second walk time (i.e. 14.59) is bigger than the mean of the first walk time (i.e. 11.66), therefore the null hypothesis can be rejected and the practitioner can conclude that the *Healthy Living* programme does improve exercise tolerance as evaluated by the length of time that patients can comfortably walk.

Independent Samples t-test

An *independent samples t-test* can be applied to the same data as the *Mann-Whitney U* non-parametric test, but with the added condition that it fulfils the requirement of being normally distributed. If the data are normally distributed then the *t*-test is more powerful than the *Mann-Whitney U test*, in that it is more likely to detect a difference between the samples if one is present. An *independent samples t-test* is performed on data from unrelated groups. The structure of the experimental design will mean that participants have been randomly assigned to experimental groups, which may therefore differ in their sizes. Furthermore, as a consequence of the random allocation of research participants, the groups may have a similar spread of data or exhibit quite different patterns of spread. As such, there are two forms of the *independent samples t-tests* available in order to cope with these different situations, which necessitates a check on the spread of the data – in addition to the normality checks – before further analyses are undertaken.

The check for similarity of spread – or statistically this is known as *homogeneity of variance* – normally appears as part of the output if you perform your *independent samples t-test* using a statistical package. One such check is *Levene's test for homogeneity* (or equality) *of variance* (Levene, 1960). The test applies a null hypothesis that the population data are similarly spread (i.e. the test assumes that if there is no difference in the variance of the two samples, then the populations have the same pattern of spread). The test is a form of *t*-test which is performed on the amounts by which data differ or deviate from the mean (i.e. $[x - \overline{x}]$), or the square of these differences (i.e. $[x - \overline{x}]^2$), and therefore returns a *t* statistic (or an *F* statistic for more than two groups; refer to chapter 9). Thus, if this statistic has a probability value greater than 0.05 (i.e. p > 0.05), this would indicate homogeneity or similarity of variance. There are many similar tests that compare two groups, or more than two groups, though we have only considered one such test here. For alternative tests and a critique of their application refer to *Using Statistics in Sport and Exercise Science Research – Book 2*.

Calculation Box 8.5   The Independent Samples *t*-test

Used with two independent samples that are normally distributed, and when computing by hand the homogeneity of variance condition must also be satisfied. Homogeneity of variance is assessed in terms of whether the standard deviations estimated for the population are equal – or nearly equal. Like the *paired samples t-test*, the *independent samples t-test* is concerned with exploring difference in population means based on the observed sample. The null hypothesis is that there is no difference between the population means, and the alternative hypothesis is that the population means are different.

(Continued…)

1. Calculate the means ($\bar{x}_1$ and $\bar{x}_2$) and standard deviations (s_1 and s_2) for each sample group

2. The degrees of freedom, d.f. $= n - 2$ where, n is the sum of n_1 and n_2

Samples of Equal Variance

3. Calculate the pooled variance, $S_p{}^2$, by the following formula:

$$S_p{}^2 = \frac{(n_1 - 1)s_1{}^2 + (n_2 - 1)s_2{}^2}{n_1 + n_2 - 2}$$

where, n_1 and n_2 are the sample sizes

$s_1{}^2$ and $s_2{}^2$ are the squares of the sample standard deviations (i.e. the variances) for each group

4. The test statistic t is calculated using the formula:

$$t = \frac{\bar{x}_1 - \bar{x}_2}{\sqrt{\dfrac{S_p{}^2}{n_1} + \dfrac{S_p{}^2}{n_2}}}$$ where, $\bar{x}_1$ and $\bar{x}_2$ are the sample means

5. The t statistic is compared with critical values from the t-table with the required degrees of freedom for the test (appendix: 3). If the t value is *greater than or equal to* the critical value from the t-table the null hypothesis is rejected.

Samples of Unequal Variance

6. A slightly different formula should be used if the variances of the two samples are not equal (i.e. it would be inappropriate to pool the variances where they were found to be different). This approach uses the individual group variances, instead of pooled variances, which decreases the potential for error arising from combining unequal variances. Though it is important to note that this test based upon individual group variances is not as powerful as the pooled variances test.

(Continued…)

The test statistic t for groups of unequal variances is calculated using the formula:

$$t = \frac{\overline{x}_1 - \overline{x}_2}{\sqrt{\dfrac{s_1^2}{n_1} + \dfrac{s_2^2}{n_2}}}$$

where, s_1^2 and s_2^2 are the squares of the sample standard deviations for each group

7.   The t statistic is compared with critical values from the t-table with the required degrees of freedom for the test (appendix: 3). If the t value is *greater than or equal to* the critical value from the t-table the null hypothesis is rejected.

We will now present a worked example to illustrate the application of the *independent samples t-test*. If we consider the data from the *Running Study* that we have examined in previous chapters, some of the physiological measures may be considered to be different between the male and female runners. One of the fundamental measures we may wish to check before addressing more complex analytical techniques would be to verify that the male and female runners came from the same population in relation to age. Age is one factor that is known to influence a number of the physiological characteristics reported in this data set (notably maximum oxygen uptake, VO_{2max}, which we examined in chapter 5). If the male and female runners actually come from different running populations relative to their respective age ranges, then differences that we may attribute to gender may actually be due to the age factor. By conducting an *independent samples t-test* on the age data for the male and female runners we will be able to verify that the male and female runners were drawn from the same population of runners.

The research hypotheses are:

Null hypothesis

H_o: Male and female runners are not different in age

Alternative hypothesis

H_1:   Male and female runners are different in age

The research hypotheses are two-tailed, in that if an age difference between male and female runners is present, the male age may be higher or lower than the female age. Data were collected from 40 male runners ($n_m = 40$) and 20 female runners ($n_f = 20$). The first step is to calculate the summary statistics necessary for the use in the *t*-test formula. The methods for calculating these summary statistics are presented in chapter 4. The data and summary statistics are presented in table 8.5.

Ages of Male Runners	Ages of Female Runners
26.9, 22.3, 21.2, 39.3, 24.9, 24.8, 21.0, 21.4 25.4, 24.8, 19.9, 24.2, 20.5, 24.0, 31.8, 34.5 25.8, 29.8, 25.6, 32.8, 21.7, 22.8, 25.3, 21.7 29.6, 25.6, 21.3, 32.1, 28.9, 20.0, 24.7, 25.2 26.3, 28.4, 32.8, 24.2, 24.6, 34.3, 22.4, 25.4	37.7, 26.9, 26.0, 25.8, 22.0, 22.6, 25.2, 18.7, 20.1, 20.9, 33.0, 29.1, 28.3, 26.9, 33.4, 30.4, 24.7, 25.4, 21.0, 23.1
Sample size, n = 40	**Sample size,** n = 20
Sample mean, $\bar{x}_m = 25.96$ years	**Sample mean,** $\bar{x}_f = 26.06$ years
Sample variance, $s_m^2 = 20.84$	**Sample variance,** $s_f^2 = 23.91$

Table 8.5   Age data for the male and female runners from the *Running Study*.

From observing the summary statistics, we might predict that there is unlikely to be any real differences in the ages of the male and female runners as the sample means and sample variances are very similar. As the sample variances are similar we can pool this data and conduct the more powerful statistical analysis. You will recall that a check to confirm homogeneity of variances can be performed using a *Levene's test*. A result that is not significant would lead us to accept that the variances are equal, and therefore we can apply the *independent samples t-test* that assumes equal variances. Conversely, a significant result would indicate that the variances are not equal, and we should adopt the alternative approach for samples with unequal variances. If you are undertaking your *independent samples t-test* by hand, the decision about homogeneity of variance is often made *by eye* – as was the case in this worked example. Variance is measured in squared units (i.e. squares of the sample standard deviations); therefore sample variances of 20–24, with sample means of around 26, would be considered as similar.

We lose an extra degree of freedom for initially splitting the data into two different groups; therefore the degrees of freedom for the present experimental design are given by:

$$d.f. \ = (n_1 + n_2) - 2$$
$$= (40 + 20) - 2 = 58$$

Applying the equation to calculate the pooled variance:

$$s_p^{\,2} = \frac{(n_1 - 1)s_1^{\,2} + (n_2 - 1)s_2^{\,2}}{n_1 + n_2 - 2} = \frac{((40 - 1) \times 20.84) + ((20 - 1) \times 23.91)}{40 + 20 - 2} = \frac{812.76 + 454.29}{58} = 21.85$$

Applying the formula for calculating the test statistic t for groups of equal variances:

$$t_{(58)} = \frac{\bar{x}_1 - \bar{x}_2}{\sqrt{\dfrac{s_p^{\,2}}{n_1} + \dfrac{s_p^{\,2}}{n_2}}} = \frac{25.96 - 26.06}{\sqrt{\dfrac{21.85}{60} + \dfrac{21.85}{40}}} = \frac{-0.1}{0.95} = -0.105$$

The final step is to look up the critical value for $t_{(58)}$ in the t-tables (note – the negative sign can be ignored as we are only interested in the size of the value), the critical value for d.f. = 58 at the 5% level is 2.002 (interpolated between d.f. of 55 and 60 in appendix: 3). As the t value (i.e. –0.105) is not greater than the t-table critical value (i.e. 2.002) we accept the null hypothesis. This analysis confirms our initial prediction that the male and female runners are drawn from the same population with respect to age. Furthermore, this means that we can have more confidence in any subsequent tests performed on the data that reveal gender-related differences. If the analysis had been undertaken on a computer, the software would generate an exact probability for the test statistic of $t_{(58)}$ = –0.105, and should therefore be reported as ($t_{(58)}$ = –0.105, p = 0.935). As p > 0.05, we would accept the null hypothesis and conclude that there is no evidence of a difference between the ages of the male and female runners.

Chapter Decision Tree

Figure 8.2 presents an overview of the questions you should ask prior to undertaking tests for differences in two groups, and the resulting decision processes as described in this chapter.

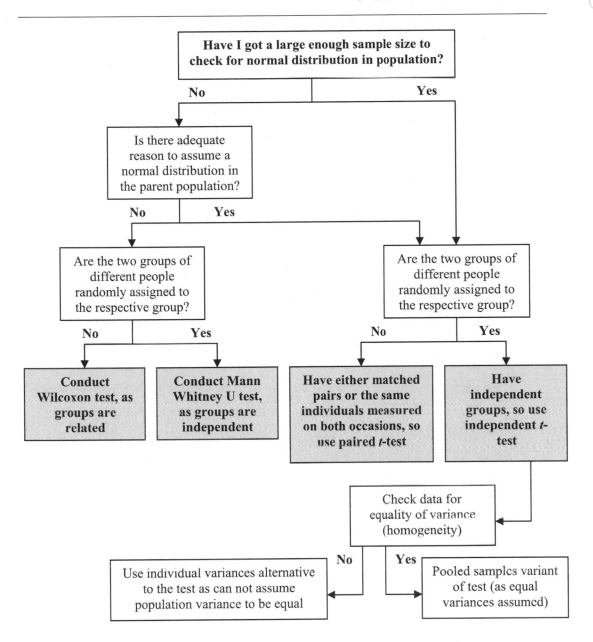

Figure 8.2   Decision tree for tests of differences in two groups.

Summary/Key Points

1. In evaluating possible differences in groups it is important that you are measuring and comparing the *same* variable, that is you must be comparing *like* with *like*.

2. The more sensitive parametric statistics are able to detect smaller differences between observations made on two populations in comparison with less sensitive non-parametric tests. This is because parametric tests are able to apply known population parameters to assist in identifying real differences in data sets; thus, parametric tests have more power by virtue of their greater sensitivity.

3. The data must initially be checked for normality, and we must also carefully consider the design of the data collection, as these will inform our choice of analytical approach.

4. The *Mann-Whitney U test* (independent groups) and the *Wilcoxon test* (related groups) are non-parametric tests of differences that compare the medians of two sample groups.

5. Two-tailed hypotheses describe an outcome where differences can occur through two alternatives with no preconceptions of the outcome. Two-tailed hypotheses require the adoption of two-tailed (2-tailed) test procedures.

6. If prior reading or experienced provides evidence to suggest that one treatment would be better (or worse) than another, then one-tailed hypotheses – which look for directional patterns in the data – would be tested using one-tailed (1-tailed) test procedures.

7. The model underlying a *t*-test assumes the data are derived from normal distributions with equal variance. Problems will arise: if the assumptions of normality are not met, if outliers are present, if there is marked skewness; or if there is considerable disparity of variances. The *t*-test will tolerate some violation of assumptions provided the samples are not too small, do not contain outliers, and are of equal or nearly equal size.

8. The *one sample t-test* tests one sample of data against a known population parameter to se if the sample is different from the population with respect to that particular factor (e.g. comparisons of height and body mass with national averages or 'desirable' values).

9. The *paired samples t-test* looks for differences between two sets of related data that follow normal distribution parameters. These related samples could be carefully matched pairs of research participants or repeated measures of a variable (e.g. over time or over condition) taken on the same research participants.

10. The *independent samples t-test* (for equal or unequal variances) looks for differences between two sets of data that are unrelated and follow normal distribution parameters. In addition to checks of normality, a check for the similarity of spread (e.g. *Levene's test for homogeneity of variance*) must also be made prior to further analyses.

9

Looking at Differences in
More Complex Experimental Designs

Chapter Objectives

- To recognise when analysis of variance (*ANOVA*) is an appropriate technique to use
- To identify alternative processes, if possible, when assumptions for *ANOVA* are violated
- To identify when it is necessary to conduct further analyses
- To apply *post hoc* testing or pre-planned comparisons appropriately when further analyses are necessary.

Introduction

In the previous chapter we examined analysis techniques for comparing up to two groups of data. Of the approaches discussed, the *t*-test was regarded as being the most powerful test under conditions that conformed to the assumptions of normality. However, the *t*-test cannot be applied to more complex designs that result in more than two groups of data. If we needed to explore differences between three groups we would need to apply three separate *t*-tests. Exploring differences between four groups would require six tests in order to compare every pair of variables. Every time another group for comparison is added the number of tests required to compare every pair increases considerably. By the time we arrived at a situation involving six groups we would need fifteen different *t*-tests.

You will recall that the foundation of this type of statistical analysis is probability theory and the notion of statistical significance. The application of each statistical test has the potential to introduce error to the decision making process. When we work at the 5% significance level, this suggests that we are prepared to set the chances of rejecting a null hypothesis wrongly (i.e. a type-I error) at 5%, or one chance in twenty. Conducting repeated tests on the same data will further multiply the chances of making the wrong decision. It is not acceptable to undertake data analyses that increase the probability of error to such a degree that the value of the research is compromised. Such an increase in error as a result of repeated analyses is referred to as *family-wise error*. Thus, performing repeated *t*-tests is not only time consuming, but it increases the risk of at least one of the comparisons being statistically significant – or deemed to be important – by chance alone. For example, in a study involving eight groups (e.g. male and female research participants measured across four different time points), 28 statistical tests would be required giving rise to *at least* one error occurring when testing at the 5% (i.e. one in twenty) level for each test. This means that we may find a difference because the associated p-value would be less than 0.05 (i.e. $p < 0.05$), but this would be occurring purely by chance!

There are both parametric and non-parametric statistical techniques that can accommodate evaluating more than two groups within one process. These techniques remove the need for conducting repeated tests and therefore still work with the 5% risk of a type-I error. Parametric tests are able to cope with highly complex experimental designs, while non-parametric equivalents are more limited. However, there are some situations where parametric tests are the only approaches to evaluating particular structures of data. The parametric tests of analysis of variance (*ANOVA*) is a collection of data analysis techniques particularly useful when more than one independent variable is included in an experimental design. Whilst *ANOVA* are relatively robust to violations, (i.e. provide reliable results even when data are not normally distributed), it is appropriate to explore the data and verify whether they do actually conform to normal distribution parameters. If violations are present, the data need to be checked in order to subjectively evaluate their potential effect. It is necessary to check that any such violations do not arise in every group; the more violations there are, the less likely the *ANOVA* test will yield reliable results. Estimates of power and effect size (chapter 3) can help with evaluating the usefulness of the *ANOVA* result under circumstances where violation of assumptions has occurred.

Non-parametric tests of difference between more than two groups are easier to explain than the more complex *ANOVA* techniques, but can only be applied to one factor (or one-way) designs. This means that although we can have more than three groups, each group should be decided by one criteria only. For example, within sports therapy we may have the need to evaluate the efficacy of a number of treatments for managing a particular condition. As discussed previously, treatment of injury is one situation where we would not be able to impose a cross-over experimental design; it would not be possible, or ethical, to identically re-injure a research participant in order to evaluate further courses of treatment! Thus, each treatment approach would be applied to a different group of individuals, and the outcome of the different therapies would need to be evaluated by a singular representative measure – such as a muscle soreness scale – that would be appropriate for all courses of treatment. Table 9.1 presents an analysis model for this design, where a number of groups (two treatment groups and a control group) are evaluated on one factor (or one-way). In this example, the therapist measured the patients' responses to the muscle soreness scale 48 hours post-exercise (where the exercise model was designed to evoke soreness in the muscle group of interest). Had the sports therapist decided to evaluate the rehabilitation process over time by measuring muscle soreness at two different time points (e.g. 48 hours post exercise and 6 days post-exercise), the analysis would be described as two-way, or two factor. In this more complex situation there would be six different groups, as described in table 9.2, necessitating the use of parametric tests of difference for multiple groups.

This chapter will examine non-parametric and parametric approaches to exploring differences in data from more complex experimental designs involving more than two groups.

	Control Group	Treatment Group-1	Treatment Group-2	Analysis Approach
Muscle Soreness Score (Time – 1)	1	2	3	**One-Way** **One Factor:** Treatment
Analysis	*Differences in treatment group as evaluated by muscle soreness scores*			*Non-Parametric, or Parametric test*

Table 9.1   Illustration of one-way (one factor) experimental designs as applied to different treatment approaches to the *Muscle Soreness* study.

	Control Group	Treatment Group-1	Treatment Group-2	Analysis Approach
Muscle Soreness Score (Time – 1)	1	2	3	**One-Way** **One Factor:** Treatment
Muscle Soreness Score (Time – 2)	4	5	6	**Two-Way** **Two Factors:** Treatment Time
Analysis	*Differences in treatment group as evaluated by muscle soreness scores over time*			*Parametric test*

Table 9.2   Illustration of two-way (two factor) experimental designs as applied to different treatment approaches to the *Muscle Soreness* study.

Non-parametric Tests of Difference Between More Than Two Groups

We will consider two non-parametric one-way tests for experimental designs involving more than two groups, depending on whether the groups are independent or related. The *Kruskal-Wallis test* examines differences in independent samples, and the *Friedman test* examines differences in related samples.

The Kruskal-Wallis Test

The *Kruskal-Wallis test* is comparable to the *Mann-Whitney U test* we discussed in relation to experimental designs involving two groups. It makes no assumptions about the distribution of the population from which the data were drawn. The test is concerned with hypotheses relating to whether the samples were from the same population or not, and this is addressed by exploring differences in the group medians.

Calculation Box 9.1   The Kruskal-Wallis Test

Calculation of the *Kruskal-Wallis test* involves the following steps:

1.   Rank all scores regardless of which group they came from; tied (the same) values are dealt with by giving an average rank for the positions.

2.   Calculate the sums of ranks for each group, R_i, where i represents each group.

3.   The tests statistic, H, is derived as follows:

$$H = \frac{12}{N(N+1)} \sum_{i=1}^{k} \frac{R_i^2}{n_i} - 3(N+1)$$

where, k is the number of groups

n_i is the number of values (observations) in group i

N is the total sample size (i.e. $\Sigma\, n_i$)

R_i is the sum of ranks for group i

4.   Compare H for significance using the χ^2 distribution with $(k-1)$ degrees of freedom (appendix: 2). The null hypothesis is rejected if the calculated value for H is greater than the tabulated $\chi^2_{(k-1)}$ value.

To present a worked example of the *Kruskal-Wallis test* we will refer back to the *Muscle Soreness* study described in the previous section. A sports therapist was interested in the efficacy of two different muscle soreness treatments – heat treatment and ultrasound treatment. The research participants were required to complete a course of exercise to induce muscle pain. The participants were then divided into three experimental groups: a control group who received no treatment for the muscle soreness; a group who received heat treatment daily for a period of five days; and, a group who received ultrasound treatment daily for a period of five days. Participants were then required to complete a 10-point pain scale questionnaire (0 – no pain; 10 – extreme pain) on day six of the study. The form that statistical analyses should take for this study would be to evaluate the differences between the three groups, to examine whether either treatment is more effective than time alone in promoting recovery from muscle soreness. All groups were only measured on one variable (i.e. muscle soreness), and were grouped based on one factor (i.e. treatment). Thus, the analysis will be a one factor, or one-way, analysis. The data collected with respect to this one factor using the 10-point pain scale questionnaire will be at the ordinal level of measurement. The scale is subjective and each individual reports their pain level relative to the level they perceived their pain to be earlier in the week, before and during the treatment period. The hypotheses for this example could be articulated in terms:

Null hypothesis

H_o: Muscle soreness treatments over five days do not reduce perceived pain

Alternative hypothesis

H_1:   Muscle soreness treatments over five days reduce perceived pain

The data for this example are presented in table 9.3; the rank position, regardless of group, is presented in italics. Data will be evaluated at the 5% significance level of testing.

Control Group	Ranks R_1	Treatment Group-1 Heat	Ranks R_2	Treatment Group-2 Ultrasound	Ranks R_3
4	8	3	4.5	6	15.5
6	15.5	4	8	4	8
6	15.5	5	12	5	12
5	12	4	8	4	8
1	1	2	2.5	3	4.5
		6	15.5	2	2.5
	$\Sigma R_1 = 52$		$\Sigma R_2 = 50.5$		$\Sigma R_3 = 50.5$

Table 9.3   Muscle soreness scores (and *ranks*) in response to no treatment (Control Group), heat treatment (Group-1) and ultrasound treatment (Group-2).

From calculation box 9.1, the four pieces of information we require before commencing our analyses are:

- The number of groups
- The sizes of the samples
- The total sample size
- The sum of ranks for each group (factor).

Thus, for the present investigation: the number of groups (k) = 3; the sample sizes are n_1 = 5, n_2 = 6 and n_3 = 6; the total sample size (N) = 6 + 6 + 5 = 17; and the sum of ranks for each group are ΣR_1 = 52, ΣR_2 = 50.5 and ΣR_3 = 50.5. We are now in a position to calculate our H statistic using the equation from calculation box 9.1:

$$H = \frac{12}{N(N+1)} \sum_{i=1}^{k} \frac{R_i^2}{n_i} - 3(N+1)$$

$$H = \frac{12}{17(18)} \left(\frac{52^2}{5} + \frac{50.5^2}{6} + \frac{50.5^2}{6} \right) - 3(17+1)$$

$$H = \frac{12}{306}(1390.88) - 54 = 0.544$$

The final step is to compare the derived value for H (i.e. 0.544) for significance using the χ^2 distribution with $\{(k-1) = 3 - 1 = 2\}$ degrees of freedom (appendix: 2). At the 5% significance level the critical value is 5.99. As our calculated value for H is less than 5.99, we accept the null hypothesis and conclude that the treatments did not improve perceived pain any more than time alone.

As the null hypothesis was accepted in this example, this would be the end of the statistical analysis stage and we would progress to presenting these findings within our chosen format for report writing (refer to chapter 11). However, if we had found that a difference did occur between the groups we would then need to continue our data investigation to explore where the difference, or differences, might be located; a significant result obtained from the *Kruskal-Wallis test* will show that there is a difference between *any* of the groups, but it will not identify between which groups the difference occurs. It is also necessary at this further investigation stage to see whether any differences were due to changes in the right direction, given that the hypotheses were worded in terms of *a reduction* in pain (i.e. 1-tailed). The *Kruskal-Wallis test* does not look at one-tailed testing.

If required, further analysis would use *Mann-Whitney U tests* to explore each pair of groups for differences. However, this further analysis may incur the problem of inflating the probability of an error arising as discussed in this chapter's Introduction in terms of *family-wise error*. To control for this possibility a procedure called *Bonferroni adjustment* is made to the significance level of the tests. This means that we divide the significance level (i.e. α) by the number of tests we need to conduct in order to make the necessary comparisons. In the case of our worked example, we would need to use *Mann-Whitney U* tests to compare the three sets of paired results (i.e. control vs. heat treatment, control vs. ultrasound treatment, and heat treatment vs. ultrasound treatment).

Under individual circumstances we would have applied the customary significance level of 0.05 to each of these three tests. To make the *Bonferroni adjustment* to this significance level we would divide α by the number of comparisons to be made (i.e. $\alpha \div 3 = 0.05 \div 3 = 0.0167$). Therefore for each of these comparisons we will operate at a significance level of 0.0167 rather than 0.05. The practical importance of this is that the decision making process is much more conservative to account for the higher risk – with multiple comparisons – of incurring an error by chance. By looking at all three tests together we will not go above a total α level of 0.05. When reporting these results it is usual to state the follow-up testing process that has been undertaken (i.e. *Mann-Whitney U tests*), and that the results have been modified using a *Bonferroni adjustment*. At this stage numeric results are usually tabulated as actual values and an explanatory sentence identifying the pairs that are significantly different at $p < 0.05$ is provided. The p-value of 0.05 is reported, as this is the *combined* significance level of these follow-up tests.

Friedman's Test for More Than Two Related Samples

The *Friedman test* is comparable to the *Wilcoxon matched pairs test* we discussed in relation to experimental designs involving two related groups, and makes no assumptions about the distribution of the population from which the data were drawn. The test is concerned with hypotheses relating to whether the related samples were from the same population or not, and this is addressed by exploring differences in the medians. The null hypothesis assumes that there is no difference in the populations, and is then tested using ranked data. In conducting our analyses we would expect there to be good correlations between the groups because the data are related.

Calculation Box 9.2   Friedman's Test

Calculation of *Friedman's test* involves the following steps:

1.   Rank each matched group of data separately (so if there are three groups of data the only possible ranks are 1, 2 and 3). This will normally be *across* a row of data in a table.

2.   Calculate the sum of ranks for each group, R_i, where i represents each group (this will usually be *down* the columns of data in a table).

3.   Calculate *Friedman's* χ^2 statistic as follows:

$$\chi_F^2 = \frac{12}{nk(k+1)} \sum_{i=1}^{k} R_i^2 - 3n(k+1)$$

where, n is the number of participants

k is the number of conditions (groups)

R_i is the sum of ranks for the ith condition (or group)

4.   As with the *Kruskal-Wallis test*, compare χ_F^2 for significance using the χ^2 distribution with $(k-1)$ degrees of freedom (appendix: 2). The null hypothesis is rejected if the value calculated for χ_F^2 is *greater than* the tabulated $\chi^2_{(k-1)}$ value.

An example from the sport and exercise science, where *Friedman's test* might be applied to the research data, would be a study of different road race cycling routes – of similar distance – but our question would be whether they were also of equal difficulty. Assuming we had a fairly homogenous group of race cyclists – in terms of physical fitness and cycling experience – who competed over each route, under similar environmental conditions, one measure we might take in order to explore the difficulty of each route could be their average race speed (km.h^{-1}). The race distance, the difficulty of the course, and the cyclist's final race time, will determine average race speed. Provided all races were conducted over a fairly short period of time so that the cyclists' training status would not change – though adequate time was allowed to ensure that the cyclists were fully recovered – and the order of circuits was randomised for the cyclists, it should be the case that if each circuit was of equal difficulty then fluctuations in average speed would be down to chance. The hypotheses for this example could be articulated in terms:

Null hypothesis

H_o: There will be no difference in average speed for the three courses

Alternative hypothesis

H_1:   There will be a difference in average speed for the three courses

As each cyclist will complete each course, the experimental/research design is one of taking repeated measures on the same individuals and therefore a test that accounts for some correlation between the data in the groups, in this case road race cycling routes, is required. There are not enough data observations in each group to be sure that data can be reliably tested for normal distribution parameters, so we shall use the non-parametric *Friedman test* for related samples to analyse the data. Table 9.4 presents the average race speed (km.h^{-1}) for each race and the rank of each average speed for each cyclist. Thus, each cyclist will have three scores ranked from $1 - 3$ from the fastest to the slowest.

From calculation box 9.2, the three pieces of information we require before commencing our analyses are:

- The number of participants
- The number of conditions (groups)
- The sum of ranks for the each condition (or group).

Thus, for the present investigation: the number of participants (n) = 10; the number of conditions (groups) (k) = 3; and the sum of ranks for each group are $\Sigma R_1 = 15$, $\Sigma R_2 = 21$ and $\Sigma R_3 = 24$.

Race–1 Average Speed (km.h⁻¹)	Rank R₁	Race–2 Average Speed (km.h⁻¹)	Rank R₂	Race–3 Average Speed (km.h⁻¹)	Rank R₃
52.7	*2*	51.6	*3*	52.8	*1*
47.4	*1*	45.2	*2*	43.1	*3*
49.9	*3*	51.8	*1*	50.6	*2*
37.7	*1*	33.4	*3*	33.7	*2*
51.2	*2*	52.1	*1*	48.6	*3*
46.2	*2*	50.3	*1*	44.1	*3*
49.8	*1*	47.1	*2*	40.3	*3*
48.7	*1*	38.8	*3*	40.1	*2*
48.1	*1*	33.3	*3*	33.7	*2*
47.8	*1*	41.8	*2*	33.8	*3*
	ΣR₁=15		*ΣR₂=21*		*ΣR₃=24*

Table 9.4   Average race speed (km.h⁻¹) for each race, and the rank of each average speed, for the racing cyclists.

We are now in a position to calculate our χ^2 statistic using the equation from calculation box 9.2:

$$\chi^2_F = \frac{12}{nk(k+1)} \sum_{i=1}^{k} R_i^2 - 3n(k+1)$$

Thus,

$$\chi_F^2 = \frac{12}{10 \times 3 \times 4}\left(15^2 + 21^2 + 24^2\right) - \left(3 \times 10 \times 4\right)$$

Therefore,

$$\chi_F^2 = \frac{12}{120}\left(225 + 441 + 576\right) - 120 = 0.1(1242) - 120 = 124.2 - 120 = 4.2$$

The final step is to compare the derived value for χ^2 (i.e. 4.2) for significance using the χ^2 distribution with $\{(k - 1) = 3 - 1 = 2\}$ degrees of freedom (appendix: 2). At the 5% significance level the critical value is 5.99. As our calculated value for χ^2 (i.e. 4.2) is less than 5.99, we accept the null hypothesis and conclude that the average speeds of the cyclists were not different across the three race routes ($\chi^2_{(2)} = 4.2$, $p > 0.05$). As no differences have been identified in this example, there is no requirement for follow-up comparisons. However, if difference had been found, the appropriate follow-up analyses – similar to the previous example for independent samples – would involve the application of *Wilcoxon matched pairs tests* for related samples, with *Bonferroni adjustment*, to identify the location of the difference(s).

We might therefore assume that there is no difference in the difficulty of the cycle road race courses. Though notably, this can only be the case if the order of completion was randomised between the cyclists. If all the cyclists had completed each route in the same order, or on the same day, then other factors than course difficulty might influence their performance (e.g. weather conditions, order effect of improving on previous performances, growing knowledge and reduced uncertainty about the experimental/research demands).

Analysis of Variance (*ANOVA*)

Parametric tests for difference are based on a range of approaches that explore variability of data from the mean. The model underlying *analysis of variance* assumes the data to have been derived from normal distributions with equal variance, so as discussed in chapter 8, these assumptions need to be checked during a preliminary exploration of the data. *Analysis of variance* explores variability of data, both between and within experimental groups – that is the differences from group to group, and the differences present within a group. These within group differences will contribute to the error that is present in all experiments, which will tend to obscure the differences between the groups. It is the variances (chapter 4) *between* groups, in relation to the size of the error *within* groups, which gives rise to the *ANOVA* test statistic. Thus, this test statistic is a ratio of variances. Ratios of variances have the *F* distribution, and this distribution has been tabulated like the *t* distribution we discussed in chapter 8 (appendix: 7). The null hypothesis is rejected when the value of the *F* ratio is *greater than or equal to* the critical value given in the corresponding look up table. As before, if the test is conducted using a computer, the *ANOVA* test statistic is accompanied by a probability (i.e. p-value) that is then compared to the level of significance (usually $p < 0.05$ as previous).

The *F* ratio is derived by dividing the *between group variation* by the *within group variation*. That is:

$$F\text{-ratio} = \frac{\text{Between Group Variance}}{\text{Within Group Variance}}$$

The *within group variance* is made up of errors that cannot be quantified and are assumed to occur randomly within the data; these would include measurement error and day-to-day fluctuations in research participants' mental and physical status. The *between group variance* will include the same sources of error as the *within group variance*, but will also include potential differences between the groups as a result of the experimental treatments/interventions or research conditions. Thus:

$$F\text{-ratio} = \frac{\text{Between Group Variance}}{\text{Within Group Variance}} = \frac{\text{Treatment Effects+Individual Variation+Random Error}}{\text{Individual Variation+Random Error}}$$

If the treatment has little or no effect, then the difference between the groups will be down to experimental error, and the value of F can be computed as follows:

$$F\text{-ratio} = \frac{\textbf{NO} \text{ Treatment Effects} + \text{Individual Variation} + \text{Random Error}}{\text{Individual Variation} + \text{Random Error}}$$

Therefore,

$$F\text{-ratio} = \frac{\text{Individual Variation} + \text{Random Error}}{\text{Individual Variation} + \text{Random Error}} = 1.0$$

From the above calculations we can deduce that if F is equal to 1.0, or is approaching 1.0, you can be fairly certain that the treatment is having *no effect*. However, as well as F needing to be greater than 1.0 to show an effect, the experimental design needs to be taken into consideration, this is because the numbers of participants involved in each condition/treatment/group will affect the F-ratio. For this reason the degrees of freedom are reported as part of the outcome data, because the statistical significance of the F-ratio is partly determined by the degrees of freedom of a specific experimental design. Thus, with an F-ratio there are two degrees of freedom that are included with the statistic in coordinate format (e.g. $F_{(1, 5)} = \ldots$). The first degree of freedom is one less than the number of groups being considered at a particular stage of the analysis, and the second is an error degree of freedom. The complexity of the interaction[9.1] of these degrees of freedom is commensurate with the complexity of the experimental/research design being analysed. So for a simple design where a group of 40 research participants, divided into 3 groups for analyses on a particular variable, the degrees of freedom would be determined as follows:

Total d.f. $= (40 - 1) = 39$ Group d.f. $= (3 - 1) = 2$ Error d.f. $= (39 - 2) = 37$

The F-ratio would therefore be reported ($F_{(2, 37)}$ = calculated value of the test statistic).

[9.1] *Interaction* is the combined effect of two or more independent variables acting simultaneously on a dependent variable.

The largest (hypothetical) value for the F statistic is infinity[9.2] (denoted by the symbol ∞), where there would be no, or very little, individual variation or random error. That is:

$$F\text{-ratio} = \frac{\text{Treatment Effects} + \textbf{NO Individual Variation} + \textbf{NO Random Error}}{\textbf{NO Individual Variation} + \textbf{NO Random Error}}$$

Therefore,

$$F\text{-ratio} = \frac{\text{Treatment Effects} + 0 + 0}{0 + 0} = \infty$$

The practical importance of this observation is that the greater the value of *F*, the more likely the effects of a treatment/experimental condition will be recognisable above potential error. Therefore, it would be less likely that the differences observed in the data were due to chance variation.

One-Way (One Factor) Analysis of Variance

The simplest form of *ANOVA* is the one-way or one factor design, where only one source of variation, or factor, is investigated. It is an extension to three or more samples of the *t*- test for two independent samples.   Typically, this statistical approach might be applied to test the null hypothesis that three or more treatments are equally effective. The experiment is designed such that the treatments are randomly assigned to the research participants or objects upon which the measurement of a response variable is to be made. The design is therefore called a completely randomised experimental design. The number of research participants in each group does not need to be the same unless the design is looking for changes *within subjects* (i.e. there are repeated measures on the same research participants – this is discussed below).

[9.2]   *Infinity* is a concept in mathematics of a value greater than any finite numerical value.

The null hypothesis will state that the means of the populations from which each of the samples were drawn are the same. The experimental hypothesis would state that at least one pair of means would be different. The null hypothesis would be rejected when the value of the calculated F ratio is greater than or equal to the critical value reported in the tabulated values of the F distribution.

One-Way Analysis of Variance with Repeated Measures

The simplest repeated measures *ANOVA* design is one in which the same, or carefully matched individuals, are observed or measured. The reason for using the same people more than once or for the very careful matching is to reduce the individual variability as much as possible. From the explanation of the F-ratio above, reducing the individual variation allows the treatment effect to be more reliably isolated. This form of experimental design is termed a *one-way within subjects design* or a *one-way repeated measures design*. It is usually the case that each subject receives each of the treatments; the order in which the subjects are exposed to the treatments is randomised, where possible, to control for order effects such as learning or fatigue.

The experimental model assumes that the measured data value x_{ij} (i.e. the measurement for the ith subject, having the jth treatment), is the result of adding three specific terms to a fixed constant. These three terms are:

- Effect due to the *participant* (i.e. individual variation)
- Effect due to the *treatment* (i.e. treatment variation)
- Effect due to random *error*.

You will recall from chapter 8 that the variability of scores can be measured by the *sum of squares* (i.e. the sum of the squared deviations from the mean). The total variability, or total sum of squares, can be partitioned (divided) into three components, where each is attributed to either treatments (SSTr), participants (SSP), and errors (SSE).

The assumptions underpinning this process are as follows:

- The participants under consideration form a simple random sample from a population of similar participants
- Each observation is an independent simple random sample of size 1, from each of $\{k \times n = kn\}$ populations, where n is the number of participants and k is the number of treatments to which each participant is exposed
- The *kn* populations potentially have different means but they all have the same variance
- The *k* treatments are fixed; that is they are the only treatments in which we have an interest and we do not wish to make inferences about a larger set of treatments
- There is no interaction between treatments and subjects.

The test statistic for this comparison is the variance ratio, *VR*, which is calculated as follows:

$$VR = \frac{\text{Treatment Mean Square}}{\text{Error Mean Square}}$$ where, the mean squares are the ways in which the variances are quantified

If the null hypothesis is true the test statistic will follow the *F* distribution, though the structure of the experiment in terms of degrees of freedom will also have to be taken into account. This is because the same value for the variance ratio – the *F* test statistic – is dependent on the number of research participants measured or observed across the number of treatments or groups. For example, 30 research participants, divided into 3 experimental groups, would provide more information about the groups than if the same 30 participants were divided between 5 groups. Thus, the test statistic could be statistically significant for some experimental structures, but not for others, depending on the complexity of the design and the numbers of research participants.

Calculation box 9.3 summarises the calculation steps for a *one-way ANOVA*, though this is best illustrated in the example on the following page.

Calculation Box 9.3   One-way Analysis of Variance

The calculation steps for a one-way analysis of variance are as follows:

1. Calculate the overall mean for the research data as follows:

$$X_{TOT} = \frac{(X_1 \times n_1) + \ldots + (\overline{X}_k \times n_k)}{N}$$

where, n is the number of participants in each group

$\overline{X}_k$ is the mean of each group

k is the number of groups (treatments)

N is the total number of participants

2. Calculate the total sum of squares (SS_{TOT}) by:

    • Subtracting the overall mean from each data observation

    • Finding the square of the result

    • Finding the sum (add) of the resulting values

3. Calculate the sum of squares for the treatment (SS_{TREAT}):

$$SS_{TREAT} = \frac{(\Sigma x_1)^2}{n_1} + \ldots + \frac{(\Sigma x_k)^2}{n_k}$$

4. The treatment sum of squares (SS_{TREAT}) and the error sum of squares (SS_{ERROR}) combine to give the total sum of squares (SS_{TOT}). Thus, we can apply the following formula to determine the error sum of squares (SS_{ERROR}):

$$SS_{TOT} = SS_{TREAT} + SS_{ERROR}$$

Thus, $SS_{TOT} - SS_{TREAT} = SS_{ERROR}$

5. Determine the degrees of freedom: For the error, $d.f._{ERROR} = N - k$

For the treatment $d.f._{TREAT} = k - 1$

6. Determine the mean square error by dividing the sum of squares for the error by the degrees of freedom for the error:

$$MS_{ERROR} = \frac{SS_{ERROR}}{d.f._{ERROR}}$$

(Continued...)

---

7.   Similarly, determine the treatment mean square by dividing the sum of squares for treatment by the degrees of freedom for treatment:

$$MS_{TREAT} = \frac{SS_{TREAT}}{d.f._{TREAT}}$$

8.   The *F*-ratio can now be calculated as follows:

$$F\text{-ratio} = \frac{MS_{TREAT}}{MS_{ERROR}}$$

9.   Using look up tables, compare the calculated *F*-ratio with ({treatment}, {error}) degrees of freedom with the critical value for F at the 5% level of significance. If the *F*-ratio is *greater than* the critical value, the *ANOVA* has found difference. As such, it is necessary to conduct further tests to locate the difference(s).

The calculations presented in calculation box 9.3 will now be illustrated in a worked example. This example is taken from a subset of data; the group sizes are not really large enough to tolerate this form of analysis, but they are sufficient to illustrate how the calculations for this analysis are conducted – without losing sight of what is actually happening with the data. Data were collected from three groups of male hockey players who took part in observational trials in which a three-dimensional analysis of shooting technique was undertaken. Each player was videoed by two cameras as they performed shots into an unguarded goal. The best trial of fifteen attempts was used for the final analysis, as it was deemed to be the optimum for that player. The *best* trial was judged on a subjective assessment of accuracy and high ball speed. The film footage was then digitised for analysis of fourteen variables, including ball velocity. A subgroup of the ball velocity data is reproduced in table 9.5, which reports shots taken from three different positions.

Shooting Position		
$-1-$ **Ball Velocity** (ms^{-1})	$-2-$ **Ball Velocity** (ms^{-1})	$-3-$ **Ball Velocity** (ms^{-1})
16.3	17.1	12.4
20.4	17.1	17.3
18.2	16.7	16.3
16.5	14.6	13.9
20.1	16.2	15.5
$\Sigma x_1 = 91.5$	$\Sigma x_2 = 81.7$	$\Sigma x_3 = 75.4$
$\overline{X}_1 = 18.3$	$\overline{X}_2 = 16.34$	$\overline{X}_3 = 15.08$

Table 9.5   Three-dimensional analysis of shooting technique   ball velocity (ms^{-1}) data from three different shooting positions $(n = 5)$.

The group means for the 3 shooting positions are presented in table 9.5; the overall mean for the research data can be calculated as follows:

$$\overline{x} = \frac{\left(\overline{X}_1 \times n_1\right) + \left(\overline{X}_2 \times n_2\right) + \left(\overline{X}_3 + n_3\right)}{N} = \frac{(18.3 \times 5) + (16.34 \times 5) + (15.08 \times 5)}{15} = 16.57$$

Despite the simplification of the calculation, it is still relatively long and therefore raises the potential for calculation error. This is also the case in determining the total sum of squares, which in this example is given by:

$$SS_{TOT} = (16.3–16.57)^2 + (20.4–16.57)^2 + (18.2–16.57)^2 + (16.5–16.57)^2 + (20.1–16.57)^2$$
$$+ (17.1–16.57)^2 + (17.1–16.57)^2 + (16.7–16.57)^2 + (14.6–16.57)^2 + (16.2–16.57)^2$$
$$+ (12.4–16.57)^2 + (17.3–16.57)^2 + (16.3–16.57)^2 + (13.9–16.57)^2 + (15.5–16.57)^2$$

$$SS_{TOT} = 0.0729 + 14.6689 + 2.6569 + 0.0049 + 12.4609$$
$$+ 0.2809 + 0.2809 + 0.0169 + 3.8809 + 0.1369$$
$$+ 17.3889 + 0.5329 + 0.0729 + 7.1289 + 1.1449$$

$$SS_{TOT} = 60.7295$$

The sum of squares for the treatment is calculated as follows:

$$SS_{TREAT} = \frac{\left(\sum X_1\right)^2}{n_1} + \frac{\left(\sum X_2\right)^2}{n_2} + \frac{\left(\sum X_3\right)^2}{n_3} - \frac{\left(\sum X_{TOT}\right)^2}{N} = \frac{91.5^2}{5} + \frac{81.7^2}{5} + \frac{75.4^2}{5} - \frac{248.6^2}{15} = 26.33$$

The calculation of the sum of squares for the error is relatively long, and therefore again there is a high risk of mistakes being made in its calculation. However, as discussed previously the treatment sum of squares and the error sum of squares combine to give the total sum of squares, where the total sum of squares is a relatively easy calculation to perform:

$$SS_{TOT} = SS_{TREAT} + SS_{ERROR}$$

By rearranging, the error sum of squares can be calculated as follows:

$$SS_{TOT} - SS_{TREAT} = SS_{ERROR}$$

$$SS_{ERROR} = 60.73 - 26.33 = 34.4$$

The degrees of freedom for this worked example experimental design are calculated as follows:

$$\text{d.f.}_{ERROR} \quad = N - k \qquad 15 - 3 = 12$$
$$\text{d.f.}_{TREAT} \quad = k - 1 \qquad 3 - 1 = 2$$

Having determined the overall mean, the treatment sums of squares, the error sums of squares, the error degrees of freedom and the treatment degrees of freedom, we are now in a position to calculate the F ratio for this example. To determine the mean square error, divide the sum of squares for the error by the degrees of freedom for the error:

$$MS_{ERROR} \quad - \quad \frac{SS_{ERROR}}{\text{d.f.}_{ERROR}} \quad = \quad \frac{34.4}{12} \quad = \quad 2.87$$

To find the treatment mean square, divide the sum of squares for the treatment by the degrees of freedom for the treatment:

$$MS_{TREAT} \quad = \quad \frac{SS_{TREAT}}{\text{d.f.}_{TREAT}} \quad = \quad \frac{26.33}{2} \quad = \quad 13.17$$

Thus, the *F*-ratio can now be calculated as follows:

$$F\text{-ratio} \quad = \quad \frac{MS_{TREAT}}{MS_{ERROR}} \quad = \quad \frac{13.17}{2.87} \quad = \quad 4.59$$

From look-up tables of the *F*-distribution, the critical value for *F* with (2 {*treatment*},12 {*error*}) degrees of freedom is 3.89 at the 5% level of significance. As 4.59 is *greater than* 3.89 the result is significant (i.e. the *ANOVA* has found difference), but does not indicate where that difference(s) may arise. As such, it is necessary to conduct further tests to locate the differences. If we want to check all possible differences (note – in the example data the difference(s) might be located between position-1 vs. position-2, position-2 vs. position-3, or position-1 vs. position-3), further testing must be applied. Through *post hoc*[9.3] testing, analysis of all available locations of difference is conducted, and an adjustment to the significance level is included within the test to prevent an inflation of *family-wise error*. The procedure of *post hoc* testing is therefore only advisable if it makes experimental sense to compare *all* possible pairs. The problem being that an adjustment to the significance level could make the statistical test so stringent (i.e. unlikely to find a difference unless it is really large), that it may not be of sufficient sensitivity to detect and locate the differences identified in the *ANOVA*. A discussion of several commonly applied *post hoc* tests, and when they should be used, is presented at the end of this chapter. The approach that is applicable to this example is the *Tukey HSD* test, which is appropriate for independent groups of equal or similar size. The *Tukey HSD* test involves a further test formula and a look-up table (appendix: 8) using a number of the values that have already been calculated in the *ANOVA*. Determination of the *Tukey HSD* test is presented in calculation box 9.4.

[9.3] *Post hoc* refers to the option of evaluating all possible pair-wise comparisons to locate any sources of difference that have been identified as being present by the first over-arching test. When the term *post hoc* is applied, it indicates that no decisions were made before analysis with respect to where we will look for differences, so it is a comprehensive procedure. The term is often misapplied, as almost always some of the comparisons undertaken are totally inappropriate (i.e. do not make practical sense), but nevertheless these are corrected for in the calculation process (cf. *a priori*, which indicates pre-planned comparisons of only the pairs that it is meaningful to consider).

Calculation Box 9.4   Tukey Honestly Significant Difference (HSD) Test

The *Tukey HSD* test should be used when the null hypothesis has been rejected and the location of differences needs to be determined. In order to calculate the formulae the following questions need to be answered for your data:

1.   How many means are being compared (k)?
2.   How many values make up each mean (n)?
3.   What are the error degrees of freedom (defined as d.f.$_{ERROR}$)?
4.   What is the value of Mean square error (MS_{ERROR})?
5.   Look up the value of q from the *Tukey* table (appendix: 8) using the error degrees of freedom and the number of means being compared
6.   Compute the *Tukey HSD* test score using the formula:

$$Tukey\ Score = q\sqrt{\frac{MS_{ERROR}}{n}}$$

The groups that are different can be located by looking to see which pairs of groups have differences between their means *greater than* the value of the *Tukey* Score. Often the best way to do this is to tabulate the differences between means on a grid.

Applying the *Tukey HSD* test to the worked example, the derived data (as detailed in calculation box 9.4) is:

1.   3 means are being compared
2.   5 values make up each mean
3.   error degrees of freedom are 12
4. MS_{ERROR} has been calculated as 2.87
5.   from the Tukey table, q for 3 means and 12 degrees of freedom can be read as 3.77

Computing the *Tukey HSD* test score using the formula from calculation box 9.4:

$$Tukey\ Score = q\sqrt{\frac{MS_{ERROR}}{n}}$$

Therefore,

$$Tukey\ Score = 3.77\sqrt{\frac{2.89}{5}} = 3.77 \times 0.76 = 2.87$$

Using a table to calculate the differences between the means (table 9.6):

	Position – 1	Position – 2	Position – 3
Position – 1	---	----	---
Position – 2	18.3 – 16.34 = 1.96	---	---
Position – 3	18.3 – 15.08 = 3.22	16.34 – 15.08 = 1.26	---

This value is the only one that exceeds the *Tukey* score of 2.87 and so is the only location of significant difference between the groups

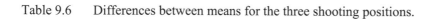

Table 9.6   Differences between means for the three shooting positions.

We have now completed the investigation of the data collected to explore the ball velocity of shots at goal from three different positions. Initially we tested the null hypothesis for differences between the three mean velocities. The *ANOVA* compared all three means in one calculation, and therefore did not increase the potential for error. The outcome of the test indicated significant difference *somewhere* in the data but did not indicate where this might be. As we had no reason to look at specific locations within the data, as it made sense within the experiment to compare all three groups for potential differences, we conducted a *post hoc Tukey HSD* test to determine where the differences were. Through this procedure we were able to unravel the research problem, and find a difference between the mean ball velocities for position-1 and position-3, and that they are likely to be so in future tests ($p < 0.05$). While differences between position-2 and either of position-1 or position-3 are likely to be down to chance fluctuations in the data rather than shooting position.

Two-way Analysis of Variance (ANOVA)

Two-way *ANOVA* is an extension of the *ANOVA* technique that allows consideration of more than one factor in our analyses. The most straightforward experimental design involving two-way *ANOVA* is where a different group of research participants are involved for each possible combination of the factor levels. This is called a *between-subjects design*.

Figure 9.1 presents a schematic representation of *Two-Way Analysis of Variance*, which serves to illustrate that once there are more factors to consider in your experimental design, there are more effects to consider:

- If the analysis shows a difference in the *marginal means* (i.e. those for each group when calculated on one factor only), there is a *main effect* difference, as differences occur between the levels of individual factors

- If inspection of the *interaction* or *cell means* within the table shows differences, then an *interaction effect* may be present (i.e. one level of one of the factors is having a different effect across levels of the other factor).

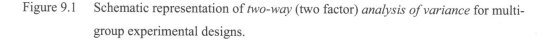

		Factor-1			
		Level-1	*Level-2*	*Level-3*	
Factor-2	*Level-1*		**INTERACTION** **(OR CELL)** **MEANS**		**MARGINAL** **MEANS**
	Level-2				
		MARGINAL MEANS			

Figure 9.1   Schematic representation of *two-way* (two factor) *analysis of variance* for multi-group experimental designs.

Main effects and *interaction effects* are different data outcomes; therefore it is possible to have significant main effects without significant interaction effects, or to have significant interaction effects without any main effects being statistically significant. Interaction can be assessed visually using a diagram to illustrate the cell means (where the 'patterns' of data will differ over the different levels), and this approach often helps in understanding what the results are actually telling us.

We will not present a full worked example to illustrate the steps in conducting a two-way *ANOVA* as this analysis approach involves a large number of repetitive calculations, and you will certainly benefit from entering your data into a computer software package in terms of speed and avoidance of calculation errors. We will however use an example through which the *process* can be examined, and we will evaluate the results from a computer output table. The data presented in table 9.7 was collected to compare the effects of two different tennis-coaching programmes and three different group sizes. The data reflect scores given by an assessor over a series of skills competency tests at the end of the coaching course. The scores were aggregated into a final percentage score.

	Group Size		
	Individual	**4 People**	**8 People**
Programme 1	80, 81, 87, 83, 70, 90, 100, 85, 75, 89, 95, 79, 91, 84, 86	81, 90, 84, 76, 60, 75, 90, 80, 85, 75, 95, 90, 60, 100, 59	74, 69, 70, 77, 81, 78, 75, 80, 72, 74, 75, 70, 80, 74, 76
Programme 2	70, 75, 85, 93, 75, 70, 75, 70, 60, 75, 90, 78, 85, 65, 80	70, 83, 77, 74, 65, 65, 70, 75, 69, 67, 70, 63, 72, 90, 68	50, 53, 71, 68, 70, 57, 61, 62, 65, 65, 69, 72, 59, 55, 58

Table 9.7   Skill test scores following two coaching programmes delivered to three group sizes.

In this research study: the *independent variables* or factors are the coaching programme and the group size; and the *dependent variable* is the skills test score that each coaching course participant achieved at the end of the course. Thus, there are two factors: the *programme factor* has two levels (programme-1 and programme-2); and the *group size factor* has three levels (individual, 4 people and 8 people). The structure of this experiment could therefore be described as a *two-by-three factorial design* (or 2 × 3). To clarify terminology:

- The mean of the scores in the bottom right hand box (i.e. participants coached on programme 2 in a group of 8 people) would be a *cell mean*
- The mean of all the scores for programme 2, regardless of group size, would be a *marginal mean*

Each box (or cell) represents a specific treatment condition, and each condition had its own separate sample, thus this example is an *independent-measures design*. The design has 2 factors, which are measured over independent samples, and one dependent variable, so *ANOVA* is the appropriate statistical approach for the data analysis. The test will consider three different hypotheses based on:

1.   The main effect of coaching programme (factor A)
2.   The main effect of group size (factor B)
3.   The interaction between the factors

These general hypotheses can be described in terms of three pairs of specific research hypotheses that would be investigated by the *ANOVA* analyses:

1.   *Null hypothesis*

H_o: The coaching programme will not affect achievement in a skills competency test

Alternative hypothesis

H_1:   The coaching programme will affect achievement in a skills competency test

2.   *Null hypothesis*

H_o: Group size will not affect achievement in a skills competency test

Alternative hypothesis

H_1:   Group size will affect achievement in a skills competency test

3.   *Null hypothesis*

H_o: A combination of group size and coaching programme will not affect achievement in a skills competency test

Alternative hypothesis

H_1:   A combination of group size and coaching programme will not affect achievement in a skills competency test

Before commencing your analyses, we should established our level of significance at which differences are deemed to be important (we will set this at the 5% level of significance), and the data should be checked for the following assumptions:

- The observations within each sample should be *independent*
- The populations from which the samples are drawn should be *normal* (refer to chapter 5)
- The populations from which the samples are drawn should exhibit *homogeneity* (equality) *of variance* (refer to chapter 8)

If the sample size is relatively large the assumption of normality is not generally a cause for concern, but the equality of variance is more important. In this example inspection of the variance indicates that we cannot be certain that we have equality of variance. However, there is no other analysis that is as suitable as *ANOVA* for this situation, and the violation is considered to have a small effect within the analysis. As discussed in chapter 8, statistical software packages will often inspect data for equality of variance between groups using a statistical test called a *Levene's test* (if the groups are independent). If this test gives a result that is *not significant* at the 5% level (i.e. if the computer gives a probability value of *more than* 0.05, $p > 0.05$), the data can be said to show equality of variance. When the data in this example were entered into the computer, the analysis gave a probability of 0.035. This is less than 0.05, but not so much as to make the analysis impossible as *ANOVA* is fairly robust to a violation of its assumptions. That is, it will be able to cope with less than ideal circumstances as long as those less than ideal circumstances are not too great. However, it is important to know that a violation of its assumptions is present, and that we should be cautious in interpreting results that are either just significant, or just not significant, at the test level. This knowledge will help us to temper our decision making, and further emphasises the importance of thorough data exploration prior to any form of statistical analysis. As *ANOVA* tests the *means* and *variation from the means* of sample groups, such data exploration should include plotting graphs to examine the shape of the data distributions, as well as calculation of the means and standard deviations – visualising the data will assist in understanding the data through subsequent data analyses (figure 9.2).

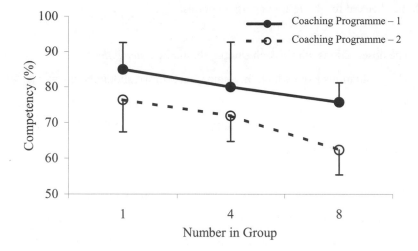

Figure 9.2   Mean scores for achievement in a skills competency test with Coaching Programmes 1 and 2, delivered individually or in groups of 4 or 8 people.

In this *tennis coaching* example, the data analysis was conducted using a computer as the length of the calculations – to be undertaken by hand – would be inappropriate and open to calculation errors. There is little added value in completing calculations by hand as long as you can apply the underlying theory of the statistical analyses to the figures and output data from a statistical software package. Exemplar computer output for the *tennis coaching* example is presented in table 9.8; whilst the information is relatively consistent between software packages, the layout and method of reading the output may differ. For example, you may find that your statistics software will present this table with the columns and rows of table 9.8 switched around as the rows and columns respectively. That is, 'Programme', 'Group Size', and 'Interaction' results are reported as rows, and the sums of squares, degrees of freedom, mean square, error of sum of square, the *F*-ratio and probability are reported as columns. This is purely a presentational preference; what is essential is that you understand the processes underpinning the table and its contents, such that changes in order of presentation do not become confusing.

(Column-1)	(Column-2)	(Column-3)	(Column-4)
			Interaction Between Coaching Programme & Group Size Results
	Programme Results	**Group Size Results**	
Sums of Squares – Treatment	2270.044	2064.422	127.489
Degrees of freedom – Treatment	1	2	84
Mean Square – Treatment	2270.044	1032.211	63.744
Error sum of Squares = 6057.600	Error Degrees of Freedom = 84	Mean Square Error = 72.114	
Variance Ratio, – Test statistic, *F*	31.478	14.314	0.884
Probability	0.0005	0.0005	0.417

Table 9.8   Exemplar computer *ANOVA* output for the *tennis coaching* example.

The output results from the computer software package can be related back to the research hypotheses, and reported in the conventional format. With respect to the first set of hypotheses addressing the affect of the coaching programme on achievement in a skills competency test (column 2, table 9.8), we can reject the null hypothesis and conclude that the coaching programme does have an effect on the skills competency test outcomes ($F_{(1, 84)}$ = 31.478, p = 0.0005). The differences in achievement in a skills competency test are seen to be as a result of the specific coaching programme and not down to chance. In this example we do not need to undertake further testing, as there are only two coaching programmes and therefore the difference must be located between the programmes. This is further verified by examining the graph of the mean data, we can see that the mean scores for programme-1 are consistently higher than programme-2 (figure 9. 2). However, this analysis does not take into consideration any potential class size influence (hypotheses-2).

For the second set of hypotheses that examined the influence of class size on achievement in a skills competency test (column 3, table 9.8), we can again reject the null hypothesis and conclude that group size does have an effect on the skills competency test outcomes ($F_{(2, 84)}$ = 14.314, p = 0.0005). However, this time it is necessary to conduct a test to follow up the results as there were 3 group sizes giving rise to 3 possible comparisons. As we have no preconceived ideas with respect to the source of difference(s), a *post hoc* test is appropriate. *Tukey HSD tests*, conducted as before, indicated that achievement in a skills competency test where the group size is 8 people would be different from achievement scores when coaching was undertaken individually (p < 0.01) or when group size was 4 people (p < 0.01). However, the difference in achievement between individual coaching sessions and sessions with 4 people in a group was not seen as significant and could therefore be happening by chance.

This analysis does not take into consideration the possible influence of the coaching programme (hypotheses-1). The third set of hypotheses examined the combined effect of class size and coaching programme on achievement in a skills competency test (column 4, table 9.8). The output data from this final set of analyses show that we can accept the null hypothesis and conclude that the combination of group size and coaching programme does not affect the skills competency test outcomes ($F_{(2, 84)}$ = 0.884, p = 0.417). This means that although there are differences in relation to the coaching programme and the group sizes, the way that each coaching programme improves achievement in a skills competency test is *the same across* the group sizes (i.e. there are no interaction effects). Both coaching programmes achieve the poorest competency scores with class sizes of 8 people, therefore it is not that one programme is better for one class size and the other programme is better for a different class size. With this non-significant outcome there is no requirement for further data analyses.

More Complex ANOVA Designs

Most studies resulting in data that would appropriately be analysed by *ANOVA* require that we understand the behaviour of two and often three factors, and their possible interaction effects, in order to answer the research question. A standard two-by-two (i.e. 2×2) *ANOVA* approach can be further developed to answer more complex hypotheses if a repeated measure is introduced on one or more of the variables.

Designs we have described so far in this chapter include:

- One factor designs, or *one-way*, where one variable (with one set of data scores) is looked at in relation to two or more groupings. Interest is in the *difference between the groups*, and the total variability is considered *between* the groups and within the *groups*
- A development of the one-way design is the *repeated measure design*, where the groups being tested are measured *more than once* on the independent variable (or factor) of interest. In this case, the *difference within the group or groups over the repeated measures* (i.e. it is the within-group variability) that is of interest. The *within-group variability* is considered in terms of *between subject variability* (i.e. how individuals fluctuate) and the *residual variability* (i.e. the error term)
- The 2×2 *design*, where there are *two factors* which divide the *between group variability* into *main effect* and *interaction variability*.

These three general *ANOVA* structures provide all the required methodology needed for more complex *ANOVA* research designs. Nevertheless, the more complex designs require careful consideration of what you are actually trying to achieve in your data comparisons, and therefore how you should appropriately apply the rules from the more simple designs. Research designs known as *mixed designs* are frequently used in studies in the sport and exercise sciences. Their structure is such that there might be an *independent grouping type factor*, and then *a second independent factor* upon which *repeated measures* are taken. Designs like this need two error terms:

- One error term for the *main effects* of the *between group factor* – this error is the *within group variance*
- Another error term for the *main effects of the repeated measure* – this error is the *residual variance*.

Further extensions of this approach involve designs where there are repeated measures on both factors being considered. For example, this might be when the same group of research participants undertake two exercise conditions and are measured before and after exercise on both occasions. In this example there would be two factors – exercise condition and time of measurement – and every participant would undergo each measurement. When using this type of design every research participant will experience four different times of measurement (refer to figure 9.3 (a)), and it is therefore necessary to make sure that performance on some conditions is not affecting performance on others (unless this is an explicit aim of the testing process). The *ANOVA* test structure for this would be described as *within subjects* or *repeated measures*, consistent with the one-way test but it is also important to identify the number of factors involved. In the present example where there are two exercise conditions and two time points, this would be described as a *two-way (*i.e. *two-by-two* or *2 × 2) repeated measures* design[9.4]. If only one of the factors was repeated, such as if male and female participants were tested on exercise condition-1 only – before and after exercise – the structure of the design would look like the model presented in figure 9.3 (b). Each participant would experience two different times of measurement, and the ANOVA test structure would be described as a *two-way mixed design ANOVA*.

[9.4]   Two-way shows two factors and two-by-two (i.e. 2 × 2) shows two levels for each factor.

Care is needed when designing this type of experiment due to the complex combination of conditions. Furthermore, when it comes to performing the data analyses using computer software, you must make sure that the identification of *within subject factors* and the number of measurement *levels* is completed properly to reflect the structure of the study. Unless there are many combinations of factors, the best way to ensure that output is clear and decipherable is by carefully naming and labelling variables. You also need to give careful consideration to which condition will be assigned to each factor level.

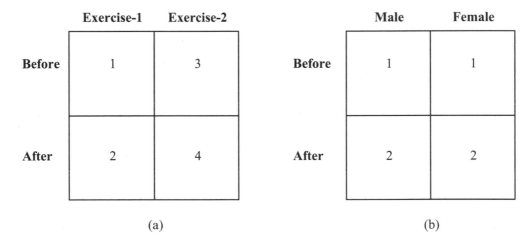

(a)   (b)

Figure 9.3   Schematic representation of a *within subjects* or *repeated measures* ANOVA test structure (a), and a *two-way mixed design ANOVA* test structure (b).

When examining results from more complex *ANOVA* designs, such as the *two-way repeated measures* design described above, careful attention is also needed in assigning the correct degrees of freedom to their corresponding groups. Normally analyses of this complexity are rarely conducted by hand, as the process is excessively time consuming and highly prone to calculation error. Whilst it is highly appropriate to use computer software packages, these must be used intelligently and with a thorough understanding of the underlying statistical operations. This entails checking that data input to the computer is correct to enable the software to analyse the data in the way that you intend. Furthermore, once the computer has completed the statistical analyses, you will also need to consider the processes of the simple *ANOVA* calculations illustrated earlier in this chapter in order to read computer output and question whether the values in the output are reflective of what would be expected from the data. For a more in-depth discussion of *ANOVA* approaches please refer to Roberts and Russo (1999).

Potential Sources of Error When Applying ANOVA

In chapter 3 we emphasised the importance of considering data analyses at the design stage of your research study.   This early consideration is essential if you are intending to apply *ANOVA* approaches to your data analyses; if the factors have more than two levels, there can be problems with selecting appropriate follow-up tests. Simple main effects are evaluated if the design is a two-by-two (i.e. 2 × 2) *ANOVA*, but *post hoc* tests, planned comparisons or linear contrasts are needed to test these simple main effects when more than 2 levels are present. Different error terms are used *for each factor* and *for the interaction* in a within-subjects design, and therefore care is needed to report the correct degrees of freedom for the specific result you are discussing. This is different from the factorial *ANOVA* design, where the same error term is used in each *F*-ratio.

Post hoc tests or pre-planned (*a priori*) comparisons are two approaches to further exploring the data and are necessary to locate differences if significant results are found in situations where there are more than two levels. If *ANOVA* analyses identify that difference is present in the data, if there are only two levels of a factor then the result suggests that it is these two means that are significantly different.   With between participant factors, where we may not have any preconceptions as to where difference might be located, a *post hoc* test should be applied. If repeated measures are involved then it is usually the case that every comparison is *not* desirable. There will be locations within the *ANOVA* structure where comparison does not make experimental or practical sense, and would therefore have little value. In situations like this a widely used method is to use pre-planned *t*-test comparisons. This means that the researcher decides where it would be *sensible* to look for differences, before performing the *ANOVA* analyses, given the hypotheses that are driving the experimental design. If the outcome results from the *ANOVA* are significant, then the pre-planned *t*-tests are carried out between the relevant pairs with the *Bonferroni adjustment* (i.e. significance level divided by the number of tests being performed) to control for error in the procedure. A paired samples *t*-test is applied when the means being compared are from related groups, whilst independent samples *t*-tests would be applied to unrelated group means.

Post Hoc Testing

From the above discussion it is evident that there is normally the need to follow-up *ANOVA* analyses with further statistical techniques. The *ANOVA* alone simply indicates whether there is an important difference in the means of the data, but not the location of that difference or differences. Follow-up testing provides this specific detail, which will allow us to make a more comprehensive interpretation of the research data. It may not always be clear in advance where to look for differences; in this case you will want to compare each mean with every other mean – or many sets of pairs – to try to locate the differences. There are a variety of *post hoc* tests that would be useful in this situation, though notably they are less powerful than pre-planned comparisons.

FISHER LSD

The *Fisher LSD* is one of the most liberal *post hoc* tests; it will locate any suggestion of a difference, and therefore is not often recommended. There must be statistical significance in the *F*-ratio from the *ANOVA* before it can be applied. The *Fisher LSD* is useful with unbalanced designs, but many researchers feel that the test is too lenient (i.e. too ready to suggest a difference), and therefore it is not often used in the sport and exercise science literature.

THE SCHEFFÉ TEST

In contrast to the Fisher LSD test, the *Scheffé test* is much more frequently applied in the sport and exercise sciences and we have therefore included its calculation steps for in this text (calculation box 9.5). The *Scheffé test* is relatively conservative (i.e. it will not show a difference unless the evidence is substantial), this is true to such an extent that there is no point using the *Scheffé test* if the original *F*-ratio was not highly statistically significant. It is the most flexible of the commonly applied approaches, but it is really an adjustment so that once performed there is no limit to the number and complexity of comparisons that can be made. It works by applying a *t*-test with a new critical value that is calculated to make significance harder to achieve – similar to the way that the *Bonferroni adjustment* works – but operates across all possible comparisons. It is this that makes it less likely to find significance than pre-planned *t*-tests with *Bonferroni adjustment*.

Calculation Box 9.5   The Scheffé Test

The *Scheffé test* requires the following steps to be performed to find the required values for each pairwise comparison:

1. How many groups are being compared (k)?
2. What are the error degrees of freedom (d.f.)?
3. What is the means square error (MS_{ERROR})?
4. What is the value of the first group mean to be compared (X_1)?
5. What is the size of the first sample (n_1)?
6. What is the value of the second group mean to be compared (X_2)?
7. What is the size of the second sample (n_2)?
8. A 'protected *t* statistic' is calculated using the formula:

$$t = \frac{\bar{x}_1 - \bar{x}_2}{\sqrt{MS_{ERROR}\left(\dfrac{1}{n_1} + \dfrac{1}{n_2}\right)}}$$

9. Calculate t^2 (i.e. $t \times t$)
10. Record the critical value of F from the F tables using $(k - 1)$ degrees of freedom
11. Multiply this F score by $(k - 1)$ to determine the *Scheffé* critical value, c
12. If $t^2 > c$ then the two means are significantly different

Steps 1–12 need to be repeated for each pair of means to be compared for differences.

TUKEY HSD TEST

The *Tukey HSD test* is a relatively stringent test that works best if groups are approximately equal in size, follow a normal distribution, and have similar variances. If data deviate from these conditions, a correcting factor may need to be applied. The *Tukey HSD test* is powerful when testing a large number of means, but is less powerful than the *Bonferroni adjustment* when examining a small number of pairs. The test procedure conducts all pair-wise comparisons between the groups and adjusts the error rate in the light of the design. The size of the experimental design is therefore of importance. Refer to calculation box 9.4 for a description of the procedures for completing the *Tukey HSD test*.

Post-Script on Post Hoc Testing…

To be statistically sound, always plan for further analyses to be undertaken and identify the appropriate follow-up or *post hoc* tests for your experimental design before conducting any data analyses. Never be tempted to compare the outcomes of several tests and chose that approach which best suits your purpose. This would be poor analytical practice; robust research is based upon setting appropriate robust rules …and sticking to them!

Chapter Decision Tree

Figure 9.4 presents an overview of the questions you should ask prior to undertaking difference tests when there are more than two groups, and the resulting decision processes as described in this chapter.

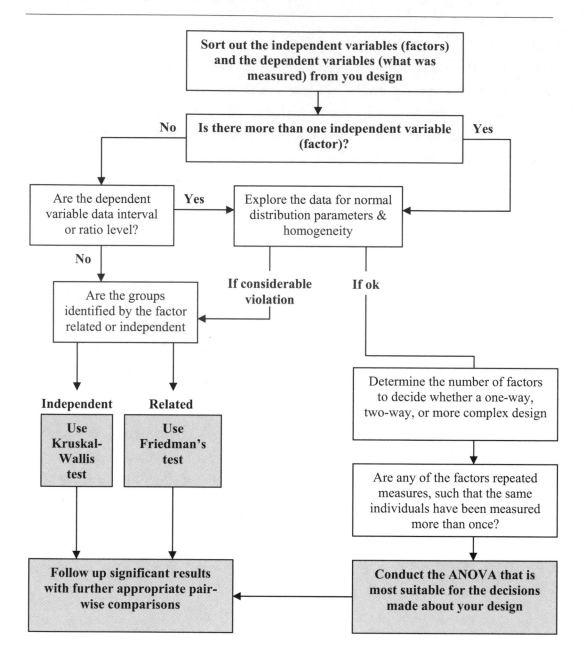

Figure 9.4   Decision tree for tests of differences for more than two groups.

Summary/Key Points

1. With more complex research designs involving more than two groups, conducting repeated statistical tests on the same data would multiply the chances of making a wrong decision; this is referred to as *family-wise error*. It is not acceptable to undertake data analyses that increase the probability of error.

2. Non-parametric tests for difference for experimental designs involving more than two groups include the *Kruskal-Wallis test* (independent samples) and the *Friedman test* (related samples), both tests are based on examinations of the medians.

3. These tests will identify whether there is a difference in the groups of data; follow-up analytical techniques are then required to identify the location of any differences. For the *Kruskal-Wallis test* further analysis should involve *Mann-Whitney U tests*, and *Wilcoxon tests* might be applied following the *Friedman test*, for pair-wise comparisons.

4. To control for *family-wise error* a procedure known as *Bonferroni adjustment* is made to the significance level of the tests. The level of significance is divided by the number of comparisons undertaken during the follow-up analyses. The practical importance of this is that the decision making process is made much more conservative to account for the higher risk of incurring an error by chance as a consequence of multiple comparisons.

5. Parametric tests for difference are based on a range of approaches that explore variability of data from the mean (i.e. analysis of variance, *ANOVA*). It is the variance between groups, in relation to the error within groups, which gives rise to the *ANOVA* test statistic – the *F*-ratio – that is a ratio of variances.

6. The assumptions underpinning *ANOVA* include: observations within each sample are independent; sample is drawn from a population that conforms to the normal distribution; and, this population exhibits homogeneity of variance. However, *ANOVA* is fairly robust to violations of its assumptions, it will be able to cope with less than ideal circumstances as long as those less than ideal circumstances are not too great.

7. If *F* is equal to 1.0, or is approaching 1.0, we can deduce that a treatment is having no effect. The greater the value of *F*, the more likely the effects of a treatment will be recognised. Reducing individual variability, and error variability, allows the treatment effect to be more reliably isolated and a *real* difference identified.

8.   *ANOVA* will find a difference in data but will not indicate where that difference may arise, necessitating further tests to locate the differences.

9.   This will take the form of *post hoc* testing (i.e. analysis of all available locations of difference – examples include the *Tukey HSD test*, the *Fisher LSD* and the *Scheffé test*) or pre-planned comparisons (i.e. analysis of locations where it would be sensible to look for differences – commonly through the application of *t*-tests).

10. More complex research designs may require the application of two-way *ANOVA*, which allows consideration of more than one factor in our analyses, where each factor may have a number of levels. The main effects arise as a consequence of the treatments/conditions (as determined by the factors), and the interaction effects reflect the outcome form the combined action of two or more factors acting simultaneously on a dependent variable.

10

Pulling It All Together:

A Worked Example

Chapter Objectives

- To present a worked example of the research process
- To articulate the active steps of the planning, experimental and analysis stages through the worked example
- To discuss the reasoning supporting the decisions taken at each stage.

Introduction

Using Statistics in Sport and Exercise Science Research has taken you on a journey through the practical processes of conducting a research project. This journey began by examining the pragmatics of translating an inquiring thought into a worthwhile research question, a research question with both scientific merit and value. Being satisfied that our research question will add to knowledge and understanding, we then discussed how we could take a relatively general question and operationalise it into specific 'testable' research hypotheses. The research hypotheses help to identify the structure of our research question, which in turn will inform our choice of an appropriate research design. Leading on from the research planning process of question-hypothesis-design, is the activity of selecting your research sample such that the findings from your study may be confidently generalised back to the wider population, or to a specific population of interest. Approaches to sampling were discussed in chapter 3, as were some of the very practical issues concerning power and effect size, data collection and conformity to accepted standards of professional practice. We then went on to examine organising and exploring raw data, as well as a number of approaches to analysing association and difference in data sets that reflected a variety of experimental designs. Whilst case examples drawn from the sport and exercise sciences have been included in the relevant chapter sections to illustrate key concepts and calculations, these have provided only part of the picture. It would now be useful to demonstrate the whole research process in action. In this chapter we will take you step-by-step through a small-scale research project. We will start at the planning stage, identifying a research question of merit and operationalising this question into research hypotheses. We will continue through deciding on an appropriate experimental design to address this question, constructing an appropriate sample, data collection, data organising and exploration, statistical analyses, finally culminating at the formulation of appropriate and substantiated research conclusions. The approach taken to articulate this process will be that *actions* (i.e. *what* you do) will be described in 'Action Boxes', and additional background information (i.e. *why* you do it) will be given as a commentary in the text. Whilst we accept that such an approach makes for a very dry treatment of what can be a very imaginative process, it will illuminate the progression of stages – and the reasoning behind this progression – at this formative stage in your research training.

The example presented will draw directly on subject knowledge from the sport and exercise sciences sub-disciplines of sports psychology, exercise physiology, exercise biochemistry and sports nutrition. However, the research project will be presented, as far as possible, in a generalised approach in order to demonstrate the application of the main themes presented through this book to a real research project.

The Planning Stage

The first step in the research process is deciding what it is that you wish to examine. This choice may be relatively free (as in the case of a dissertation, an independent project or a personal study), or it may be constrained (as in the case of contract research, commercial research, or work-based research). When you have a general idea of the theme of your research, it is important to gain background knowledge to the context of this idea and – in relation to the subject matter of this text – the underlying science. From chapter 2 you will recall that this first step in the planning stage is concerned with *articulating the problem*. Once you have gained related and background knowledge of the area, it is time to become more specific in *developing a research question*. The research question will help to define more specifically the subject matter and provide direction to your research project, but before you can proceed further with confidence you must first *determine the intellectual merit of your research question*. Primarily through reading relevant scientific literature, or through gaining insights founded on practice- or experience-based evidence, you must determine whether your question is scientifically sound, has intellectual and/or practical relevance, and (in relation to postgraduate doctoral and contractual/commercial research) has not been comprehensively examined previously. Once this process has been completed and merit has been demonstrated, the next step provides direction and focus to your project through the *formulation of research hypotheses*. Your research hypotheses, in turn, will help determine your *research design* and the structure of your *research sample*.

Case Example Planning Step-1: Articulating the Problem

Sport and exercise performance is limited by the availability of appropriate fuels to the muscles performing work and the maintenance of an appropriate fluid balance. Performance will further be compromised if the event or activity is taking place in an adverse environment (e.g. high or low temperature, high or low humidity, or high altitude or sub sea-level). Limited fuel availability and/or a negative fluid balance (i.e. dehydration), will be associated with a deterioration of sport/exercise performance and the onset of fatigue. In recent years both sports performers and workers employed in physically demanding occupations have looked to the field of nutrition to provide the means by which the onset of fatigue may be delayed, and thereby improve exercise capacity and/or mental function.

This is far from being a new area of scientific enquiry; indeed the link between what we eat and how we perform was demonstrated in a series of studies undertaken during the early part of the twentieth century (Christensen and Hansen, 1939). Interest in this field of enquiry was given a tremendous boost with the measurement advances of the Scandinavian scientist, Jonas Bergstrom, and the development of an improved needle biopsy technique (Bergstrom, 1962). This technique allowed researchers to examine tissue from active, healthy individuals, and therefore more directly evaluate the relationship between diet and performance. Much of the scientific interest during the 1960s, 1970s and early 1980s focussed upon dietary macronutrients, namely carbohydrate, fat and protein, as the principle energy providers during exercise. However, a number of groups were also examining the roles of equally important micronutrients – dietary constituents required in relatively smaller amounts – that were essential for both sustained exercise performance and the maintenance of good health. One such micronutrient that has gone on to spawn innumerable scientific investigations and a multi-million pound industry is the amino acid, creatine (Harris et al., 1992).

From an exercise biochemistry perspective, creatine (Cr) and phosphorylcreatine (PCr) are found in a variety of the body's tissues that are all characterised by a capability to rapidly increase their rate of energy breakdown (where energy is provided in the form of the chemical adenosine triphosphate, ATP). The presence of creatine and phosphorylcreatine facilitates high rates of ATP (energy) breakdown and provides some protection against the accumulation of metabolic products – such as adenosine diphosphate (ADP) – that will interfere with normal tissue function. The greater part of scientific interest in creatine supplementation in the sport and exercise sciences has focussed upon skeletal muscle, and its role in maintaining muscle contraction during high-intensity fatiguing exercise. Brain tissue has many similarities to muscle tissue in that it has a high creatine content, large carbohydrate reserves, and the capability to rapidly increase its rate of energy breakdown. Muscle requires energy in the form of ATP to fuel contractile activity, where as the brain requires energy to maintain appropriate electrochemical gradients between different brain regions, and to send electrical and chemical messages to target tissues that ultimately control the functioning of the whole body. Thus, like muscle, the brain can similarly experience fatigue if the supply of energy (ATP) is reduced.

Action box 10.1 summarises the line of argument discussed above, and how this argument might be developed to give rise to the *inquiring thought* from which our research project will evolve.

Action Box 10.1   **Articulating the Problem**

1.   Sport/exercise performance is limited by the availability of appropriate energy to active tissues...

2.   This energy is ultimately derived from an individual's diet...

3.   Impaired energy provision is associated with the onset of muscle fatigue...

4.   Skeletal muscle energy turnover is facilitated by the presence of creatine, such that providing creatine reduces fatigue...

5.   There are similarities between muscle tissue and brain tissue in terms of their capabilities for energy turnover...

6.   Therefore, energy turnover in the brain might equally be facilitated by the presence of creatine...

7.   Such that fatigue will be reduced and brain function better maintained.

Therefore, an *inquiring thought* from this line of argument might go something like this:

> *If creatine supplementation holds benefits for skeletal muscle tissue in terms of maintaining performance in the face of reduced energy availability, might such a dietary strategy also have benefits for maintaining brain function, where brain is a tissue that is equally susceptible to compromised energy availability?*

Case Example Planning Step-2: Developing a Research Question

You will recall that the next step is to take this relatively general thought and to translate it into a focussed and specific research question. We will now take the 10-step process described in chapter 2 and apply each step to the present example, articulating the thought process in response to each step (action box 10.2).

Action Box 10.2   Developing a Research Question

1.   **Conceptualise your thoughts into a 'directed' way of thinking...**

In Planning Step-1, we suggested the following inquiring thought:

> *If creatine supplementation holds benefits for skeletal muscle tissue in terms of maintaining performance in the face of reduced energy availability, might such a dietary strategy also have benefits for maintaining brain function, where brain is a tissue that is equally susceptible to compromised energy availability?*

To provide 'direction' to this thought, it might be suggested that, under conditions that would give rise to an energy deficiency – or compromised energy provision – in brain tissue, creatine supplementation may assist in maintaining brain function (i.e. increase creatine provision, increase brain function).

2.   **State your research problem in one sentence; what is the key issue?**

In this example, one of the key issues is the circumstances under which there is a physiological rationale for this supplement to play a role – that is, a state of energy deficiency or compromised energy provision. This state may arise under conditions of 'limited rest', where energy availability to the brain may be reduced.

(Continued...)

A further key issue to consider is the possible form a performance outcome will take under conditions of limited rest. In the question presented below, we have suggested that 'limited rest' would be associated with increasing levels of mental fatigue and an impaired ability to concentrate. Thus, the sentence may take the form of the following:

"Under conditions of limited rest, where brain function may be compromised, is oral creatine supplementation associated with reduced mental fatigue and improved concentration?"

3. **Can this key issue be reduced to a single question?**

In this example we have reduced our inquiring thought into a single question, though there are two components to this question. This in itself is not a problem, however we must consider how we might measure and evaluate the state of 'mental fatigue' and the ability to 'concentrate'. One approach adopted in sports psychology to evaluate mental functioning – under conditions such as increasing fatigue – is to measure reaction time. A rationale for adopting reaction time as our composite[10.1] measure of mental fatigue and concentration is that limited rest would be associated with increasing mental fatigue, which in turn would be associated with a decrease in the ability to concentrate and impaired (i.e. increased) reaction time. Thus, we might reduce the sentence stated in (2) to the following:

"Under conditions of limited rest, where brain function may be compromised, is oral creatine supplementation associated with the maintenance of reaction time performance?"

4. **… Or are there a number of questions?**

There may be a number of associated questions, but to raise these here would distract our focus…

(Continued…)

[10.1] A *composite measure* refers to one that is made up of, or composed of, separate parts. This reflects in this instance that performance in a reaction time task will be influenced by both the state of mental fatigue and the ability to concentrate. Though in this example we will not discriminate the degree to which these two attributes influence reaction time performance.

5. **If there are a number of questions, are they of equal relevance or importance?**

    In making this decision we have already decided that, whilst there are a number of questions surrounding this issue, they are not of equal relevance or importance.

6. **Identify the most important question and order the remaining (if appropriate).**

    We have therefore identified the most important question and, for the present, not addressed other possible questions…

7. **Review the quality with which this question or framework of questions encapsulates your initial thoughts as described in (1), and has intellectual merit in terms of previous research.**

    In reviewing the quality with which the question in (2), and modified in (3), encapsulates our initial thoughts we can conclude:

    a. we have clearly defined the *circumstances* (i.e. limited rest)

    b. we have identified the *intervention* (i.e. creatine supplementation)

    c. we have described the *proposed outcome* (i.e. reduced mental fatigue and improved ability to concentrate such that reaction time performance is maintained)

    In the next section we will describe an approach to collecting evidence to determine whether our research question has intellectual merit in terms of previous research…

8. **Abort your research question if there is no intellectual merit or practical significance.**

    The culmination of this process of collecting evidence will be this decision concerning whether to abort our research question if there is no intellectual merit or practical significance…

9. **Or if you are confident in the 'worthwhileness' of your research question, modify your research question if necessary**…

10. **…Or continue**…

From the above process, our research question for this case example is:

> *"Under conditions of limited rest, where brain function may be compromised, is oral creatine supplementation associated with the maintenance of reaction time performance?"*

Case Example Planning Step-3: Determining the Intellectual Merit of our Research Question
Having articulated our research question we must now verify that it is indeed worthwhile and would add to current scientific knowledge and understanding. From the above discussion there is an intuitive logic to the line of argument presented in action box 10.1. However, we must now search for evidence in the current body of scientific literature to further support each step in this argument. In addition, we must also assess the amount of work that has already been conducted in this area; if a wealth of studies is reported in the literature, addressing every facet of this question, there is probably less value in performing more investigations. That is not to say that if other researchers have already investigated a specific research question there is no additional value in replicating these studies. It just means that we must be very clear of our motives for conducting our study – what is the *purpose* of our investigation? Under circumstances where previous work has been conducted it would be inappropriate to introduce our study as a 'groundbreaking' investigation, when really we are verifying, or clarifying, or supplementing the earlier work of others.

Not that many years ago, a search of the scientific literature would have been a labour intensive process, involving sifting through large volumes of indexed abstracts and then performing some detective work to link together fragments of information into a much larger picture. Since the widespread availability of personal computers and the Internet, literature searches can largely be completed from the comfort of your desk through accessing a number of subject appropriate electronic indexes. Increasingly these indexes will include abstracts of the cited scientific investigations, and depending upon your licence rights you may even be able to download the full scientific paper. There will always be a need to read the full paper in order to verify that the study provides strong and appropriate evidence. Popular electronic indexes commonly accessed during literature searches in the sport and exercise sciences include PubMed (http://www.ncbi.nlm.nih.gov) and MedScape (http://www.medscape.com). The aim of these searches are two-fold: first we are assessing the extent and the strength of the body of published literature that directly, or indirectly, has relevance to our research question; and second we are seeking evidence to support the steps in our argument giving rise to our research question. In the case of the latter, we are ensuring that the research question is grounded in sound scientific principles. Whilst in the case of the former, we are contextualising our study within the work that has been completed previously. The processes involved in determining the intellectual merit of our research question are presented in action box 10.3.

Action Box 10.3   Determining the Intellectual Merit of our Research Question

1.   Identify 'key words', or defining words relevant to your research question (e.g. creatine supplementation, brain energy metabolism, mental fatigue, mental/psychological performance, ability to concentrate, reaction time)

2.   Apply these key words in a search of subject indexes (either as hard-copy volumes or more likely – and quicker – as electronic indexes).

3.   You may have knowledge of workers already researching in your area of interest, or as you work through your search the names of active workers will start to become apparent and will be repeated in multiple search entries.

4.   Identify investigations providing evidence to support the steps in your argument underpinning your research question as detailed in action box 10.1, and…

5.   Try to get a feel for the extent and the strength of the body of relevant published literature.

6.   Be aware that your initial choice of key words may not be immediately successful and you may therefore need to revisit (1) and repeat your search.

(Continued…)

7. Even if your initial choice of key words proves to be appropriate this first search will rarely be exhaustive; review the scientific papers cited in response to this preliminary key word search and identify further papers worth following up.

8. Through experience you will appreciate when you have arrived at a point in this process where you feel that you have substantive evidence both to support the worthiness of your research question and to support the rationale of your line of argument.

With reference to the worked example, at the time of writing a key word search identified a wealth of scientific literature to support the use of oral creatine supplementation to improve skeletal muscle function, but far less literature describing the use of creatine in maintaining brain function. There was evidence that reduced levels of creatine in the right medial temporal lobe of the brain was associated with increased incidence of panic disorders (Massana et al. 2002). Furthermore, like skeletal muscle tissue, the creatine content of brain tissue may be increased through supplementation (Dechent et al. 1999). Watanabe et al. (2002) demonstrated that dietary supplementation with creatine reduced mental fatigue when research participants repeatedly performed a simple mathematical calculation.

Whilst none of these studies specifically addresses the question being raised in the present case example, they are all consistent with the general line of enquiry. That is:

1. Whole body fatigue arising from increased energy utilisation and/or inadequate rest/recovery, will lead to…

2. Reduced rate of energy metabolism in body tissue – including skeletal muscle and brain tissue – which may lead to increased fatigue in muscle as well as increased mental fatigue and loss of concentration.

3. Dietary/oral creatine supplementation (at a rate equivalent to 8 g.day^{-1} for 5 days) has been associated with increased creatine content in brain tissue…

4. And reduced mental fatigue, reduced panic disorders and improved abilities to concentrate.

As we start to give structure to our research study through developing an initial thought into a research question, supported by a logical line of argument and evidence from the scientific literature, elements of the required experimental design will also start to become apparent. These elements will gain further in structure as we now move to formulating our research hypotheses.

Case Example Planning Step-4: Formulating Research Hypotheses

Being satisfied that our research question has scientific merit and will add to current knowledge and understanding, the next step is to translate the research question into specific, testable research hypotheses. The research hypotheses will assist, in turn, the decision making process that gives rise to an appropriate research design. The processes involved in formulating research hypotheses from a research question are described in action box 10.4.

Action Box 10.4   Formulating Research Hypotheses

1.   Re-consider the research question:

> *"Under conditions of limited rest, where brain function may be compromised, is oral creatine supplementation associated with the maintenance of reaction time performance?"*

2.   Define the conditions (i.e. limited rest) that remain constant, and the conditions (i.e. with or without creatine supplementation) that will change (i.e. the *independent variables* – refer to chapter 3).

3.   Identify the primary characteristics, responses, or behaviours of interest that may change (i.e. in this example reaction time). This is the *dependent variable*.
   (Continued...)

---

4. List the possible outcomes assuming, in this example, creatine supplementation has no effect and if it did have an effect. In this way we develop our research hypotheses:

Null hypothesis

H_o: Under conditions of limited rest where brain function may be compromised, oral creatine supplementation does not affect reaction time performance.

Alternative hypothesis

H_1:   Under conditions of limited rest where brain function may be compromised, oral creatine supplementation improves reaction time performance

Note: Whilst in our research question we are suggesting that creatine supplementation will contribute to reduced mental fatigue, improved ability to concentrate, and hence maintenance of reaction time, these hypotheses refer to a comparison of a no creatine and a creatine trial.

With reference to action box 10.4, the null hypothesis describes an outcome of *no effect* on reaction time performance as a consequence of oral creatine supplementation. The alternative hypothesis describes a situation where there is *an effect* of oral creatine supplementation on reaction time performance. Thus, we have given focus and direction to our research question, and have identified an aspect of human activity that may be influenced by creatine supplementation, and we should now explore how we might go about translating these hypotheses into a sound experimental design.

Case Example Planning Step-5: Developing a Research (Experimental) Design

If we now examine our research question in the context of the conditions giving rise to our experimental situation, we will first be aware that the research participants must undergo a research intervention involving some form of "…limited rest" that will be associated with

"...compromised brain function". For the purposes of this worked example, we will take as our research population undergraduate and postgraduate students at the University of Chichester, Chichester, United Kingdom. This provides a group of research participants who are routinely involved in high-level academic study, often working long hours associated with reduced sleep duration and impaired sleep quality, and as such may experience "...limited rest".

An intervention that would yield the required level of mental fatigue, and has relevance both to the research participants and for occupational groups who work long hours or who undergo shift work, would be sleep deprivation. Prolonged sleep deprivation is associated with mental fatigue probably in association with reduced brain tissue energy metabolism and reduced ability to concentrate. One way to implement this would be to have research participants attend the laboratory for a 24-h period, during which they would be prohibited from sleeping. Whilst this would be relatively mild sleep deprivation in the context of sleep studies reported in the literature, it would be adequate for an initial examination of the research hypotheses and would be ethically more acceptable in the first instance.

With respect to the experimental design, we need to consider those elements of research design that would allow us to control as many variables as possible that might affect the ability to see *real* differences between a control group and a creatine supplemented group. The treatment in this case example required research participants to supplement their diet with creatine, and from previous literature an appropriate dose rate would be equivalent to 8 g.day^{-1} for 5 days. The most powerful design for examining the influence of a treatment or intervention is a *randomised cross-over design*, with all research participants undertaking a control trial and a treatment or intervention trial. This reduces the between-trial error variation arising from differences in the participants regardless of any treatment/intervention differences: this source of error variation is *minimised* if the *same* individuals undertake *all* conditions; but is *maximised* if *different* individuals are involved in the separate trials. In chapter 3 we discussed the problems arising from treatments or interventions that were non-reversible, or at least non-reversible over the short term. Creatine supplementation is one such treatment, where a relatively long 'wash out' period of several weeks is required for the restoration of pre-supplementation tissue creatine concentrations. Whilst this treatment is reversible, the delay for this to occur may result in changes in other aspects of human physical and mental performance that would compromise experimental control and introduce an additional source of error to the investigation. The best approach in this case would therefore be to recruit different participants for the control trial and the treatment/intervention trial, such that we would adopt an *independent groups design* for this investigation. This is a practical compromise – whilst independent groups for the different trials is not as powerful as a randomised cross-over design, the potential error incurred as a consequence of an extended interval between trials is possibly greater. A further practical problem of an independent groups design is the need to recruit a greater number of research participants. Obviously in a randomised cross-over study, all participants complete all trials; in an independent groups study, every participant completes only one trial. Therefore separate groups of participants are required for each trial (or condition), and each group must be large enough to ensure that it is representative of the population(s) of interest. An alternative approach would be to require the same group of participants to undertake the experimental procedure on two occasions, with all participants having the control trial first. However, the disadvantage of this approach would be that participants would learn from the first (control) trial, and reap the benefit during the second (treatment/intervention) trial. As a consequence, we would introduce an *order effect*, and the treatment effects of – in this example creatine – would be combined with a *learning effect,* as all participants will be supplementing with creatine prior to the second trial. Thus, it is better to have separate – independent – groups and to incorporate procedures into the experimental design for identifying group differences without supplementation before the experimental trials commence (e.g. an initial 'control' condition for all participants).

Finally, we must decide on the specific detail of our control treatment[10.2], where you will recall from chapter 3 that the control trial is one of 'no change'. In supplementation studies, such as the present case example, a common approach is to administer a placebo treatment for the control trial. This is to ensure that, whilst control participants are not actually receiving a creatine dose, they 'think' that they are receiving something and therefore do not feel psychologically disadvantaged in relation to other participants. Good practice would be for both treatments (i.e. placebo and creatine) to be administered either double blind if possible, or at least single blind (refer to chapter 3) to ensure that participant – and investigator – knowledge does not prejudice the outcome of the investigation.

In formulating our testable hypotheses from our initial inquiring thought, we have already made the suggestion that one aspect of mental performance that is likely to suffer under such conditions would be an individual's reaction time. The suggestion is that mental fatigue would be associated with a reduced ability to concentrate, and an increase in response time to a specified stimulus. This increase in response time would reflect impaired reaction time performance. For the purposes of this case example, we will assume that reaction time will be measured using an instrumented light box, where research participants respond by pressing the corresponding buttons associated with a particular sequence of lights being illuminated. The reaction time is recorded as the time delay in milliseconds (ms) between illumination of the lights and the appropriate buttons being pressed. Thus, we have a method for evaluating reaction time; we must also consider how this measurement approach will be incorporated into our experimental design over the 24-h trial period. If reaction time is to be measured only once at each time point, then there is a greater opportunity for chance results to hide the true effects of the treatment. To control for this possibility, we might undertake repeated measurements at each time point and determine a mean±SD value. This approach should provide data that are representative of the reaction time of an individual participant, but will not be enough to increase skill during the pre-sleep deprivation stage, nor increase fatigue during the final stages of the experimental protocol.

[10.2] In this chapter we have employed two levels of *control*: the control condition is undertaken initially by all participants to evaluate pre-experimental group differences; the control (placebo) trial is administered in tandem with the experimental (creatine) trial to evaluate possible treatment differences.

The experimental design that is evolving from the research question now has the following structures: there will be two independent groups made up of postgraduate and undergraduate students (a placebo – PLAC – group and a creatine – CREAT – group); both groups will attend the laboratories for a period of 24 hours on two occasions separated by a specified number of days; during each 24 hour observation (trial) period research participants will not be permitted to sleep, and their reaction time will be measured at the start of the observation period (i.e. 0900 h), and then after 6 (i.e. 1500 h), 18 (0300 h) and 24 hours (0900 h); and for 5 days prior to a second trial participants will supplement with either placebo or creatine in a randomised double blind design (i.e. neither the participants nor the investigators will be aware of who is ingesting the placebo and who is ingesting creatine) (figure 10.1). The initial control condition with no (placebo or creatine) supplementation would provide an opportunity for possible differences between the two groups to be evaluated. It is common to allow a 'recovery' period between experimental trials of approximately 7 days; this is both to allow the research participant to recover from any fatigue arising from a research intervention (but not too long as to allow training/detraining effects), and will also result in the participant attending the laboratory on the same day of the week. This approach provides the best opportunity to ensure that the activities and events immediately prior to both experimental trials will be similar. Remember that in the present example the research participants were students who operate on a weekly timetable of study commitments, work commitments, and sporting activities. Thus, we are trying to control as many external variables as possible that may influence the effect of sleep deprivation.

Action Box 10.5   **Research Design**
From the above discussion the key elements to be included in the research design of this case example are:
1.   **Research participant population:** undergraduate and postgraduate students of the University of Chichester, Chichester, United Kingdom.
(Continued…)

2. **Condition:** a situation of "…limited rest", associated with "…compromised brain function", will be induced through sleep deprivation.

3. **Treatment/Intervention (independent variable):** with or without creatine supplementation (at a rate equivalent to 8 g.day^{-1} for 5 days). As this treatment requires an extended wash out period, we will need to recruit two groups – a control (placebo) group and a treatment (creatine supplemented) group.

4. **Design:** as two different groups of research participants will be undertaking the two trials of this investigation, this is an independent groups design.

5. **Measurable dependent variable:** reaction time (ms), where an increase in response time to a light stimulus would reflect increased "…mental fatigue" and a reduced ability to "…concentrate".

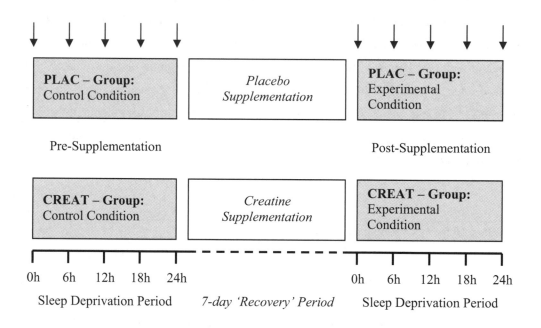

Figure 10.1   Schematic representation of the experimental procedures in the *Sleep Deprivation Study* (Note: 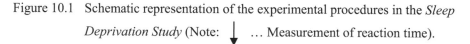 … Measurement of reaction time).

Case Example Planning Step-6: Considering Your Data Analysis

At this point in the planning stage an outline idea of the analysis techniques should be forming. It is not good research practice to complete your sampling and data collection procedures *before* identifying the form that data analysis will take. The identification of suitable analysis techniques is an important part of preliminary design considerations. In this case there are two conditions for each group, an initial control sleep deprivation (trial) condition (no placebo or creatine supplementation) and an experimental (trial) condition (following either placebo or creatine supplementation). However the control and experimental conditions do not need to be compared with each other – one is a precursor to the other – and it is likely that the data collected will be analysed in separate stages. This approach is appropriate and will not increase the potential for error as a consequence of multiple analyses, as the results are separate samples of data collected at different times. No re-use of the same data will occur in this process.

Both sets of analyses will follow the same structure, comparing two groups (PLAC and CREAT) over four periods of sleep deprivation, giving rise to four sets of reaction time data (measured at 0 h (Pre), 6 h, 18 h and 24 h). We would anticipate that 'no effects' should be evident – either in the control or experimental conditions – at 0 or 6 hours, though after 18 and 24 hours the effects of the sleep deprivation may be visible. This analysis will have two factors so immediately non-parametric procedures have to be discounted, as they do not have the complexity to handle this kind of design. However, *ANOVA* would be an appropriate approach as the hypotheses being investigated are concerned with potential differences between groups. Data should follow normal distribution parameters for ANOVA to be at its most powerful. The data we are going to collect will be reduced to a mean of forty reaction times prior to analysis; this strengthens the likelihood of the data following the normal distribution. A mathematical rule known as the *central limit theorem* shows that, regardless of the original (raw) data distribution pattern, sample means will be normally distributed around the original distribution mean. The standard error of this distribution can be calculated from knowledge of the original data (by dividing the original standard deviation by the square root of the original sample size).

The *ANOVA* will indicate whether any differences observed between the groups are happening by chance or whether they are 'likely' to occur again in the population. If a significant difference is evident from the *ANOVA*, follow up analyses will be required. It would not make sense to compare reaction times of one group after 6 h sleep deprivation with the other group after 18 h sleep deprivation, as would happen if a *post hoc Tukey test* were used to examine all possible comparisons; the sensible comparisons to make would be to compare the two groups (i.e. placebo vs. creatine) across the four commensurate time points (i.e. Pre, 6 h, 18 h and 24 h). Thus, if follow up analyses are required we will undertake pre-planned independent (i.e. different groups) *t* tests between the two groups at each time point to see where differences occur. These tests will be examining data that have already been used within the main analysis and therefore should be subject to a *Bonferroni adjustment* for the number of tests completed. Some researchers argue that this is not necessary, because under the limited (i.e. pre-planned) comparisons we wish to undertake, each subset of data will only be used once within one *t*-test. It is often the case that the importance of a type I error (i.e. reject the null hypothesis when it is true) within the context of the experimental hypotheses, is evaluated when making a decision about the use of the *Bonferroni adjustment* under these circumstances. For example, if an incorrect rejection of the null hypothesis could endanger health, while an incorrect acceptance of the null hypothesis would not cause any danger, then the *Bonferroni adjustment* would be applied to make the likelihood of wrongly rejecting the null hypothesis as stringent (i.e. strict) as possible. The comparisons identified for further analysis using independent samples *t*-tests were selected as the experimental design is one of a repeated measure on the time factor, and it does not make sense within the context of the experiment to compare *all* available time points in one group with *all* available time points in the other group.

While considering the experimental design (Step-5) and the proposed approaches to data analysis (Step-6), prior to data collection, it is important to also consider the effect size of the experiment and the power of analysis. As discussed in chapter 3, studies such as the present case example do not usually attract large numbers of research participants. However, there are direct links between participant numbers, power of analysis and experimental effect size (chapter 3). Traditionally an experimental design would have been evaluated to find the optimum compromise between these three elements to provide the strongest analysis. For example, if we state that an acceptable power is 0.6 (i.e. if the null hypothesis is false, we will obtain a significant result causing us to reject the null hypothesis 60% of the time), and an acceptable effect size is 0.5 (i.e. a *medium* effect size), then the *required sample size* could be found using a combination of power tables and a mathematical calculation. Looking at previous work in the field and deciding on a value that is at least as good, or if possible better than what has been done before, can also determine the desired power and effect size (this approach will be addressed in more detail, including calculations, in *Using Statistics in Sport and Exercise Science Research – Book 2*). For the purposes of the present example, we can apply a simple calculation – that does not take into consideration specific details of the experimental design – to provide an indication of the required power and effect size. Using a method proposed by Howell (1997), the relationship between power, effect size and sample size for equalised groups and two independent means can be evaluated by:

$$\delta = d\sqrt{\frac{N}{2}}$$

where, δ is a value for the chance of power of 0.6 at the 5% significance level
…found from a look up power table
d is the required effect size
N is the total sample size.

For the worked example, we have specified the acceptable power (i.e. 0.6 at the 5% significance level, such that δ is 2.2 – *from power tables*; Howell, 1997) and effect size (i.e. 0.5); we can therefore calculate a simple guide to the required sample size as follows:

$$\delta = d\sqrt{\frac{N}{2}}$$

Becomes… $2.2 = 0.5\sqrt{\frac{N}{2}}$

Rearranging… $2 \times \left(\frac{2.2}{0.5}\right)^2 = N = 38.72$

Thus, to achieve a power of 0.6 at the 5% significance level, with an effect size of 0.5, our sample size must be 38–39 research participants if we were only using a *t*-test approach on one factor. We have proposed *ANOVA* to look at two factors simultaneously, so <u>at least</u> 40 research participants would be needed to work towards the desired power and effect size. In this worked example, to test forty individuals would be intensive on resources and – for the required experimental design – very time consuming. Issues concerning the available resources and the available time will sometimes limit what is practically possible over what is experimentally the most desirable. In terms of studies similar to the current case example, often the best that can be achieved is to work with the numbers of participants that volunteer to participate in the study (in this worked example there were 19 volunteers). Nevertheless, to produce a retrospective estimate of the power and effect size of the investigation that has been undertaken helps to contextualise the data that has been collected, and hence helps in the formulation of conclusions. This will be undertaken during the present case example and is reported in table 10.4. Readers requiring a more comprehensive discussion of the inter-relationship between power, effect size and sample size are directed to Howell (1997).

Action Box 10.6   Proposed Data Analysis

From consideration of our experimental design the proposed analyses will be as follows:

1.   **Inspection of individual case data for fluctuation of data around the individual means**
     This will involve inspection of line graphs with error bars for each data reading to see if any individual has very erratic reaction times throughout the experiment.

2.   **Inspection of group data to compare group behaviour**
     This will require summary statistics to be calculated and the data to be graphically presented.

3.   **Testing for group differences between the 'Control Conditions' of the two groups**
     i.e. Two-way *ANOVA*, the factors being *time* and *treatment group*
     (Continued...)

4.	**Computation of difference data**
	… if the results of stage (3) showed there to be significant differences between the two groups.
5.	**Testing for group differences between the 'Experimental Conditions' of the two groups**
	i.e. A further two-way *ANOVA*, the factors being *time* and *treatment group* as in step (3)
6.	**If the *ANOVA* in step (5) is significant**
	… then differences between the two groups at each corresponding time point will be followed up with pre-planned independent samples *t*-tests (*Bonferroni adjusted*).

Case Example Planning Step-7: Constructing Your Sample

We have defined the research population for this case example as the undergraduate and postgraduate student body of the University of Chichester, Chichester, United Kingdom. As this population is relatively small in number (i.e. varying between 4000 and 5000 students), we might consider applying *random sampling* techniques to construct our research sample (Chapter 3). However, this is a relatively dynamic population, (with students changing their registration status), and as a consequence of part-time students and distance learners the population is not tightly geographically focussed. In addition, the extensive time commitment and potentially arduous and stressful nature of the research condition (i.e. sleep deprivation) would preclude participation of a number of the population on available time, health and/or personal preference grounds. Thus, the common approach to sampling in this kind of example is to publicise the study (e.g. flyers, posters, and messages on the University's internal computer website), calling for volunteers. The volunteer body will then undergo checks to ensure that they are not presently supplementing with creatine (and had not done so within the last 6 months), standard health history screening and informed consent procedures, and the resulting group of participants will form our total sample size, *N* (where the size of the total sample, and the resulting experimental groups, will be defined by the power and effect size calculations discussed previously).

The nature of the research intervention (i.e. creatine supplementation) is such that, after formulating our research sample, we will need to construct two groups of research participants. In terms of reducing error variation between these two groups, a compromise approach would be for the two groups to be made up of matched pairs. However, we will assume that, as is often the case in supplementation studies over several days in the sport and exercise sciences, the initial sample recruitment is less than optimal such that our N (total sample size) is not adequate for matching purposes. You will recall from chapter 3 that the process of matching is only effective if the matching is good; a 'near miss' on some matches will compromise the whole experiment. Thus, if we cannot be confident in our matching such that each group is made up of reciprocal matched pairs, and that each group is reflective of the population from which it was drawn, we are best to avoid this approach and simply to randomise the allocation of participants from the total sample to the placebo (control, PLAC) and creatine (experimental, CREAT) groups. Some form of *post hoc* justification and/or analysis of participant characteristics is appropriate to verify the representation and quality of your sample, and subsequently your research groups. It is important to confirm that the groups are not different (with reference to key attributes and capabilities thought to be associated with the treatment/intervention and the outcome measures) prior to the start of the investigation, such that any differences observed at the end of the investigation can be deemed to be as a consequence of the experimental treatment/intervention. Examples of analysis approaches that are appropriate for the present example would include a comparison of means for a control condition, and evaluating homogeneity of variance.

Action Box 10.6   Constructing Your Sample: Case Example

1.   Random sampling is rarely, if ever, achievable in the sport and exercise sciences.

2.   The common approach is to advertise for volunteers, possibly specifying a number of defining features (e.g. gender, age range, physical training status, sporting participation, sporting representation level/standard, injury status or disease status for clinical studies, and perhaps even such attributes as personality traits).
      (Continued...)

3.   Power and effect size calculations will provide guidance on the required size of your research sample, but always refer to your selection criteria in order to ensure homogeneity of variance in your sample.

4.   Once a sample has been recruited, it is good practice to apply some form of *post hoc* justification/analysis to verify the representation and quality of your sample and/or research groups (e.g. evaluating comparability of means and/or analysing for homogeneity of variance).

The Experimental Stage

Having completed the planning stage of the research project, it is now time to move on to the 'doing' part where we actually collect the data to address the research question. This section will provide the practical detail with reference to the research participants, what they were required to undertake, and how the data were collected and analysed.

Case Example Experimental Step-1: Research Participants

Nineteen healthy, undergraduate and postgraduate male students volunteered to participate in this investigation (age 25.1 ± 6.5 years, height 1.78 ± 0.13 m, body mass 70.1 ± 12.2 kg). All participants completed health history questionnaires, questionnaires to evaluate their normal sleep patterns, and confirmed that they were not presently supplementing with creatine (nor had done so within the last 6 months), prior to giving their informed consent. The University of Chichester Ethical Review Committee approved all procedures.

Case Example Experimental Step-2: Experimental Design

An independent groups design was adopted with the total research sample being randomly allocated to two groups. As nineteen participants were recruited, this resulted in uneven groups for the placebo (PLAC) group (n = 9) and the creatine (CREAT) group (n = 10) respectively. This is not a problem in this example, as the independent groups design can cope with uneven groups at the analysis stage. However, if we had decided upon a matched pairs design, and achieved a good level of matching across the groups, we would have had to discount the data from one of the participants in the CREAT group, as there would not have been a corresponding matched participant in the PLAC group. Equally, if we had commenced the study with matched pairs, and one participant from a pairing was unable to complete a trial, then all data associated with that pairing – including the complete data set from their matched participant – would have to be discounted.

Case Example Experimental Step-3: Procedures

Research participants reported to the laboratory at 0800 h after a12-h overnight fast. They were instructed not to undertake any strenuous exercise and not to consume alcohol or caffeine over the 48 h before the trial. Participants were also instructed to record their dietary intake over this period prior to the control condition, and to replicate this diet over the 48 h prior to the experimental condition. Adherence to pre-test instructions was verified as participants reported to the laboratory. Body mass was measured with participants wearing underwear using balance scales, and height was measured in bare feet using a wall-mounted stadiometer.

The experimental protocol is illustrated in figure 10.1. All trials were undertaken in an air-conditioned laboratory that was maintained at a temperature of 20.0±0.0°C, 30% relative humidity. After the preliminary measurements, participants were provided with a standardised breakfast consisting of breakfast cereals and toast. Water was provided, and participants were encouraged to drink *ad libitum*[10.3] throughout the 24-h sleep deprivation period. The first reaction time test (Pre) was undertaken at 0900 h in a sound proof cubicle. This test comprised forty random light pattern trials, and the mean±SD reaction time for the forty trials was recorded for each time point during the sleep deprivation period. Further reaction time tests were undertaken at 1500 h (6 h), 0200 h (18 h) and 0900 h (24 h) the following morning under the same controlled conditions. A standardised lunch (consisting of sandwiches, yoghurt and a piece of fruit) was provided at 1300 h, a standardised tea (consisting of baked potato with cheese and salad, and a piece of fruit) was provided at 1800 h, a standardised supper (consisting of sandwiches, yoghurt and a piece of fruit)

[10.3]   *Ad libitum* is a term used to denote that an activity is undertaken without restraint (i.e. freely).

was provided at 2300 h, and a standardised breakfast (consisting of cereals and toast) was provided at 0600 h. During the sleep deprivation period, participants were provided with reading material (books and magazines), videos, music and access to television and radio, as well as being encouraged to bring their own indoor (non-exercising) activities to the laboratory. As far as possible, these activities were standardised for each participant across the two conditions.

The control and experimental conditions were separated by an interval of 7-days. During five days prior to the experimental condition, the creatine group supplemented with 8 g of creatine (divided into four 2 g boluses taken in capsule form) per day and the placebo group supplemented with 8 g of placebo (i.e. glucose, divided into four 2 g boluses taken in capsule form).

Case Example Experimental Step-4: Statistical Analyses
Statistical analyses were undertaken with SPSS™ version 11.5 (SPSS™, Chicago Il, USA). Values are reported as mean±SD unless otherwise stated as mean±SEM. A two-way *ANOVA* was used to evaluate differences between the placebo and creatine groups for the control condition. Similarly a two-way *ANOVA* was used to evaluate differences between the placebo and creatine groups for the experimental condition. Pre-planned independent samples *t*-tests (*Bonferroni adjusted*) would be used if required to evaluate the significance of differences arising from the *ANOVA* analyses. Significance was accepted at the 5% level (i.e. $p < 0.05$).

Action Box 10.7   Experimental Protocol and Approaches to Data Collection

1.   Describe your research participant sample selecting population and experimentally relevant characteristics. Report any selection criteria or specific requirements for inclusion in the research sample. It is also appropriate to describe the form of pre-experimental health assessments and tests of suitability for undertaking the experimental procedures. Finally, you must confirm that your protocol has been expertly reviewed and identify the body that undertook the review process. Note – if the outcome of this review process was that the protocol was not approved, your study should not have progressed to the experimental stage!

2.   Identify your experimental design and describe the processes informing the formation of experimental groups.

3.   Present your research protocol and procedures, describing the specific detail of your research treatment/intervention if appropriate. Describe the form of all measurements, the methods of measurement and the conditions surrounding the taking of measurements, and the sequencing and/or timing of these measures. A diagram is particularly useful to clarify this detail. All steps taken to ensure trial standardisation and experimental control – maximising measurement sensitivity – should be clearly articulated.

4.   A description of the preferred approaches to analysing and evaluating the data should be presented. These approaches should be compatible with the experimental design, which in turn will be informed by the research hypotheses. A statement of the level of significance should be included.

The Analysis and Review Stage

Case Example Analysis and Review Step-1: The Raw Data

The raw data for this case example reflect the means of forty reaction time trials at each time point during the sleep deprivation period in the control and experimental conditions, such that the data

---

presented in tables 10.1 and 10.2, for the control and experimental conditions respectively, are reported as mean±SD.

	Placebo Group				Creatine Group			
	Control – Sleep Deprivation				Control – Sleep Deprivation			
Subject	Pre	6 h	18 h	24 h	Pre	6 h	18 h	24 h
1	393±55	367±59	392±80	393±55	395±53	408±84	402±67	357±76
2	376±53	363±49	381±87	376±53	353±47	419±71	391±56	374±56
3	391±52	346±43	327±50	391±52	419±78	388±53	436±62	382±48
4	374±39	356±36	396±107	374±39	438±93	430±76	427±72	416±54
5	400±55	422±50	397±42	400±55	398±60	397±70	418±100	407±69
6	347±60	379±68	411±70	347±60	376±60	355±75	379±52	347±52
7	359±72	386±88	449±85	359±72	388±58	374±55	384±63	369±60
8	415±69	455±67	453±86	415±69	386±69	398±66	370±68	343±64
9	382±84	360±70	395±65	382±84	366±42	400±46	422±74	379±48
10					373±49	395±58	399±63	360±73

Table 10.1   Reaction times (ms) for participants undertaking the *Sleep Deprivation Study* in the placebo and creatine groups during the control condition (mean±SD).

	Placebo Group				Creatine Group			
	Experimental – Sleep Deprivation				Experimental – Sleep Deprivation			
Subject	Pre	6 h	18 h	24 h	Pre	6 h	18 h	24 h
1	337±46	355±54	365±71	387±98	348±81	370±77	360±83	390±99
2	358±52	378±49	353±34	405±48	346±59	380±34	364±35	350±72
3	331±65	339±69	298±55	347±63	406±42	394±50	346±55	414±47
4	343±38	331±37	334±46	358±89	387±75	382±57	369±53	354±84
5	350±55	387±57	385±43	382±60	362±55	388±91	405±100	347±69
6	339±62	391±71	359±89	359±70	338±67	368±66	348±57	326±67
7	381±84	433±118	425±78	429±128	334±41	383±56	374±58	366±61
8	427±56	445±81	446±91	399±52	344±69	400±91	341±55	336±53
9	340±67	373±59	349±57	327±51	339±37	383±57	379±47	344±76
10					368±37	372±54	374±48	339±36

Table 10.2   Reaction times (ms) for participants undertaking the *Sleep Deprivation Study* in the placebo and creatine groups during the experimental condition (mean±SD).

Case Example Analysis and Review Step-2: Data Organisation and Exploration

As identified earlier, the first place to start with any data that have been collected is to organise the data into a structure that can easily be inspected for patterns and anomalies. After tabulating your data in a way that is appropriate and relevant to your particular experimental design, you will then be in a position to start to explore the data for any obvious patterns.

Samples for studies like the present example are usually small due to such factors as research and participant expense, technical resourcing, the labour intensive nature of data collection, participant discomfort, participant inconvenience and their ability to take 24 hours out of normal life on two occasions within a short period of time. With small samples a good place to start is to look at the behaviour of each individual. Graphs of the mean and standard deviation reaction time for each participant over time will provide an indication of whether the data have large or small individual variation. It will answer the question of how representative of individual performance is the mean reaction time. Thus, initial inspection of this small data set should begin with inspection of individual participant data, to see if there are any individuals who show erratic or atypical values (this would be evident as large standard deviations at each time point). If any individual has erratic values across all time points then their data will not be representative of the effects of sleep deprivation on reaction time, and they may mask any treatment effects. The problems caused by erratic values is exaggerated in small samples, as each participant has a greater proportional influence on the behaviour of the sample than would be the case if the sample was larger.

Graphs like the one presented in figure 10.2 illustrate individual behaviour well. These data are for research participant – 1 in the placebo group; the graph indicates that reaction time performance starts to fluctuate more widely at the 18 h data collection point, and this is a consistent finding across both conditions. This consistent observation is good; this research participant was not supplementing with creatine, which we have hypothesised would affect their reaction time performance and perhaps would be associated with less variation at this stage in the sleep deprivation period. Whilst you may plot individual graphs for each participant in your laboratory book, it is unlikely that they will ever find their way into a final report. That is unless they serve to illustrate a particular finding of interest, for example where an atypical response had wider relevance for the population as a whole or is of unique scientific importance. The report would describe all exploratory work undertaken to verify underlying assumptions of any tests that were completed as part of the main analysis. Nevertheless, this exploration stage is essential if you are to know your data thoroughly, and be able to explain and discuss the differences or similarities in your data in an informed way, and should therefore not be passed over quickly.

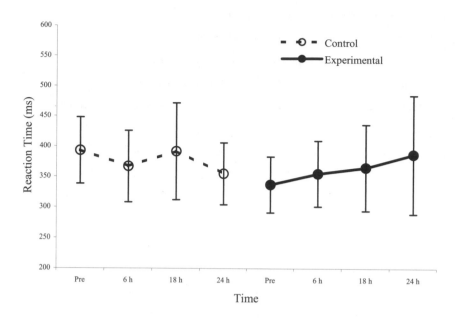

Figure 10.2   Reaction times for Participant-1 (PLAC) during the control and experimental conditions of the *Sleep Deprivation Study* (mean±SD).

Following inspection of individual participant data, the second stage of data exploration is to compare the behaviour of the sample groups. This is best achieved through the calculation of summary statistics, group by group, and the drawing of graphs. Computers are a huge benefit in this area, as they are able to process large volumes of data very quickly to produce summary statistics and graphical presentations of the data. Table 10.3 presents the summary statistics of the reaction times (ms) of the placebo and creatine groups for the control and experimental conditions.

		Control Condition				Experimental Condition			
		Pre	6 h	18 h	24 h	Pre	6 h	18 h	24 h
Placebo Group	Mean	381.89	381.56	400.11	388.44	356.22	381.33	368.22	377.00
	SD	20.82	35.35	37.31	37.60	30.43	38.65	45.21	31.98
	SEM	6.94	11.78	12.44	12.53	10.14	12.88	15.07	10.66
Creatine Group	Mean	389.20	396.40	402.80	373.40	357.20	382.00	366.00	356.60
	SD	25.12	21.29	22.21	23.89	23.64	10.27	18.90	26.81
	SEM	7.94	6.73	7.02	7.56	7.48	3.25	5.98	8.48

Table 10.3   Summary statistics of the reaction times (ms) of the PLAC and CREAT groups for the control and experimental conditions during the *Sleep Deprivation Study*.

Presenting summary statistics allows for any differences found during the *ANOVA* to be visually verified in relation to the sample groups. Whilst graphically presenting the data allows an opportunity to evaluate the possible locations of differences between the sample groups before we commence our statistical analyses to assess whether such differences are generalisable to the wider population. Figures 10.3 and 10.4 present the mean±SE reaction times for the placebo and creatine groups during the control condition and experimental condition respectively. Histograms of group data will illustrate patterns of data distribution, and will often be important precursor checks of assumptions underpinning various aspects of data analysis (e.g. evaluating normality of a data distribution). In this case example, tests of normality are not essential, for as discussed previously the data being analysed are means of data readings. The *sample means* are the means of the forty readings from each individual at each time point. Given that our mean data are unlikely to violate assumptions of normality, we are in a position to proceed with our proposed two-way *ANOVA* tests, where interpretation is made easier by having the summary statistics and corresponding figures to hand.

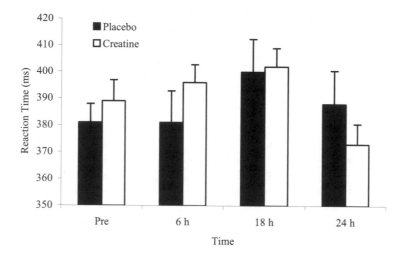

Table 10.3   Reaction times (ms) for participants undertaking the *Sleep Deprivation Study* in the placebo (black bars) and creatine (grey bars) groups during the control condition (mean±SE).

Examining figure 10.3, the standard errors (as indicated by the error bars extending from each bar of the histogram) for each group mean overlap. This suggests that it is unlikely that a statistical difference is present between the placebo and creatine groups at any time point during the control condition. This is a good finding, as we need to provide evidence that the groups did not have different reaction time performances before the supplementation period.

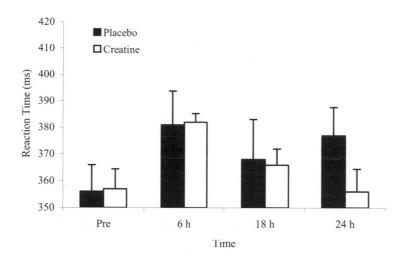

Table 10.4   Reaction times (ms) for participants undertaking the *Sleep Deprivation Study* in the placebo (black bars) and creatine (grey bars) groups during the experimental condition (mean+SE).

If we now consider figure 10.4, which presents the reaction time data for the two groups during the experimental condition, the pattern of data distribution and the overlapping of the standard errors is also indicative of no differences between the means. Nevertheless, we will now progress to the statistical analyses in the form of two-way *ANOVA*, which will provide an indication of how we might expect the two groups to behave in the wider population. It is worth noting at this point that a research project is not a failure if it does not provide evidence to reject the null hypothesis. You have still found something – even if it is that there is no difference or no effect – that will contribute to further developing knowledge and understanding.

Action Box 10.8   Organising and Exploring Your Data

1.   Tabulate raw data in a way that is appropriate and relevant to the experimental design.

2.   It is helpful at this stage to examine individual participant data – possibly by plotting data on graphs – to identify atypical or anomalous values …or perhaps even data entered incorrectly!

3.   Tabulate summary statistics again in a way that is appropriate and relevant to the experimental design. These will assist in verifying differences identified through *ANOVA*.

4.   Plotting groups mean data (with SD to illustrate data range, or SEM to provide an indication of measurement error) assists in locating potential differences between groups. Select the most appropriate format for pictorially presenting your data depending upon the nature of your data and the specific detail of your experimental design – remember that figures are not to make your report attractive; they are drawn to help you more clearly identify patterns in the data.

Case Example Analysis and Review Step-3: Statistical Analyses

In the planning stage we discussed how elements of the experimental design should inform the choice of analytical approaches. Even at such an early stage in the research process, before the first participant has been recruited and the first measures taken, we should be considering the form of data that we will be collecting and how we should organise and evaluate these data to allow us to make decisions. This is *not* to say, "…How do I analyse my data to show what I want it to show"? Rather, it is to consider the forms of analyses that will allow you to appropriately interrogate all elements of the research design, such that informed and evidence-based decisions can be made with respect to the research hypotheses.

The design of the analysis can be described as follows:

- There are two sets of data (i.e. the control condition and the experimental condition)
- …for each group (i.e. the placebo group, PLAC, and the creatine group, CREAT)

The main focus of the analysis is to evaluate the effect of creatine supplementation, and we must therefore control for any further external, influential variables that may reduce our ability to evaluate this effect. As discussed during data exploration, the first step in the data analysis is to verify that the two groups initially behaved comparably to the challenge of sleep deprivation alone. Practically we will be analysing the progressive effect of sleep deprivation over time without supplementation, and how different individuals may respond differently in this situation (i.e. a comparison of the placebo vs. control group during the control condition). We have previously evaluated this visually by plotting the data for the placebo and creatine groups on a graph and examining their patterns of response over the 24-h sleep deprivation period of the control condition (figure 10.3). Similarly, calculating means for comparative time points in the two groups, and examining the variance at these time points, provides a mathematical approach to comparing the data sets (table 10.3).

We have previously decided that the preferred approach for conducting this analysis would be to undertake a two-way *ANOVA*, where the factors are *time* and *treatment group*. The *ANOVA* will only indicate whether any differences observed between the groups are happening by chance or whether they are 'likely' to occur again. A non-significant result would not necessarily mean that the two groups could be considered the same, only that any differences between them could be down to chance. Nevertheless, this would strengthen the analysis for a comparison between the groups during the experimental condition; if the only differences during the control condition are due to chance, then any significant differences during the experimental condition (i.e. those not due to chance) can be attributed to treatment effects.

A problem arises if there are significant differences between the groups during the initial control condition. If there are differences at this stage, where participants have undergone the same treatment (i.e. no supplementation), then it would be difficult to attribute any differences you may observe following the experimental condition to treatment (i.e. creatine) effects. If there are differences at the outset, it is likely that there will be differences at the end, regardless of treatment. If this arises, the only real course of action is to examine the *differences* between the control and experimental conditions in the placebo and creatine groups respectively. That is, we will analyse the *changes* in reaction time (often referred to as the *delta* value, and denoted by the Greek letter Δ) for the two groups, where we will be evaluating whether creatine results in a different pattern of change in comparison with the placebo group. We will not address this issue further here, as one of the dangers of analysing *changes* is that sometimes these values can be so small that the analysis procedure is not powerful enough to identify *real* changes in the data; this would result in a type-II error.

The two-way *ANOVA* for the control condition was undertaken using a statistical software package, and the following values for the effect of *group* and *group changes over time* (i.e. the interaction effect) were obtained. Figure 10.5 provides a schematic representation of the *ANOVA* analysis for the control condition. The computer analysis also gave results for the effect of *time* alone, but this is not reported; whether there were changes in reaction time – ignoring the group effect – is not of issue in our research project, and is more or less an 'intuitive finding' (i.e. it is highly likely that all participants will experience a change in reaction time the longer they are deprived of sleep). The important point to note is that a computer is very useful for completing tedious calculations quickly, but it has no concept of the application of the data that it is processing. A computer will conduct every element of the analysis that you instruct it to undertake, whether this would be practically sensible or not. When faced with extensive computer output, you must develop the ability to discriminate between relevant findings that have real value, and irrelevant findings that have no value. Thus, knowledge and appreciation of the analytical processes underpinning the computer operations is essential if you are to make sensible decisions on your data.

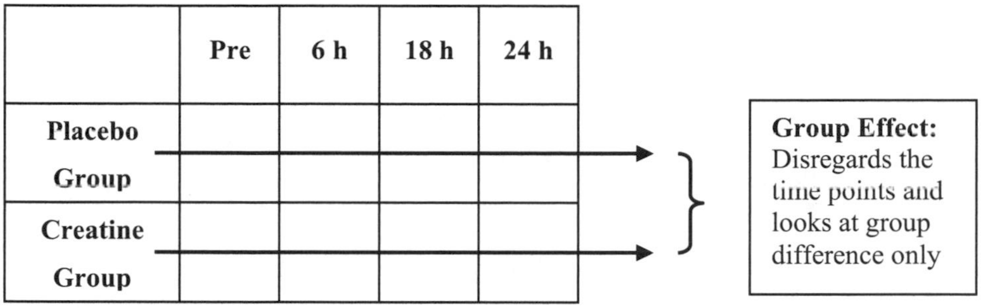

	Pre	6 h	18 h	24 h
Placebo Group				
Creatine Group				

Group Effect: Disregards the time points and looks at group difference only

Figure 10.5   Schematic representation of the two-way *ANOVA* for the placebo and creatine groups for the control condition.

Refer to calculation box 9.3 (chapter 9) for an overview of the *ANOVA* calculation.   You will recall:

$$SS_{TOT} = SS_{TREAT} + SS_{ERROR}$$

where, SS_{TOT} ... total sum of squares

SS_{TREAT} ... treatment sum of squares (or 'group' in this example)

SS_{ERROR} ... error sum of squares

For the present example: SS_{GROUP} ...113.732

SS_{ERROR} ...34227.400

These data are derived from the group data, and are presented as part of the output from an *ANOVA* test performed on a statistical software package.

The 'sum of squares' were divided by the degrees of freedom (i.e. 1 for the groups and 17 for the error) to give the mean squares:

$$MS_{GROUP} \; = \; \frac{SS_{GROUP}}{d.f._{GROUP}} \; = \; \frac{113.732}{1} \; = \; 113.732$$

$$MS_{ERROR} \; = \; \frac{SS_{ERROR}}{d.f._{ERROR}} \; = \; \frac{34227.400}{17} \; = \; 2013.376$$

The mean square values, in turn, provide the test statistic (i.e. the *F*-ratio) as follows:

$$F\text{-ratio} \; = \; \frac{MS_{GROUP}}{MS_{ERROR}} \; = \; \frac{113.732}{2013.376} \; = \; 0.056$$

The *F*-ratio with (1 {*group*}, 17 {*error*}) degrees of freedom is 0.056, which is then compared to the F-distribution (appendix: 7) to determine the corresponding p-value. The outcome of this comparison is reported as:

$$F_{(1, 17)} = 0.056, \, p = 0.815$$

You will recall that when a computer undertakes the analysis, it includes an accurate calculation of the exact two-tailed probability of a test statistic. This is the *equivalent* of using the look up tables, but actually using the look up tables only provides you with the ability to specify 'greater than' or 'less than' a chosen significance level (i.e. normally $p < 0.05$), not to calculate an exact probability. The comparison is still made with the significance level identified for a specified experimental design in order to draw an appropriate conclusion. In this example $p = 0.815$, therefore $p > 0.05$, so we accept the null hypothesis that there is no difference in the population during the control conditon.

The effect of the group and time interactions (i.e. potential differences arising between each subgroup of [placebo at Pre, 6 h, 18 h and 24 h] and [creatine at Pre, 6 h, 18 h and 24 h]) can also be reported from the same value sources as group alone. Figure 10.6 provides a schematic representation of the two-way *ANOVA* for the group and time interactions for the control condition.

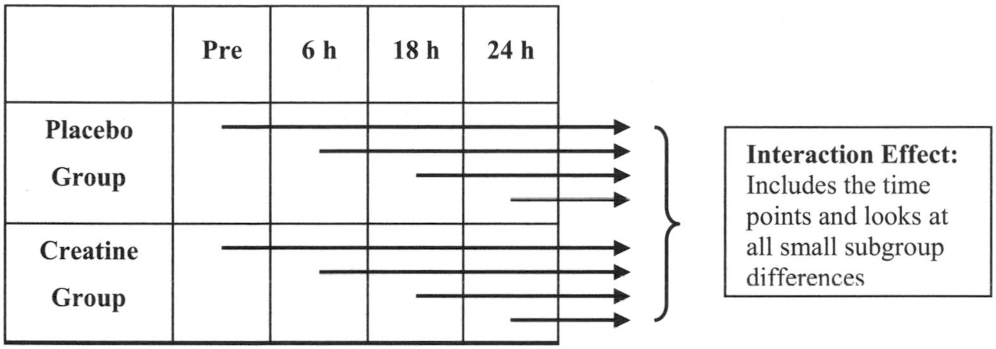

Figure 10.6   Schematic representation of the two-way *ANOVA* for the group and time interactions for the control condition.

The outcome of this analysis is ($F_{(3, 51)} = 1.852$, p = 0.149). As p > 0.05, we accept the null hypothesis that there are no differences in the way the treatments affect reaction times. This means that we can continue with our analyses and undertake the same comparisons for the experimental condition.

Again from the analyses, ignoring the *time alone* effect as it is not of interest within the context of this study, the remaining results indicate that there were no treatment based differences (i.e. $F_{(1, 17)} = 0.215$, p = 0.648 for the group effect, and $F_{(3, 51)} = 1.364$, p = 0.264 for the treatment group by time interaction). We already suspected that this would be the outcome of the statistical analyses based on the graphs we obtained during the data exploration stage. Both probabilities are greater than 0.05 and so the null hypotheses would be accepted.

To put the results from this case example into context, retrospective estimates of power and effect size for each reported result were calculated. Computer software packages are likely to calculate a more complex effect size than the one we used at the preliminary stage; η^2 (i.e. eta squared) is calculated for *ANOVA* structures. The estimates for the reported *ANOVA* results are presented in table 10.4. From table 10.4, it is evident that the retrospective estimates are not as good as we would have liked (i.e. pre-experiment estimated power = 0.6 and effect size = 0.5). However, our sample size of 19 falls well short of the number of research participants we would have liked to recruit for this study.

Control Condition		Experimental Condition		
Power	**Effect Size**	**Power**	**Effect Size**	
0.056	0.003	0.072	0.013	**Group**
0.452	0.098	0.341	0.074	**Group by Time**

Table 10.4   Power and effect size estimates for the control and experimental conditions in the *Sleep Deprivation Study* derived from η^2.

Action Box 10.9	Analysing Your Data

You will recall that your data analysis is identified during the planning stage, and was articulated in action box 10.6. You should endeavour to keep to your proposed plan of analysis as far as is sensible to do so. Obviously, it would not be sensible to do so if your data identified some new and unsuspected findings that you had not considered prior to undertaking the study. However, any deviations from you initial plan must be carefully considered, founded in objective reasoning, and must not merely be based on trying to find an analytical approach that gives you a 'statistically significant' observation.

Case Example Analysis and Review Step-4: Research Conclusions

The final stage in the research process is that of formulating your research conclusions based on the evidence that you have collected during the course of your research project. By this time, the main conclusions should be fairly self-evident: there was a difference ...or not; there was a relationship ...or not; and so forth. The big danger is one of over-speculating; especially if your study did not provide the outcome you had hoped for! The advice here is to only make statements for which you can provide supporting objective evidence. A good starting point is to return to your research hypotheses, which for the present example were:

Null hypothesis

H_o: Under conditions of limited rest where brain function may be compromised, oral creatine supplementation does not affect reaction time performance

Alternative hypothesis

H_1: Under conditions of limited rest where brain function may be compromised, oral creatine supplementation improves reaction time performance

From the statistical analyses we found that there were no group effects in the control condition (which was good) or in the experimental condition (which would have been interesting). Neither were there any group by time interaction effects across the two conditions. We therefore accepted the null hypothesis. The conclusions from this investigation will therefore be one of 'no effect'. That is, in this research population (i.e. undergraduate and postgraduate students at the University of Chichester), who experienced limited rest (i.e. 24 h of sleep deprivation) where brain function may be compromised, oral creatine supplementation (i.e. at a dose rate equivalent to 8 g.day^{-1} for 5 days) does not affect reaction time performance. However, whilst the size of the research sample in this worked example is consistent with similar studies in the scientific literature, we know from our calculations of power and effect size that the current experimental design (where n = 19) may lack sufficient power. It is commonly difficult to recruit large samples in the sport and exercise sciences, especially for very arduous or demanding studies, care must therefore be taken to maximise design sensitivity (refer to chapter 3) such that correct decisions are reached when formulating your research conclusions.

Action Box 10.10   Formulating Research Conclusions

1.   Start with your research hypotheses – reflect on the statistical decisions to accept or reject the null hypothesis, and consider the level of significance with which that decision was made.

2.   …answering your research hypotheses should form the backbone to your research conclusions.

3.   Only make statements for which you can provide supporting objective evidence based on the data you have collected and the appropriate analyses of these data.

4.   A conclusion of 'no effect' or 'no relationship' is not a failed study! Negative findings are equally as informative as positive findings, that is as long as it is a *real* negative finding and not merely a lack of power in your experimental design.

Summary/Key Points

1. From an inquiring thought, articulate the problem and focus your statement into a research question.

2. Determine the intellectual merit of your research question by searching relevant scientific literature for work supporting your line of argument and to evaluate the depth of work already undertaken in the field.

3. Operationalise your research question into testable research hypotheses.

4. Your research hypotheses and specific detail from the research question (e.g. whether the treatment/intervention is reversible or not) will inform your research (experimental) design.

5. Your research design, in turn, will inform your data analyses.

6. Your research sample should be constructed so as to be representative of the population from which it was drawn, and to which the research conclusions will be extrapolated.

7. Data exploration following data collection is a key preliminary step for your subsequent data analyses, and should be undertaken comprehensively and thoroughly before any further work is undertaken on the data.

8. In undertaking your statistical analyses, always be mindful of the practical processes and comparisons you are actually executing on the data.

9. Remember, statistical analyses provide a systematic and objective approach to making decisions on your data; they allow patterns and dissimilarities, within and between data sets, to be evaluated.

10. In formulating research conclusions, only make statements for which you can provide supporting and objective evidence based on the data you have collected and the appropriate analyses of these data.

11

Presenting Your Findings

Chapter Objectives

- To identify different methods of presenting your findings to the scientific community
- To describe the different formats and critique their relative merits
- To provide practical guidance for adopting each format.

Introduction

Having identified the problem, developed your hypotheses, designed your study, collected your data, explored, analysed and evaluated your data, and provided an interpretation of these data with reference to previously published worked, it is now time to present your findings. The main formats in which to present your research to the wider scientific community are: abstract communication; oral communication; poster communication; a rapid written communication; and a scientific paper. If you are an undergraduate or postgraduate student, you may be required to write up your findings as a dissertation or a thesis (this format will not be addressed in detail here, as there are already numerous texts dedicated specifically to this task). Each approach has its own merits – for example the abstract communication (usually published in relation to conference proceedings) is a relatively rapid means by which your work can be presented in the public domain; conversely, a scientific paper affords more 'space' in which to critique and explain your research findings. But not as much space as you would have in a dissertation or thesis. Nevertheless, especially with this latter format, disciplined writing is essential for effective communication; do not say something in a hundred words if it can be said in ten! Often work may appear in more than one format over time, for example: preliminary findings might be submitted as an abstract communication for publication within related conference proceedings; the author will then go on to present their work at the conference in either an oral or a poster format; and finally, if the work has merit it is desirable that it is written up as a scientific paper, adding to the main body of understanding. Whilst it is appreciated that one of the target groups for this text are undergraduate students who may not feel ready to present their work in a public forum, the guidance presented in this chapter also has relevance to the completion of undergraduate and postgraduate assignments. Moreover, it is never too early to embrace the appropriate reporting conventions of your discipline; it is far better to start with good habits than to unlearn bad habits.

It goes without saying that, whatever format is chosen, the fundamental literacy skills of spelling, grammar and punctuation should all be addressed. A concise and succinct scientific writing style is also essential, but is something that is developed over time and with continued practise. Finally, competent and appropriate presentation skills will influence the overall impact of your report. Whilst it is not necessary for us all to be information technology experts, clearly typed and formatted text, and clear tables and figures (as appropriate), are all necessary prerequisites for successful communication. Increasingly in these days of global access to personal computers, conference organisers and publishers are requiring authors to bear a greater burden of formatting pre-publication copy. Whilst this obviously reduces publishers' costs, it also means that time to publication has been reduced substantially over recent years.

However, there is a step that we have omitted to discuss between preparing your research findings for publication and publication – that of expert peer review. All work published in the public domain *should* have undergone some form of expert review as a quality assurance mechanism, defending both scientific and professional standards.

The Process of Expert Review

On submission of a research report as an abstract, rapid written communication, or a scientific paper, the report will be scrutinised by a panel of appropriate experts. This panel is usually made up of a minimum of two scientists, with recourse to a third (or more) reviewer if there is disagreement. Their role is to examine: the worthiness of the original research question; whether the experimental design is appropriate for addressing this question; the quality of the data collection; the consistency of the data analyses with respect to the research design; the appropriateness of the conclusions drawn and whether they are supported by the experimental data; and the overall quality of the research report (i.e. does it conform to the necessary format as well as universal reporting conventions? Is it an honest reflection of the study undertaken? Is all the necessary detail presented, and is the report consistent and coherent?).

With reference to scientific papers, each reviewer will present a report comprising of general and specific comments, and will make a recommendation on the merit of the paper with respect to publication. In the worse case scenario, the reviewers may feel that the research report, or its scope, may not be appropriate for that particular conference or journal. It is rare for a paper not to be subject to some form of revision ...if at all. The extent of this revision may be substantial, such that the paper requires resubmission and must undergo the full review process again. Or the reviewers may accept the research report, but will still provide critique and make recommendations that will ultimately improve the report. Thus, this review process should be viewed as a positive step in the research process, rather than a necessary hurdle to be overcome. Normally, the review process enhances the overall quality of the final publication.

Generic Sections of a Report

All formats of scientific communications will include a title, a summary, an introduction, a methods section, the results, and a discussion that is finished off with a carefully constructed conclusion. The precise detail of these sections, with respect to required detail and wordage, will vary depending upon the required format. We will present guidance specific to the different formats of report later in this chapter. However, to avoid repetition we will now present a general critique of these sections.

Report Title

The Title should be brief, specific and informative, conveying to the reader the nature and scope of the study. It should be clear in terms of its terminology and should be accurate with respect to what was actually undertaken in the study and/or what was found. It is important to note that investigators searching the literature will initially apply key word searches (as described in chapter 10), which will be followed up be examination of the title, before moving on to the report's summary/abstract. Thus, a poorly worded title will not encourage workers to read-on. Equally, an inaccurately constructed title that does not reflect the actual scope and content of your report – such that potential readers are misled – will not help to further enhance your reputation within your field.

Report Summary or Abstract

The Abstract provides a concise summary of the investigation. Space is very limited; for a scientific paper journals will often stipulate a maximum wordage (e.g. 200–250 words is common). Details should normally be limited to the main points of the *Method* and the *principal findings*. With respect to your findings, it is always good to selectively include some of your most important data, as essentially this is the key aspect of your report – your new findings. Abbreviations (e.g. to denote experimental groups, research conditions, or protocols) may be used, but must be clearly defined – observe convention where this exists, and be logical where it does not. Electronic literature searches may allow an investigator to view the Abstract of papers resulting form their search, therefore ensure that your Abstract is clear and accurate.

Report Introduction

The aim of the Introduction is to set the scene. A research rationale is developed from the published literature, providing justification and relevance for your research question. In the sport and exercise sciences this justification and relevance may also come from clinical practice or practical coaching experience. Nevertheless, the purpose must be evidence-based, and whilst anecdotal reports may provide some substantiation for a particular research question they are rarely adequate justification on their own. In a scientific paper the Introduction has particular importance in that it sets the tone and direction of the whole report. Normally this section concludes with a clear statement of the aim or purpose of the study that has been undertaken.

Methods Section

Details of the research participants should be provided (e.g. age, height, body mass and sporting or population-specific defining measures), with details of any criteria that would select-out volunteers. All conventions attending to the safety of the participants should be reported, and details of steps taken to ensure participant standardisation.

The Methods section should provide a comprehensive description of the experimental design, detailing the protocols followed and the measures taken. Of importance here is the sequencing of measures throughout extensive protocols, and steps taken to promote tight experimental control should be noted. You must also report any information identifying the make and model of technical equipment such as ergometers and analysers, as well as specific details concerning their calibration and operation (if appropriate).

A statement of the form of data exploration and analysis is included. Though occasionally, depending upon the complexity of data handling, it may provide greater clarity if this detail – or additional detail – is included in the *Results* section. The *Methods* section should provide all the necessary information to allow the study to be replicated by a third party.

Results Section

It is good practice to be selective and precise in reporting your research findings, maintaining a clear focus upon the research question and the research hypotheses. All units and formulae should be presented in SI form. Data are normally presented as mean values ± standard deviation or standard error of the mean depending upon the nature of the data being cited. Standard deviations are reported where you wish to convey information relating to the range of your data; this might be particularly pertinent when reporting the physical characteristics of your research sample. Standard error tends to be reported when it is appropriate to provide information relating to the error of measurements about the mean; this is often the preferred approach when reporting physiological data such as blood metabolite concentrations or hormone profiles.

Present your most important data first. This is often the data that addresses your principle hypothesis or relates to the specific purpose of the study. Then present the remainder of your data in a hierarchal manner, using these secondary findings to substantiate what you would consider to be the main finding. At all times consider the story you are presenting to the reader, maintain a logical progression through the *Results* section, and ensure that you provide appropriate evidence to support a chosen line of argument that you may later present in the Discussion.

Do not replicate data presentation in different formats, unless in doing so it adds to the reader's understanding of the main findings. Note, all units and formulae should be presented in SI form. The text should provide a logical commentary, guiding the reader through the tables and figures of data. Tables should be informative and figures should be illustrative – they are not to be included in a report merely to enhance its aesthetic appeal! Rather, they should present your findings in the best way to allow you to ultimately make informed decisions in relation to your research hypotheses.

In reporting the outcome of your statistical analyses adopt standard conventions where they exist, and report in a logical order where they do not. Normally, you should present the statistic for the particular analysis being undertaken, the degrees of freedom for your experimental design, the p-value, and a judgement as to whether the outcome is significant or not. However, in undertaking your analyses remember that it is the raw data that is most important – statistical analysis approaches are measurement tools that allow you to examine patterns and discern differences in your data. Finally, be clear in your reporting what information are *results*, and what are points of discussion; no debate or valued comment on the data should be undertaken in the *Results* section.

Discussion and Conclusions

The Discussion should present a clear and concise summary of the main findings, and contextualise these findings with observations reported in the scientific literature or from clinical-, professional-, or sporting-practice. Emphasise the new and important aspects of your study, drawing links with the *Introduction* and providing comment where your data agrees or disagrees with the outcome 'expected' based on the literature. It is appropriate to provide possible explanations of your data but avoid being over-speculative, especially if your study is limited or has weak analytical power.

A clear statement of your research conclusions should be included, usually at the end of the *Discussion*. It is good practice to link your conclusions to your hypotheses or the statement defining the purpose of your study, but avoid unqualified statements not supported by the data. Provide recommendations for future work, or changes in professional practice or policy, if appropriate and supported by your data. It is appropriate to articulate any limitations of your study but avoid being overly negative – if *you* do not draw out the positives of *your* work no one will!

We will now provide some specific guidance and/or advice relating to the different formats of report presentation. This information should not be viewed as exhaustive, and should be applied in association with *local* guidance provided, for example, by your tutor, by your employer, by a conference, by a journal, by your professional organisation or by a grant awarding body. We will pay greatest attention to those formats that differ most extensively from the generic format reported earlier in this chapter, and spend less time on such formats as scientific papers which follow this generic style more closely (if a section title is not expanded further in the text, this infers that this is not too dissimilar from the generic format).

Abstract Communication

Abstract communications are the most rapid form of communicating your research findings to the wider scientific community. This form of research reporting is normally used to submit the key finding(s) of your project for consideration for presentation at a conference. Whilst the study may generate many interesting findings, you must be very selective in terms of those that are reported in your abstract communication. The maximum wordage is tightly limited to (normally) between 200 and 300 words; however this is variable and is detailed in the abstract submission information published by the conference organising committee. Also included within this information are the specific submission arrangements, which increasingly is in an electronic format. Thus, the guidelines are very specific in order to facilitate ease of publication in the conference proceedings with the minimum of additional pre-production. The Abstract will contain the sections detailed above, however they will normally be included as a single body of text often without section subheadings. The following provides general guidance of the (notional) different sections of the *Abstract*:

1.   *Title*

2.   *Author(s)/Institution(s):* All investigators who made a significant contribution to the research study should be listed and their institution(s) or organisation(s) of affiliation.

3.   *Main Body of Text:* The abstract provides a concise summary of the investigation. The opening sentence usually provides a very brief rationale and therefore defines the *purpose of the study*. A short section detailing the subjects and the main points of the method follows this. You will generally not have enough space to include all the procedures undertaken in the study; rather you will have to limit your description to those measurements generating the data specifically reported in the abstract. Equally the space available to report data is very limited, so again you must be very selective and maintain a clear focus on the main finding you wish to communicate. Space may be used more economically by integrating aspects of the *methods* and *results* sections, however this should not be undertaken at the expense of clarity. Sometimes there may be an allowance for a figure or table in the abstract; this will normally present the most important data or finding of the study. Abbreviations for key terms may be used to

further reduce space, but these should be defined in full after the first time they appear; standard scientific conventions should be adopted where they exist and the abbreviation chosen should be logical where they do not. Finally, you should finish your abstract with a concluding sentence. This will refer to the purpose of the study as stated at the outset, and be substantiated by the data evidence presented in the abstract.

4. *Acknowledgements:* Include any workers who made some contribution to the research project but whose contribution does not warrant inclusion as an author. Also acknowledge the support of any sponsors to the study.

Oral Communication

Oral communications are the primary format for presenting your research findings at conference. Unlike written formats (i.e. abstract, rapid written communication, or scientific paper), the oral communication allows for immediate feedback on your research project from the conference floor. There can be 'real time' debate between yourself and the intended recipients of your work. Oral communications are potentially very nerve wracking affairs, where you and your work are left totally exposed to the criticism of your peers in a very public forum. However, it can be extremely exhilarating to present your findings in front of established and respected scientists, especially if you have the opportunity to engage in open debate with these senior colleagues.

In making an oral communication you would be wise to seek advice from anyone involved in public speaking. Specifically consider the volume and speed of your delivery with respect to the audience's ability to absorb the detail of your study; use intonation of the voice to break up the distinct sections of the study and to add emphasis where appropriate. In addition, the following guidance notes will help balance the structure of your communication. The total time allocation is normally about 10 minutes (possibly up to 15 minutes at some conferences), with an additional 5 minutes allowed for questions from the floor. Nevertheless, conference schedules are prone to change without notice, and you may arrive for your session to be met by a last minute change in the time allocation. Therefore know your work well and be aware of those sections of your presentation that could most readily be cut if such a situation arose. Remember this is an opportunity to present YOUR work; therefore do not dwell too long on the work of others after you have articulated your rationale. YOUR methods and YOUR data are the most important sections of the presentation; the introduction might be readily cut back, as might the discussion save from a well-constructed conclusion.

Oral communications are supported by a series of slides – either prepared on the computer in PowerPoint™, as traditional photographic slides, or as overhead projector acetates – and the rule is 'less is more'. Do not be tempted to blind your audience by filling too many slides, with too much information, and racing through each slide way too quickly. In each section below we will indicate a 'ball park' estimate of the number of slides for each section and a possible time allocation from a standard 10 minute presentation (though bear in mind that this may be subject to last minute change!). The figures cited for number of slides and time allocations are, in practice, relatively arbitrary, as it does tend to very much depend upon the nature of the project being presented.

1.   *Title/Author(s)/Institution(s):* (1 slide) – Time allocation 15 seconds. In introducing yourself and your co-workers, this provides opportunity to settle your nerves, identify an appropriate level of voice projection for the public address system (if provided) or the venue (if a public address system is not provided), s-l-o-w d-o-w-n your rate of speech, and take command of the audience. This is your time, and it is up to you to make the most of this opportunity to 'sell' your study to the assembled members of the scientific community.

2.   *Introduction:* (1–2 slide) – Time allocation 1–2 minutes. Whilst it is appropriate to contextualise your work within the scientific literature and what has gone before, what is key is that you provide a logical and succinct rationale for the study being undertaken. This can normally be achieved in three or four well-chosen sentences. There is not the time to provide an extensive review of associated literature, so be very selective in citing studies from the literature; interested members of the audience will normally have knowledge of relevant literature to varying degrees.

3.   *Methods:* (1–2 slides) – Time allocation up to 3 minutes. Both the actual number of slides and the necessary time allocation will ultimately be dictated by the complexity

of your experimental design. However, it should be noted that even if the study itself was very complex, it is not necessary to provide all the different facets of your study in one oral communication; keep a focus on the main finding you wish to convey and describe the protocols and procedures relevant to the data that will support this finding. If at all possible, this is best achieved in the form of a diagram, to which you can talk through the additional detail during the presentation. Describe your research participant group (e.g. age, height, body mass, and include population-specific measures[11.1] as appropriate), and highlight key elements of standardisation and experimental control. It may be appropriate to describe how the data may be treated at this stage, or this can be left until...

4. *Results:* (up to 4 slides) – Time allocation 3–4 minutes, depending upon the complexity of data collection. Again, it is difficult to provide a slide count or a time allocation for this section, as this is totally dependent upon the number of measures recorded and the story you wish to tell. As was the case with the Methods section it is not necessary to report absolutely all the data collected; be selective and report those measures deemed appropriate to support the experimental conclusions. It is easier for the audience if the data, as far as possible, is presented as figures. *More* data can be presented in a table, but tables are difficult for audiences to interpret quickly in the course of a 10-minute presentation in an auditorium. In describing the patterns in the data bring out the data analysis to emphasise whether these patterns are statistically significant.

5. *Discussion/Conclusion:* (1–2 slides) – Time allocation up to 2 minutes. Make a statement emphasising the principle finding of your study. A brief explanation may be appropriate, but keep it short and avoid repetition of the Results section. Remember, your final statement is, in essence, your 'take home' message for the audience – make it epitomise your study, make it strong, make it memorable.

6. *Acknowledgements*

[11.1] Population-specific measures could include data relating to the training status of the research participants if working with an athletic group (e.g. VO_{2max}, f_{cmax}, running economy, peak running speed, maximum power output, etc.), or provide details of symptom limited exercise capacity in a patient group, or provide classification of disability if working with a group of disabled performers.

Poster Communication

Poster communications are another common format for presenting your research findings at conference. Like oral communications, posters allow opportunity for real time discussions, however these discussions may be more intimate, taking place around the site of your poster presentation, with those delegates who have direct interest in the work you are presenting. Depending upon the structure of the conference, you may be invited to present your poster in the form of a mini-oral communication; this should be viewed as recognition of the merit of the content and/or the quality of your work. The detailed specification of the poster area (dimensions), text font, text size, figure/table format and size will be prescribed by the conference organising committee, and you will be expected to keep, without exception, to these guidelines. However there remains tremendous scope for making your poster attractive and 'eye catching'. As was discussed in terms of the slides for the oral communication, do not be tempted to fill all available space with text and/or figures. Reflect on your main finding, and structure your poster with this as the guiding principle and focal point. In designing your poster it is always a delicate balance between over-simplification and inadequate detail on the one hand, and over-complexity and excessive detail on the other.

In structure, poster communications could be regarded as (slightly) extended abstracts, with the added luxury of several figures and/or tables in which to present and illustrate your data.

1.   *Title*
2.   *Author(s)/Institution(s)*
3.   *Introduction:* Citing <u>carefully selected</u> investigations from the scientific literature, provide a <u>brief</u> rationale for the study undertaken and articulate the purpose of the study.
4.   *Methods:* Describe the research participants (e.g. age, height, body mass and population-specific measures), the key points to the experimental design and the procedures adopted. As was the case for the oral communication, this is often best achieved with the help of a diagram. However, you will need to include a brief commentary articulating the experimental design and highlighting the key elements of

standardisation and control. Limit your description of methods to those measurements generating data specifically reported in the poster. It may be appropriate to detail the data treatment in the Methods section, or as in the oral communication incorporate this detail into the Results section.

5. *Results:* Again, you must be <u>selective</u> in the reported data, maintaining a clear focus on the main finding you wish to communicate through the poster presentation. However, there is more space to expand your data presentation with respect to secondary/supporting data beyond the main finding. Whilst there is the space to include a number of figures/tables, do not be tempted to include more and more data at the expense of poster clarity; an overcrowded poster is less attractive and will command less attention of passing conference delegates. As in the Abstract, abbreviations for key terms may be used to save space.

6. *Discussion/Conclusion:* The final main section in the poster is the Discussion/Conclusion. It is good to open this section with a statement of the main finding, followed by a short explanation as appropriate, and merited, by the study's data.

7. *References:* Details of all investigations cited in the poster should be included.

8. *Acknowledgements*

Rapid Written Communication

Rapid written (short) communications provide opportunity to present more detail of your research project in comparison with a poster presentation, but are not as expansive as a scientific paper. This form of presentation is published in a scientific journal but is normally limited to around 3 printed pages. You will also find that the number of figures and tables that you may include is also limited to possibly no more than 2. The scope of short communications tends to address specific technical/method issues, issues relating to data treatment/analysis, or perhaps provides a rapid response to a paper recently published in the journal. It might be viewed as a means of stimulating and communicating 'current' debate in a very focussed manner, and as such a succinct writing style is essential. As with previous formats, the specific details of the short communication will depend upon the target journal for publication – indeed, it should be noted that not all scientific journals accept this format of reporting; these details normally appear in the journal and on the journal's website.

1. *Title*

2. *Author(s)/Institution(s)*

3. *Abstract:* The abstract provides a concise summary of the investigation. Details should be limited to the main points of the Method, the principal findings and a clear conclusion.

4. *Key Words:* The authors are generally required to identify up to 5 key words for subject indexing of the manuscript. The key words should reflect the content of the article and should adopt the terminology that is common to the particular field of study to which the manuscript refers. Guidance for selecting key words can be obtained by referring to current indexing publications (e.g. *Index Medicus* for medical subject headings), or by applying similar principles as is evident in such publications.

5. *Introduction:* As discussed previously, the aim of the Introduction is to set the scene and to develop a research rationale, providing justification and relevance for the question being addressed in the short communication. Often the Introduction is relatively short in comparison with a scientific paper, but has paramount importance in identifying the need for this rapid communication.

6. *Methods:* If the short communication is presenting experimental data, the Methods will detail the research participants (e.g. age, height, body mass and population-specific measures), provide an account of the experimental design and procedures, and perhaps describe the form of data analysis. However, if the short communication raises a technical issue concerning methods of data collection, data treatment, or data interpretation, the balance of the content of the Methods section will reflect the specific purpose of this rapid response.

7. *Results:* Should be precise and selective, and again will reflect the specific purpose of this rapid response. As a means of saving space, details of data treatment and/or data analysis may be included with the data as it is reported in the Results section. As mentioned previously, the number of figures and tables is limited, requiring you to be

very selective and to keep a clear focus. All units and formulae should be presented in SI form.

8. *Discussion:* The Discussion/Conclusion will similarly be dictated by the purpose of the short communication, providing a clear and concise summary of the main findings and articulating their importance. An appropriate commentary of the Results is required, with comparisons being made to published work where appropriate.

9. *References:* All source material should be referenced following a standard referencing convention. However, the number of references allowed in a short communication is limited to a maximum of about 8. Therefore, be very selective in your citation choice and select contemporary original investigations of merit (though older, 'historical' citations have value, providing seminal papers in a particular field of enquiry).

10. *Acknowledgements*

Scientific Paper

Scientific papers provide greater opportunity to report the full depth of the research project that was undertaken. However, you should still maintain a succinct scientific writing style and a clear focus of the research question being addressed. The specific detail of the scientific paper format varies tremendously and will depend upon the target journal for publication (refer to individual journals or their respective website). Even within a sub-discipline there is considerable variation between the scope and content of different journals, it is therefore wise to carefully consider the most appropriate journal for your research study before starting the process of writing your scientific paper. We have listed the common sections to be included in a scientific paper, and have included additional information where this has not been discussed previously. For further guidance on the content of each section refer to the *Generic Sections of a Report* presented earlier:

1. *Title*
2. *Author(s)/Institution(s)*
3. *Abstract*
4. *Key Words*
5. *Introduction*

6.   *Methods*

7.   *Results*

8.   *Discussion*

9.   *References:* All source material cited in the text, but only these, should be referenced following a standard referencing convention. Journals vary in their preferred style of referencing from full citations in the text to numbered citations, so again refer to the relevant instructions to authors when writing your manuscript. Be focused with your reference selection and avoid dependency upon review articles and textbooks (i.e. secondary source material).

10   *Acknowledgements*

Summary/Key Points

1.   The main formats in which to present your research to the wider scientific community are: abstract communication; oral communication; poster communication; a rapid written communication; and a scientific paper.

2.   Regardless of the format chosen, the fundamental literacy skills of spelling, grammar and punctuation should all be addressed. A concise and succinct scientific writing style is also desirable, whilst competent and appropriate presentation skills will influence the overall impact of your report.

3.   A research report will normally be scrutinised by a panel of appropriate experts who will examine the worthiness of the original research question, the experimental design, the quality of the data collection and its analysis, the appropriateness of the conclusions drawn, and the general quality of the research report.

4.   This review process should be viewed as a positive step in the research process, which normally enhances the overall quality of the final publication.

5.   The chapter presents guidance notes for the preparation of research reports to be presented in the principle formats applied to the sport and exercise sciences.

12

Common Problems in Conducting Research:
Solutions and Reflections

Chapter Objectives

- To describe some general problems encountered during the research process
- To suggest possible solutions or appropriate routes of action for overcoming these problems
- To discuss advice provided by a group of experienced researchers from the sport and exercise sciences.

Introduction

Using Statistics in Sport and Exercise Science Research has taken you on a journey through the activities involved in identifying a worthwhile and answerable research question, formulating hypotheses, designing a research study, collecting, organising, evaluating, and analysing data, drawing conclusions, and finally presenting your work to the scientific community. At the outset, this journey can often seem very daunting and unmanageable, therefore the aim of this text has been to divide the research process into more manageable steps – providing explanation as to why you may wish to pursue a certain approach, and practical guidance as to how this might be achieved. You will be aware that experimental research is largely a decision making process, where each decision is fundamentally vital to the validity and integrity of the research project as a whole. Thus, a further aim of this text has been to provide you with the knowledge, which in turn will give you the confidence, to make the right decision at each step along the way – good decisions will provide a firm foundation to good research.

This final chapter will examine some of the common problems encountered by those conducting research; many of these problems – but not all – might be avoided by careful planning at the outset. The list is by no means exhaustive, and has intentionally been kept to general themes rather than addressing specific details. The purpose of this chapter is to promote avoidance of obvious potential research hazards, rather than to frighten you into an avoidance of research itself! In raising and examining these hazards or problems we will present the reflections of a number of researchers, of varied experience, drawn from a range of disciplines within the sport and exercise sciences. All of the researchers had completed their graduate studies, and were either pursuing higher research degrees or were *career* researchers. All were asked to describe, in their view, the highs and lows of research, their top tips for successful research, and the one piece of advice they wished that they had been told at the start of their research career.

In this chapter we will review the research process in terms of the planning stage, the experimental stage, the analysis stage, and the reporting stage. Within each section we will initially present a *Problem Box* detailing the issues that may adversely affect a research study at this stage. This will be followed by a commentary in which these issues will be discussed with reference to the guidance presented in *Using Statistics in Sport and Exercise Science Research*, and the observations and experiences of our group of researchers. Finally, we will present a *Solution Box* in which we will articulate advice or a possible course of action to avoid falling foul of these research hazards.

Problem Box 12.1	**The Planning Stage: Getting Started**

1.   Initial thought too vague

2.   Not focused in reducing this thought to a specific research question

3.   Hypotheses not testable/too vague

4.   Inappropriate/flawed design; poor sampling

5.   Not 'excited' by the project!

The Planning Stage: Getting Started

As discussed in chapter 2, the hardest part of research can often be the first step. Where you have the luxury of free choice in terms of what you are going to research – such as an independent project, dissertation or private study – it can be torturously difficult to come up with an idea that seems appropriate and is 'do-able'. This is not only a problem for undergraduate students in the sport and exercise sciences, but can also plague the lives of postgraduate researchers; "researcher's block" is not solely the preserve of the novice researcher. The advice in this instance is to look to the areas that interest you or that have practical relevance for you. To conduct thorough research you need to be totally engaged with the subject matter, there has to be some kind of emotional bond or personal investment in the work to be undertaken. Only then will you be "bothered" by the outcome, and consequently motivated to complete the project to the best of your abilities. With this emotional investment will come the *research buzz*, the excitement of discovery, and the satisfaction from completing the process.

With personal interest and personal relevance will come a clearer focus. The first problem of an overly vague initial thought will tend to arise through a lack of connection with the chosen area of study. This in itself should not automatically preclude the research being undertaken, but will mean that you must work harder to embed yourself within the field of enquiry relevant for the research project. This will normally involve increasing your reading in and around appropriate literature. Alternatively, if the initial thought arose from professional practice in the field, then perhaps you may need to gain a clearer insight of the issues pertaining to the research project through practical experience.

The second highlighted problem, one of a lack of focus in reducing your initial thought to a specific research question, might equally result from a lack of connection and therefore would similarly be addressed by greater reading or additional practical experience. However, this problem might also arise from an inability to identify what is central, what is the nub of the issue, what is the essence of the research project. The ability to focus upon what is important and relevant is something that does improve and develops with experience, along with a greater knowledge of the field and empathy for the subject matter. Thus, it is appropriate to take guidance if you have concerns that you are not asking the *right* questions; asking the right question is fundamental to the success of developing your research question. Experienced researchers will equally subject themselves to peer review in order to satisfy that, at this formative stage, the research question is appropriate. It is far better to be proved wrong at this point than later down the line when considerable time and expense may have been incurred in answering the *wrong* question!

The third problem refers to an inability to operationalise the research question in the form of research hypotheses. You will recall from chapter 2 that hypotheses were described as "…suggested testable explanations"; thus they are statements about measurable outcomes, and this ability to measure provides a means by which we can statistically analyse, or test, the outcome. If a hypothesis is not testable, by definition it will not be a hypothesis. Equally a vague hypothesis is likely to be an incorrect hypothesis; by their very nature hypotheses should sharpen our focus on the research aim. Remember that in conducting research we are undertaking an investigation, and like detectives we are seeking to draw together pieces of evidence to support or refute an answer to our research question. In the research context, the pieces of evidence arise from the measures we are able to undertake as part of our study. Simplistically put, our hypotheses should therefore refer to the potential outcomes of each of these measures. Thus, in focussing upon the measures we are more likely to articulate statements concerning *testable* outcomes, and consequently develop testable, and specific research hypotheses. These are often directional – from experience, practice, or background reading, we will normally be in a position to make a judgement in terms of which group will yield the higher or lower values – but this is not always the case.

The fourth general problem in relation to the planning stage is that of developing an inappropriate or flawed experimental design. Such an error will arise from a lack of knowledge, appreciation or understanding of the research process. Related, but also occurring separately, is the problem of poor sampling. Poor sampling approaches may result in a research sample that is either non-representative of the research population (i.e. in terms of individual characteristics or behaviour identified as being important in relation to the research question), or is inadequate in terms of the experimental design (refer to chapter 3 for clarification of this point). Again, knowledge, appreciation and understanding of research methods will reduce the likelihood of such an error occurring. *Using Statistics in Sport and Exercise Science Research* has sought to provide general guidance with which to address these concerns; that is, what are the steps I should be taking in this process and what are the decisions I need to make at each step? However, as a consequence of the multiplicity of research questions and their incumbent research designs, it would be impossible to provide a definitive text covering all possibilities. The important advice here, drawn from the reflections of the experienced researchers, is to know when to seek advice; knowledge is not always about what you know, it is also about knowing what you do not know!

Finally, if you are not excited at this planning stage, it is unlikely that you will have personally invested in the project. To have invested, to be engaged, to be bothered by the outcome will all motivate you to complete the project to the best of your abilities. Whilst this may appear as a lesser issue if you are just starting out in research, it was identified to be of paramount importance in the reflections of the experienced researchers. Indeed, we would argue that what differentiates good research from adequate research – good researchers from adequate researchers – is a sense of excitement about discovery, the need to find answers, a need driven by a total engagement with the subject being examined.

Solution Box 12.1   The Planning Stage: Getting Started

1.   Initial thought too vague

You need to develop a clearer understanding of the chosen area; depending upon the specific area of the sport and exercise sciences this might be achieved through greater reading to improve knowledge, or through developing 'experiential' understanding. If neither of these options is successful, it may be appropriate to change your initial thought to something in which you have greater knowledge or experience.

2.   Not focused in reducing this thought to specific research question

This may similarly be as a result of a lack of connection and therefore might be addressed through increased reading and/or gaining additional experience, or it may be due to an inability to identify what is the key issue. In the case of the latter, seek advice.

3.   Hypotheses not testable/too vague

The measures we undertake in our study will provide the pieces of evidence upon which we will base our decision concerning the research question. The research hypotheses should refer to the potential outcomes of each of these measures, which will be specific to the research question. Thus, the research hypotheses will be testable and specific.

4.   Inappropriate/flawed design; poor sampling

Knowledge, appreciation, and understanding of research methods will reduce the likelihood of such errors occurring. If in doubt, seek advice.

5.   Not 'excited' by the project!

If you have free choice, choose a different project! If there is no choice, seek to educate yourself as fully as possible about the subject matter and try looking at the project from every conceivable angle. To be excited you need to be engaged, to be engaged you have to find something that has interest and/or relevance to you.

Problem Box 12.2	**The Experimental Stage: Collecting Your Data**

1.   Inadequate standardisation or failure to standardise
2.   Inadequate control or failure to control

The Experimental Stage: Collecting Your Data

It is beyond the scope of this text to discuss the very specific issues related to data collection across the different disciplines of the sport and exercise sciences. However, it is essential that in executing the data collection stage of your research project you are mindful of the need to *standardise* and the need to *control*. Both these concepts were discussed in chapter 1; the fundamental importance of these two concepts to the research process cannot be overstated. Inadequate standardisation, or a failure to standardise, between conditions, between trials, between research participants, between research approaches, between research procedures, day-to-day, week-to-week, month-to-month will result in your study being flawed and of no real value in terms of developing knowledge and understanding. Standardisation of all aspects of the research environment will maximise the chances that the important relationship, or the important difference, in your data is as a consequence of the independent variable. As the quality of standardisation diminishes, the confidence you can have in such an assertion will equally diminish to the point of no standardisation, no confidence. The solution to this problem is meticulous planning and attention to detail; consider all extraneous factors that may impinge upon the outcome of your study and ensure that they remain constant – as far as possible – throughout your experimental trials or observation periods. Ensuring standardisation is not an easy task, but time and care invested at this stage will be rewarded in the analysis stage of the research project.

Similarly, inadequate control or failure to control will also reduce your level of confidence in the outcome of your study. Experimental control must be exerted at every stage in the research process. Assuming that, through the planning stage, we have arrived at an appropriate and valid research design, control will be evident in the rules governing: research participant recruitment and pre-study briefing; implementation of guidance concerning the research participant's pre-trial status (e.g. in terms of exercise, diet, lifestyle, and medication); every aspect of the execution of the experimental trial from preparation of the research environment and research participant, to the information and instruction provided to all participants and investigators involved in the trial; and approaches to measurement and data collection. General issues concerning measurement are discussed in chapter 2; of importance to emphasise and reflect on here are the key concepts of objectivity, reliability, validity, and relevance. On a specific level, a thorough knowledge of the measurement being taken, good technique and practical competency are all important considerations for promoting experimental control. If these concepts are adhered to in terms of the choice and execution of measurements, control in data collection will be assured.

Solution Box 12.2   The Experimental Stage: Collecting Your Data

1.   Inadequate standardisation or failure to standardise

Meticulous planning and attention to detail are essential in promoting research standardisation; all extraneous factors potentially impinging upon the study outcome must be considered and maintained constant as far as possible throughout your experimental trials or observation periods.

2.   Inadequate control or failure to control

General measurement issues concerning objectivity, reliability, validity, and relevance, as well as specific issues concerning a thorough knowledge of the measurement being taken, good technique and practical competency, are all important for promoting experimental control.

Problem Box 12.3   The Analysis Stage: Evaluating Your Data

1.   Inadequate consideration, or failure to consider, data analysis as part of the planning stage

2.   Inadequate organisation and exploration, or failure to organise and explore, data prior to initiating data analysis procedures

3.   Poor choice, or wrong choice, of analytical procedures

4.   Poor decision-making, or wrong decision-making, in evaluating your data analyses

5.   Drawing of inappropriate, over speculative, or unsubstantiated, conclusions

---

The Analysis Stage: Evaluating Your Data

Of the research process as a whole, it is generally the analysis stage that appears to cause most concern, where statistical analysis is viewed as some mystic science whose comprehension is beyond the realm of mere mortals. As discussed earlier in *Using Statistics in Sport and Exercise Science Research*, statistics are nothing more sinister than information, and statistical analyses merely provide a means of measuring and evaluating how statistics behave relative, or not, to each other. Thus, statistical analyses should simply be viewed as a tool, or an instrument, along with all the other measurement instruments you may use in your research, for examining data. Some of the very early decisions you will make before embarking on your research study, indeed decisions that will inform the formulation of hypotheses, concern the variables you should measure and the measurement tools you will apply. With this in mind, the type of statistical measurements that would be appropriate for the data you are proposing to collect should be given full consideration as an integral part of this planning stage, informing the decision making process giving rise to the research experimental design.

Once data collection is ongoing, it is time to consider organising and exploring your data. It is not necessary to wait until data collection is complete; as soon as you have a few sets of data from your research trials or observation periods you can start to explore possible patterns in the data.

This procedure is eased by the use of computer spreadsheets, or indeed downloading data directly into your computer in some measurement applications. Though one major problem to be aware of with the latter automated data transfer is that it removes an opportunity for you to engage with your data and get a *feel* for what it may be showing you. Nevertheless, once data has been written to a spreadsheet it is relatively straightforward to apply descriptive statistical calculations to determine, if appropriate for your particular research question, measures of central tendency and measures of data spread or dispersion. This early organisation of data into a spreadsheet will also assist in identifying possible problems in data collection and allow action to be taken; it is not correct, nor is it ethically sound, to continue with an approach to data collection if you know that it is inappropriate or incorrect for the research study being undertaken. The research process should always be viewed as a dynamic decision making process, where information gained at each step should be considered and inform future decisions. This is not to say that once research has been initiated you should lightly consider changing your chosen approach; any change to an agreed, and expert reviewed, protocol may require further agreement as part of an ethical review process and this will introduce delay. Nevertheless, a delay in research is obviously to be preferred over erroneous or flawed research.

In contrast to starting your data organisation and exploration early, the converse of passing quickly over – or omitting – this step of the analysis stage is another problem that might be incurred. The temptation to "…get on with the *proper* analyses" is all too great, but should be resisted. In deciding upon your approach to analysing your data during the planning stage, you will have made a series of educated guesses with respect to the possible outcomes from your investigation – that is, your research hypotheses. Nevertheless, you must always be open to the unexpected outcome or the possibility that your data may not conform to the models you hypothesised at the start of the study. Indeed, this is one of the potential dangers of analytical procedures based upon hypotheses testing as presented in *Using Statistics in Sport and Exercise Science Research* – the danger of making your data fit. This danger will be avoided through careful data exploration, and an openness to accept that data will not always behave in the ways you have predicted. It is often the unanticipated outcomes, assuming that such outcomes are underpinned by sound research technique, which generate most interest in the research literature. *Using Statistics in Sport and*

Exercise Science Research – Book 2 will explore alternative inductive approaches to examining data, that moves away from classic hypotheses testing and provide a more contemporary perspective to data analysis and interpretation.

A second issue to consider at the analysis stage is that of poor choice, or wrong choice, of analytical procedures. This will occur if there is a lack of knowledge of statistical procedures and a lack of understanding of your data. Knowledge can be acquired, whereas understanding develops over time through experience and exposure to research data. In understanding your data you will know the nature of measurements (analyses) you will need to make on these data to inform the answer to your research question. As mentioned earlier in this chapter, it is important to be aware of what you know with confidence, and what you do not know; the problem of poor choice, or wrong choice, of analytical procedures should normally not arise if guidance is sought when necessary at appropriate stages in the research process. Furthermore, you will recall from chapter 2 that at the planning stage research project proposals are submitted for expert review as part of an ethical review process. This proposal will contain a full description of the project to be undertaken, including a section detailing the data analyses, which will then be subject to scrutiny. Thus, such expert review provides a formal check to ensure that a problem of poor choice, or wrong choice, of analytical procedures does not arise.

Thirdly, we raised the potential problem of poor decision-making, or wrong decision-making, in evaluating your data analyses. As in the previous case, this would most probably be a problem born out of a lack of knowledge or lack of understanding. So equally, self-awareness of your level of expertise is the solution to this issue – knowing when it would be appropriate to seek advice. However, awareness of the statistical rules governing your choice of analytical approach will also protect you in this instance. Different analytical approaches will have different sets of rules informing the decisions to be made on the outcome of the statistical procedures. These rules will be supported by clear and robust criteria that are appropriate to the nature of data examined and evaluated by each approach. Thus, again we can see the importance of clear thinking at the planning stage of any research project, where predictions are made on the outcome of data obtained during data collection, which in turn will define the approach to data analysis, and finally the rules and criteria governing data evaluation. Knowledge, or access to knowledge and expertise, of appropriate rules and criteria will ensure good decision-making post data analysis.

The final potential problem we will consider at the analysis stage is that of drawing inappropriate, over speculative, or unsubstantiated, conclusions. This problem is overcome by maintaining a clear focus upon the original research question, and then drawing very tight lines of critical reasoning from the research question through developing your hypotheses, formulating your research design, collecting your data, exploring and analysing your data, and finally evaluating the outcome of your data analyses. From these evaluations, does your data support the null or experimental hypotheses? What is the level of confidence of this support? Has your intervention brought about a change or not? Is there an association between the variables being examined or not? Does this association allow further events to be predicted or not? Inappropriate conclusions arise from statements made that have limited or no direct relevance to the data collection. Over speculative conclusions arise from extending your comments beyond the scope of the data collected. Whilst often it is helpful to provide some speculation to contextualise your observations and perhaps provide further explanation, such comments should be clearly defined as such and should not constitute the greater part of any discussion within a research publication. Unsubstantiated conclusions arise from statements where, normally, the level of confidence in the data is relatively low.

Solution Box 12.3   The Analysis Stage: Evaluating Your Data

1.   Inadequate consideration, or failure to consider, data analysis as part of the planning stage

     Approaches to data analysis should be considered along with deciding upon an appropriate and valid experimental design – where the experimental design informs data analysis, and the data collection requirements for the required data analysis approach will inform the experimental design.

2.   Inadequate organisation and exploration, or failure to organise and explore, data prior to initiating data analysis procedures

     It is helpful to commence data organisation and preliminary exploration as soon as you start collecting data; this will allow any problems to be identified and addressed early. Data exploration should not be omitted or rushed. It allows patterns in the data to be observed more clearly and is therefore essential for confirming the suitability, or otherwise, of the chosen approach to data analysis.

3.   Poor choice, or wrong choice, of analytical procedures

     Be honest about what you do and do not know. The ethical review process provides a formal check on all aspects of the research project including the proposed analytical procedures. If you have any doubts seek advice before your proposal reaches this point in the planning stage – an ethics panel should be viewed more as a regulatory mechanism rather than an advisory mechanism.

4.   Poor decision-making, or wrong decision-making, in evaluating your data analyses

     Self-awareness of your own level of expertise and knowledge, or access to knowledge and expertise, of appropriate rules and criteria for evaluating data analyses will ensure good decision-making.

5.   Drawing of inappropriate, over speculative, or unsubstantiated, conclusions

     Maintain a clear research line from research question, hypotheses, experimental design, data collection, data exploration and analysis, to data evaluation. Comments made and conclusions drawn whilst evaluating your data should be clearly linked back to the research question at every step in the research process.

Problem Box 12.4   **The Reporting Stage: Presenting Your Work to the Scientific Community**

1.   Choice of wrong forum (i.e. specific conference or journal/periodical) for the nature and scope of the data/study being presented

2.   Choice of wrong format for the nature and scope of the data/study being presented (i.e. abstract communication, oral communication, poster communication, a rapid written communication, or a scientific paper)

3.   Poor literacy skills with respect to spelling, grammar and punctuation

4.   An excessively wordy and imprecise scientific writing style

5.   Poor presentation skills with respect to clearly typed and formatted text, appropriate choice of clearly presented tables and figures

---

The Reporting Stage: Presenting Your Work to the Scientific Community

The first major consideration once you have completed your data analysis and have evaluated the 'story' presented by your research data, is where and how should you present your exciting new findings? The answer to these questions will dictate the format your research report will take and the specific detail of the content of this report. If there were a need to get your findings out into the public domain as quickly as possible, then the faster approaches would be either to present at conference as an oral or poster communication, or to submit a rapid written communication to a scientific journal. As discussed in chapter 11, conference organising committees and journal editorial boards prescribe the detailed specification your report should follow.

Once the decision of whether you wish to present at conference or to publish in a journal has been made – which may not necessarily be exclusive activities – you must then decide which would be the best forum for your work. Conferences and journals are generally either single discipline, multi-discipline or thematic, or represent the publication mechanism of a learned society (e.g. the

American Colleges of Sports Medicine – *Medicine and Science in Sport and Exercise*, The Physiological Society – *Journal of Physiology*, or The Nutrition Society – *Journal of Nutrition*). As well as the discipline or theme of your report, the calibre of the science, the quality and complexity of the data collection and the quality of your data analyses will all influence which would be an appropriate presentation forum. Like all areas of life there is a hierarchy to conferences and journals in terms of prestige and impact upon the scientific community; highly prestigious conferences and high impact journals provide an important reference resources for the sport and exercise science community. Therefore it is appropriate to evaluate the contribution of your work to scientific knowledge and understanding, and thus at which conference or in which journal your work would most appropriately sit.

Having decided upon the forum (i.e. conference or journal) and the format (i.e. abstract communication, oral communication, poster communication, a rapid written communication, or a scientific paper), the overall impact of your research report will be dependent upon sound presentational skills. Even the most groundbreaking work will have reduced impact on the scientific community if careful attention is not given to ensuring the quality of fundamental presentational skills. Perhaps some of the most annoying errors for editors and readers are those resulting from poor literacy skills with respect to spelling, grammar and punctuation. This is especially true in this computer era where word-processed reports can be automatically checked, and corrected, for incorrect spellings, poor grammar, and inappropriate punctuation.

A further presentation problem would be that of excessively wordy reports and/or reports adopting an imprecise scientific writing style. Both of these failings reflect a lack of discipline in your writing approach; a direct, focused report will convey the main findings of your work far more clearly and unambiguously. All forums for presenting your work will have limits either of time (i.e. oral communication), space/area (i.e. poster communication), or wordage (i.e. abstract communication, rapid written communication or a scientific paper). Submissions in excess of these limits will be returned to their authors, which at the very least will delay the publication process or may even result in non-inclusion of your work if a deadline is missed. Whilst learning to adopt a more direct and focused approach may initially result in a very dry writing style, in the longer term your work will benefit from clearer thinking and a resulting improvement in report clarity. In chapter 2 we introduced the adage 'Keep it Simple...' in relation to developing your initial research question; this adage is of equal relevance to the final stage in the research process, that of presenting your findings to the scientific community.

Finally, you should consider the specific structure of your research report with respect to clearly typed and formatted text, and appropriate choice of clearly presented tables and figures. As mentioned earlier, conference organising committees and journal editorial boards prescribe the detailed specification with respect to the format your report should take. This specification will normally include information relating to:

1. Printing areas (i.e. left, right, top and bottom of page margins or state A4)
2. Inclusion and formatting of headers and footers (e.g. page number, running title, etc.)
3. Preferred typing font (e.g. *Times New Roman* is a commonly adopted font)
4. Print size (e.g. 10-point or 12-point are common type sizes)
5. Line formatting (e.g. double-spaced or 1.5-line spacing)
6. Report sections and titles format
7. Formatting of data and units (SI units) in the main body of text
8. Reference formatting in the text and Reference section (e.g. number system, Harvard system)
9. Formatting of tables and figures
10. Author details for correspondence

Failure to adopt specified writing directions is another source of editorial irritation, and is a presentation error that *should not* arise. In addition, duplication of information should not arise. This sometimes occurs when data has been tabled, but may also appear in a figure; choose one format – that which best illustrates the point being made from the research data.

Solution Box 12.4   **The Reporting Stage: Presenting Your Work to the Scientific Community**

1.   Choice of wrong forum (i.e. specific conference or journal/periodical) for the nature and scope of the data/study being presented

This will be influenced by whether your work needs to be rapidly disseminated or not, the scientific discipline(s) or theme which underpins your research project, and a judgement on the quality and complexity of your work.

2.   Choice of wrong format for the nature and scope of the data/study being presented (i.e. abstract communication, oral communication, poster communication, a rapid written communication, or a scientific paper)

Your chosen forum for presenting your work will dictate the format of your research report and the detailed presentation specification/guidelines prescribed by the conference organising committee or journal editorial board.

3.   Poor literacy skills with respect to spelling, grammar and punctuation

If this is a known personal weakness, make sure you activate the automatic spelling, grammar and punctuation checkers on your word-processor/computer. If this option is not open to you, ensure that all your work is proof read by a colleague with good literacy skills before submission.

4.   An excessively wordy and imprecise scientific writing style

Keep it Simple – be direct, be focused, be succinct!

5.   Poor presentation skills with respect to clearly typed and formatted text, appropriate choice of clearly presented tables and figures

Observe and act upon conference organising committee or journal editorial board presentation specifications/guidelines for submitting your research report.

The "Highs" and "Lows" of Conducting Research

Once engaged in a research project you will soon become aware that it is a roller coaster of emotions, where the elation of a break through might be rapidly thwarted by the disappointment of any number of research difficulties. This is especially true in the sport and exercise sciences, where most research projects will focus upon the actions, behaviours, views or emotions of human beings, and how these might interact with the social context in which they live, work, compete or play. Humans are characteristically unpredictable relative to other physical phenomenon we might choose to study, and – under normal circumstances – also have the capacity for *free* thought and therefore *free* action. In research terms, at the very least this will contribute to the *variability* in our measurements, but equally might provide a source of *measurement error*. Increased variability in our measurements would occur if our research participants failed, for example, to adhere to pre-test guidelines or to follow a prescribed research intervention. Added frustration may arise from the fact that we may not know for sure if they have followed these instructions – our research participants might actually lie! Both these examples represent aspects of standardisation and control in our research study; the 'humanness' of our subject of study in the sport and exercise science is often at the root of thwarted standardisation and reduced experimental control. When research fails to go to plan, especially as a consequence of phenomena outside our control, this can be a major source of disappointment or a major research *low*. Equally, when a project runs smoothly in response to extensive and meticulous planning, this can provide a real research *high*.

You will recall from the Introduction to this chapter that our group of researchers were asked to describe, in their view, what they would consider to be their highs and lows from conducting research. Their responses are presented in table 12.1; we have semi-organised the data into general groups to avoid over repetition of similar or related themes. The researchers were very candid in their responses, and where the highs serve to illustrate the tremendous feelings of justifiable satisfaction that can be attained from a project well done, the lows will leave you in no doubt that this satisfaction is hard won.

Research Highs	Research Lows
Identifying a problem/research question and working out a research design that allows an answer to be provided	The 'hoops' you have to go through, and paperwork, to get work started; Paperwork related to ethics is onerous; Some procedures are overly bureaucratic and impede research; Organisational difficulties with other agencies (e.g. research participants, other researchers, providers of facilities/resources etc.)
Data analysis – the "Eureka moment!"; Seeing the final results for the first time	Research participant recruitment; Collecting data from reluctant participants; Research participants not turning up
Writing a coherent piece of work; Ability to develop constructive arguments which allow academic debate with research colleagues	Pace of project being slowed by factors beyond your control; Problems of equipment failure
Developing knowledge in a specific area; Increased knowledge and understanding of a specialist area; The process of developing new skills/knowledge; Gathering new and original information; The breakthroughs in grasping something new; Finding interesting results	Number crunching; Formatting your work to comply with journal requirements; Writing the final report
Contact with the community of researchers in the same field; Recognition/belonging (e.g. presentation of a paper, publication); Getting work published; Working with leading members within your field of research; Collaborating with like-minded colleagues; In-depth relationship and knowledge/partnership with colleagues or students; Dealing with bright people	When data does not appear to lead to a clear/definite result; Retrospective realisation of a poor design or flawed approach
Clarifying complex results for non-scientists so that they make sense in practice; Seeing your work used in an applied/practical setting; Application of knowledge to real life; Making outcomes useful to others; Finding the solutions to real problems; Seeing the results of your study changes the way something is done in practice	The need for systematic analysis can be very time-consuming; Never having enough time to do what you want to do; There is always a deadline that is difficult to meet when other responsibilities are high
Completing the whole process – uncovering information and identifying more questions which require answering	Not being recognised – low prestige of researchers and lack of promotion opportunities; Poor salary; Occasional unnecessary rivalry between research groups – Academic arrogance!
	Moments of insecurity about ability to complete

Table 12.1   Summary of research "Highs" and "Lows" as described by a group of researchers.

Post-Script: "Advice I Wish I'd Been Told at the Start of My Research Career"

Having looked at the potentially good and bad aspects of conducting research, it would be remiss of us not to leave you with some strategies and approaches to avoid problems occurring, or to deal with problems that will *inevitably* occur as you undertake a research project. Thus, as a fitting end to this chapter, we asked our researchers what their top tips were and the one piece of advice they wished they had received at the start of their research careers.

Researchers' Top Tips

When the researchers were asked what their 'top tips' would be for novice researchers, or those still in their early stages of a research career, the usual initial remark was "Don't!" This reflects the frustration you will undoubtedly experience at some point in – or even most of the way through – your research project. Some of the tips and pieces of advice do not specifically relate to conducting an undergraduate dissertation, independent project, or personal study, they refer to more general themes associated with conducting research or indeed researching as a career. Nevertheless, it was felt that such comments should be included, as they reflect a way of thinking that informs a process. Too often, our attention is focussed upon the outcome such that the process – in this instance the process of conducting research – is not given the necessary consideration. As discussed previously, careful consideration and sound evidence-based decisions made at each step in the research process will provide a firm foundation to good research. Table 12.2 presents the researchers' top tips for the planning stage, experimental stage, analysis stage, and reporting stage of the research process.

The Planning Stage	The Experimental Stage	The Analysis Stage	The Reporting Stage
Always take time to think – this is undervalued and underrated			
Make sure your supervisor, or line manager, asks for weekly progress discussions			
Choose a topic which will be fun to research, do not do it unless you are interested and believe in it; research on any scale will dominate your life... and may define your future	Start your work early – it always takes longer than expected – but do not try to do too much in one go	Keep the 'science' strong – it can be devalued	Put research back into context – how has this furthered our understanding, what are its implications, and how can we apply it?
Start reading early (now) and read widely	Be a research participant – experiencing the process from the other side is often very illuminating for you data collection!	Remain objective at all times during the data analysis – set your objective criteria/rules and stick to them	Continue to read as many research articles as you can, regardless of how relevant they are to your work – good writing skills can rub off this way
Do not be afraid to contact others researching in the field; discuss extensively BEFORE starting; if unsure or do not know, seek help	Good pilot studies are invaluable to ensure your measures are appropriate and that you are executing them competently		Write-up as you go along
Concentrate on developing a clear research question, well controlled experimental design, spend time ensuring your measures are the best available, and know exactly what analyses you are going to apply before you start	Focus upon what you are researching, as your data can always lead you to more questions that might require further investigation		

Table 12.2   Top tips for the planning stage, experimental stage, analysis stage, and reporting stage of the research process.

- Choose something that really interests you
- Choose something with which you can connect – either professionally or experientially... preferably both
- Concentrate on a specific programme of research and do not try to do too much too quickly
- ...do not try to do too much!
- Don't rush into a research project without first doing extensive research and preparation
- Read, read, read... and when your through reading, read some more
- ASK lots of questions, and LISTEN to the answers
- I had plenty of good advice... but acting upon it was more of a problem
- Do not believe everything you are told!
- Asking for help or guidance is not a sign of weakness... it's common sense!
- If you can explain your project to a non-practitioner or a lay person and they understand, you can be confident you've got a good handle on what you are supposed to be doing
- You can never over-plan; you can never over-prepare
- Make sure you are confident, and competent, in all aspects of your study before you start collecting your data
- At some point you've just got to make a start, and if you make a mistake it's ok as long as you learn from it!
- Most research is about thinking; take time to think
- Keep good reference records as you go along – electronically is quicker – saves a lot of time and trouble at the end
- Keep a sense of perspective and enjoy it!

Table 12.3   The one piece of advice that the researchers wished they had received at the start of their research careers.

Advice Born of Experience…

Many of the tips presented in table 12.2 support comments made earlier in this chapter; these are comments born out of practice and experience. This is equally true of the comments presented in table 12.3, which provides a collation of the responses of the researchers when asked what would be the one piece of advice that they wished they had received at the start of their research careers. Again there is repetition with what has been suggested earlier in this chapter and what is presented in table 12.2. However, we felt that it was appropriate, and essential within the context of *Using Statistics in Sport and Exercise Science Research*, to report the main themes that the researchers kept returning to when discussing research in general, and the research process in specific.

Synthesising the themes from the researchers' top tips and advice, we would suggest that a maxim you may wish to consider as you continue on your research career would be:

"Take time to read – Take time to think – Take time to plan"

References

British Association of Sport and Exercise Sciences (2000) Code of Conduct. http://www.bases.org.uk/newsite/accredditation.asp (Aug. 2005).

Bergstrom J. (1962) Muscle electrolytes in man. *Scand. J. Clin. Lab. Invest.* 14(Suppl. 68): 11–13.

Christensen E.H., Hansen O. (1939) Hypoglykamic, arbeitafahighkeit und ermundung. *Skand. Arch. Physiol.* 81: 160–175.

Cochran W.G., Cox G.M. (1957) *Experimental Design.* New York, USA: John Wiley and Sons.

Cohen J. (1988) *Statistical Power Analysis for the Behavioural Sciences (2nd Edition, revised).* Hillsdale NJ, USA: Erlbaum.

Dechent P., Pouwels P.J., Wilken B., Hanefeld F., Frahm J. (1999) Increase of total creatine in human brain after oral supplementation of creatine-monohydrate. *Am. J. Physiol.* 277(3, Part 2): R698–704.

Drowatzkky J.N. (1996) *Ethical Decision Making in Physical Activity Research.* Champaign IL, USA: Human Kinetics.

Harris R.C., Soderlund K., Hultman El (1992) Elevation of creatine in resting and exercised muscle of normal subjects by creatine supplementation. *Clin. Sci.* 83: 367–374.

Howell D.C. (1997) *Statistical Methods for Psychology*. Florence, Ky, USA: Wadsworth.

Kerlinger F.N. (1966) *Foundations of Behaviour Research: Educational and Psychological Inquiry*. New York, USA: Holt, Rinehart and Winston.

Levene H. (1960) Robust Tests for the Equality of Variance. In: I. Olkin (Ed.) *Contributions to Probability and Statistics*. Palo Alto, Ca: Stamford University Press.

Lorr M. (1984) *Profile of Mood States – Bipolar Form (POMS-BI) Manual*. San Diego, USA: Educational and Industrial Testing Service.

Massana G., Gasto C., Junque C., Mercader J., Gomez B., Massana J., Torres X., Salamero M. (2002) Reduced levels of creatine in the right medial temporal lobe region of panic disorder patients detected with (1)h magnetic resonance spectroscopy. *Neuroimage* 16(3, Part 1): 836.

McMorris T. (1986) *An investigation into the relationship between cognitive style and decision making in soccer*. Doctoral Thesis, University of Southampton, Southampton, United Kingdom.

Morrow J.R., Jackson A.W., Disch J.G., Mood D.P. (1995) *Measurement and Evaluation in Human Performance*. Champaign, IL, USA: Human Kinetics.

Ntoumanis N. (2001) *A Step By Step Guide To SPSS™ For Sport And Exercise Studies*. London, UK: Routledge.

Ritchie J., Lewis J. (2003) *Qualitative Research Practice*. London, UK: Sage.

Roberts M.J., Russo R. (1999) *A Student's Guide to Analysis of Variance*. London, UK: Routledge.

Shultz B.B., Sands W.A. (1995) Understanding measurement concepts in statistical procedures. In: Maud P.J., Foster C. *Physiological Assessment of Human Fitness*. Champaign IL, USA: Human Kinetics.

Tabachnick B., Fidell L. (1996) *Using Multivariate Statistics (Third Editon)*. New York, USA: Harper Collins.

Thomas J.R., Nelson J.K. (1990) *Research Methods in Physical Acivity (Second Editon)*. Champaign IL, USA: Human Kinetics.

Tukey J.W. (1977) *Exploratory Data Analysis*. Reading, Ma, USA: Addison-Wesley.

Tuckman B.W. (1978) *Conducting Educational Research (Second Edition).* New York, USA: Harcourt Brace Jovanovich.

Vincent W. (1995) *Statistics in Kinesiology.* Champaign IL, USA: Human Kinetics.

Watanabe A., Kato N., Kato T. (2002) Effects of creatine on mental fatigue and cerebral hemoglobin oxygenation. *Neurosci. Res.* 42: 279–285.

Appendix: 1 –   Data from the *Running Study*.

Gender	Age (yrs)	Height (m)	Mass (kg)	V_{Emax} (l.min^{-1})	$f_c$max (b.min^{-1})	VO_{2max} (ml.kg^{-1}.min^{-1})
M	26.9	1.75	65.5	113.9	195	53.4
M	22.3	1.87	83.3	146.5	199	62.3
M	21.2	1.74	65.8	150.9	187	76.5
M	39.3	1.66	63.2	108.7	178	65.8
M	24.9	1.76	73.2	119.9	179	66.1
M	24.8	1.88	74.7	164.3	185	69.9
M	21.0	1.63	66.8	124.3	186	63.0
M	21.4	1.76	70.7	119.1	182	63.2
M	25.4	1.81	62.9	135.2	174	72.1
M	24.8	1.74	73.5	139.2	199	57.6
M	19.9	1.71	65.7	144.8	178	74.4
M	24.2	1.75	83.1	136.6	201	58.2
M	20.5	1.81	75.2	145.2	191	63.0
M	24.0	1.89	79.6	134.1	183	67.2
M	31.8	1.80	74.6	132.2	188	60.2
M	34.5	1.63	67.1	123.5	193	67.5
M	25.8	1.74	73.3	123.1	209	47.8
M	29.8	1.70	66.3	112.2	187	52.9
M	25.6	1.80	73.0	133.2	195	63.0
M	32.8	1.80	75.2	139.2	171	58.9
M	21.7	1.82	68.3	132.7	197	67.1
M	22.8	1.77	82.1	109.7	191	56.7
M	25.3	1.75	88.5	134.0	207	49.9
M	21.7	1.69	57.2	91.5	207	59.2
M	29.6	1.80	74.5	133.4	209	62.4
M	25.6	1.81	73.6	123.8	196	59.0
M	21.3	1.81	83.2	156.3	176	61.3
M	32.1	1.74	60.2	121.3	198	67.1
M	28.9	1.69	65.3	125.4	201	60.4
M	20.0	1.72	67.7	103.7	202	50.2
M	24.7	1.74	68.7	131.9	197	58.9
M	25.2	1.76	66.5	100.4	183	53.4
M	26.3	1.82	76.5	116.6	181	54.1
M	28.4	1.90	73.9	126.4	189	63.3

Appendix: 1 –   Data from the *Running Study* (Continued).

Gender	Age (yrs)	Height (m)	Mass (kg)	$V_E$max $(l.min^{-1})$	HRmax $(b.min^{-1})$	VO_2max $(ml.kg^{-1}.min^{-1})$
M	32.8	1.63	68.6	120.0	184	64.0
M	24.2	1.79	72.5	111.3	188	59.0
M	24.6	1.70	68.9	110.4	192	58.4
M	34.3	1.87	81.4	119.3	195	63.4
M	22.4	1.83	67.4	130.7	196	65.4
M	25.4	1.79	72.4	121.8	195	58.0
F	37.7	1.67	50.6	84.9	192	54.7
F	26.9	1.61	61.4	107.5	193	59.7
F	26.0	1.71	52.1	91.4	193	57.2
F	25.8	1.59	60.3	105.4	195	58.5
F	22.0	1.62	47.8	92.4	186	49.9
F	22.6	1.77	65.1	93.9	197	45.2
F	25.2	1.59	62.0	94.2	203	45.9
F	18.7	1.65	58.9	86.5	180	44.4
F	20.1	1.70	59.3	96.4	198	54.0
F	20.9	1.58	58.3	83.5	186	42.1
F	33.0	1.62	58.8	78.7	183	44.8
F	29.1	1.56	57.3	76.6	191	45.4
F	28.3	1.70	55.3	92.6	183	56.1
F	26.9	1.69	56.9	83.0	194	42.2
F	33.4	1.67	51.3	79.3	181	49.2
F	30.4	1.65	63.9	99.6	186	53.1
F	24.7	1.65	58.0	82.5	190	46.0
F	25.4	1.61	59.8	103.1	197	58.5
F	21.0	1.60	58.6	84.0	190	44.6
F	23.1	1.59	48.4	94.5	195	50.0

Appendix: 2 – Values of the Chi-Square (χ^2) Distribution.

df	0.05	0.01	df	0.05	0.01	df	0.05	0.01
1	3.84	6.64	34	48.60	56.06	67	87.11	96.83
2	5.99	9.21	35	49.80	57.34	68	88.25	98.03
3	7.82	11.35	36	51.00	58.62	69	89.39	99.23
4	9.49	13.28	37	52.19	59.89	70	90.53	100.42
5	11.07	15.09	38	53.38	61.16	71	91.67	101.62
6	12.59	16.81	39	54.57	62.43	72	92.81	102.82
7	14.07	18.48	40	55.76	63.69	73	93.95	104.01
8	15.51	20.09	41	56.94	64.95	74	95.08	105.20
9	16.92	21.67	42	58.12	66.21	75	96.22	106.39
10	18.31	23.21	43	59.30	67.46	76	97.35	107.58
11	19.68	24.73	44	60.48	68.71	77	98.49	108.77
12	21.03	26.22	45	61.66	69.96	78	99.62	109.96
13	22.36	27.69	46	62.83	71.20	79	100.75	111.15
14	23.69	29.14	47	64.00	72.44	80	101.88	112.33
15	25.00	30.58	48	65.17	73.68	81	103.01	113.51
16	26.30	32.00	49	66.34	74.92	82	104.14	114.70
17	27.59	33.41	50	67.51	76.15	83	105.27	115.88
18	28.87	34.81	51	68.67	77.39	84	106.40	117.06
19	30.14	36.19	52	69.83	78.62	85	107.52	118.24
20	31.41	37.57	53	70.99	79.84	86	108.65	119.41
21	32.67	38.93	54	72.15	81.07	87	109.77	120.59
22	33.92	40.29	55	73.31	82.29	88	110.90	121.77
23	35.17	41.64	56	74.47	83.52	89	112.02	122.94
24	36.42	42.98	57	75.62	84.73	90	113.15	124.12
25	37.65	44.31	58	76.78	85.95	91	114.27	125.29
26	38.89	45.64	59	77.93	87.17	92	115.39	126.46
27	40.11	46.96	60	79.08	88.38	93	116.51	127.63
28	41.34	48.28	61	80.23	89.59	94	117.63	128.80
29	42.56	49.59	62	81.38	90.80	95	118.75	129.97
30	43.77	50.89	63	82.53	92.01	96	119.87	131.14
31	44.99	52.19	64	83.68	93.22	97	120.99	132.31
32	46.19	53.49	65	84.82	94.42	98	122.11	133.47
33	47.40	54.78	66	85.97	95.63	99	123.23	134.64
						100	124.34	135.81

The first example in chapter 6 has 2 df at 0.05 level of significance to give a critical value of 5.99

Appendix: 3 –   Values of the *t* Distribution (1 and 2-tailed tests).

df	2-tailed 0.05	2-tailed 0.01	1-tailed 0.05	1-tailed 0.01	df	2-tailed 0.05	2-tailed 0.01	1-tailed 0.05	1-tailed 0.01
1	12.706	63.657	6.314	31.820	31	2.040	2.744	1.696	2.453
2	4.303	9.925	2.920	6.965	32	2.037	2.738	1.694	2.449
3	3.182	5.841	2.353	4.541	33	2.035	2.733	1.692	2.445
4	2.776	4.604	2.132	3.747	34	2.032	2.728	1.691	2.441
5	2.571	4.032	2.015	3.365	35	2.030	2.724	1.690	2.438
6	2.447	3.707	1.943	3.143	36	2.028	2.719	1.688	2.434
7	2.365	3.499	1.895	2.998	37	2.026	2.715	1.687	2.431
8	2.306	3.355	1.860	2.897	38	2.024	2.712	1.686	2.429
9	2.262	3.250	1.833	2.821	39	2.023	2.708	1.685	2.426
10	2.228	3.169	1.813	2.764	40	2.021	2.704	1.684	2.423
11	2.201	3.106	1.796	2.718	42	2.018	2.698	1.682	2.418
12	2.179	3.055	1.782	2.681	44	2.015	2.692	1.680	2.414
13	2.160	3.012	1.771	2.650	46	2.013	2.687	1.679	2.410
14	2.145	2.977	1.761	2.625	48	2.011	2.682	1.677	2.407
15	2.131	2.947	1.753	2.603	50	2.009	2.678	1.676	2.403
16	2.120	2.921	1.746	2.584	55	2.004	2.668	1.673	2.396
17	2.110	2.898	1.740	2.567	60	2.000	2.660	1.671	2.390
18	2.101	2.878	1.734	2.552	65	1.997	2.654	1.669	2.385
19	2.093	2.861	1.729	2.540	70	1.994	2.648	1.667	2.381
20	2.086	2.845	1.725	2.528	75	1.992	2.643	1.665	2.377
21	2.080	2.831	1.721	2.518	80	1.990	2.639	1.664	2.374
22	2.074	2.819	1.717	2.508	85	1.988	2.635	1.663	2.371
23	2.069	2.807	1.714	2.500	90	1.987	2.632	1.662	2.368
24	2.064	2.797	1.711	2.492	95	1.985	2.629	1.661	2.366
25	2.060	2.787	1.708	2.485	100	1.984	2.626	1.660	2.364
26	2.056	2.779	1.706	2.479	125	1.979	2.616	1.657	2.357
27	2.052	2.771	1.703	2.473	150	1.976	2.609	1.655	2.351
28	2.048	2.763	1.701	2.467	175	1.974	2.604	1.654	2.348
29	2.045	2.756	1.699	2.462	200	1.972	2.601	1.653	2.345
30	2.042	2.750	1.697	2.457	∞	1.960	2.576	1.645	2.326

The first example in chapter 6 has 18 df at 0.05 significance level to give a critical t value of 2.101

Appendix: 4 –   Values of the Wilcoxon T Distribution (2-tailed test).

Sample Size	0.05	0.01
1	-	-
2	-	-
3	-	-
4	-	-
5	-	-
6	0	-
7	2	-
8	3	0
9	5	1
10	8	3
11	10	5
12	13	7
13	17	9
14	21	12
15	25	15
16	29	19
17	34	23
18	40	27
19	46	32
20	52	37
21	58	42
22	65	48
23	73	54
24	81	61
25	89	68
26	98	75
27	107	83
28	116	91
29	126	100
30	137	109

The example in chapter 8 has a sample size of 13 so at 0.05 level of significance the critical T value is 17

Appendix: 5 –   Decimal Percentage of Scores Under the Normal Curve, ±Z score (2-tailed).

± Z	0.00	0.01	0.02	0.03	0.04	0.05	0.06	0.07	0.08	0.09
0.0	0.0000	0.0080	0.0160	0.0239	0.0319	0.0399	0.0478	0.0558	0.0638	0.0717
0.1	0.0797	0.0876	0.0955	0.1034	0.1113	0.1192	0.1271	0.1350	0.1428	0.1507
0.2	0.1585	0.1663	0.1741	0.1819	0.1897	0.1974	0.2051	0.2128	0.2205	0.2282
0.3	0.2358	0.2434	0.2510	0.2586	0.2661	0.2737	0.2812	0.2886	0.2961	0.3035
0.4	0.3108	0.3182	0.3255	0.3328	0.3401	0.3473	0.3545	0.3616	0.3688	0.3759
0.5	0.3829	0.3899	0.3969	0.4039	0.4108	0.4177	0.4245	0.4313	0.4381	0.4448
0.6	0.4515	0.4581	0.4647	0.4713	0.4778	0.4843	0.4907	0.4971	0.5035	0.5098
0.7	0.5161	0.5223	0.5285	0.5346	0.5407	0.5467	0.5527	0.5587	0.5646	0.5705
0.8	0.5763	0.5821	0.5878	0.5935	0.5991	0.6047	0.6102	0.6157	0.6211	0.6265
0.9	0.6319	0.6372	0.6424	0.6476	0.6528	0.6579	0.6629	0.6680	0.6729	0.6778
1.0	0.6827	0.6875	0.6923	0.6970	0.7017	0.7063	0.7109	0.7154	0.7199	0.7243
1.1	0.7287	0.7330	0.7373	0.7415	0.7457	0.7499	0.7540	0.7580	0.7620	0.7660
1.2	0.7699	0.7737	0.7775	0.7813	0.7850	0.7887	0.7923	0.7959	0.7995	0.8029
1.3	0.8064	0.8098	0.8132	0.8165	0.8198	0.8230	0.8262	0.8293	0.8324	0.8355
1.4	0.8385	0.8415	0.8444	0.8473	0.8501	0.8529	0.8557	0.8584	0.8611	0.8638
1.5	0.8664	0.8690	0.8715	0.8740	0.8764	0.8789	0.8812	0.8836	0.8859	0.8882
1.6	0.8904	0.8926	0.8948	0.8969	0.8990	0.9011	0.9031	0.9051	0.9070	0.9090
1.7	0.9109	0.9127	0.9146	0.9164	0.9181	0.9199	0.9216	0.9233	0.9249	0.9265
1.8	0.9281	0.9297	0.9312	0.9328	0.9342	0.9357	0.9371	0.9385	0.9399	0.9412
1.9	0.9426	0.9439	0.9451	0.9464	0.9476	0.9488	0.9500	0.9512	0.9523	0.9534
2.0	0.9545	0.9556	0.9566	0.9576	0.9586	0.9596	0.9606	0.9615	0.9625	0.9634
2.1	0.9643	0.9651	0.9660	0.9668	0.9676	0.9684	0.9692	0.9700	0.9707	0.9715
2.2	0.9722	0.9729	0.9736	0.9743	0.9749	0.9756	0.9762	0.9768	0.9774	0.9780
2.3	0.9786	0.9791	0.9797	0.9802	0.9807	0.9812	0.9817	0.9822	0.9827	0.9832
2.4	0.9836	0.9840	0.9845	0.9849	0.9853	0.9857	0.9861	0.9865	0.9869	0.9872
2.5	0.9876	0.9879	0.9883	0.9886	0.9889	0.9892	0.9895	0.9898	0.9901	0.9904
2.6	0.9907	0.9909	0.9912	0.9915	0.9917	0.9920	0.9922	0.9924	0.9926	0.9929
2.7	0.9931	0.9933	0.9935	0.9937	0.9939	0.9940	0.9942	0.9944	0.9946	0.9947
2.8	0.9949	0.9950	0.9952	0.9953	0.9955	0.9956	0.9958	0.9959	0.9960	0.9961
2.9	0.9963	0.9964	0.9965	0.9966	0.9967	0.9968	0.9969	0.9970	0.9971	0.9972
3.0	0.9973	0.9974	0.9975	0.9976	0.9976	0.9977	0.9978	0.9979	0.9979	0.9980
3.1	0.9981	0.9981	0.9982	0.9983	0.9983	0.9984	0.9984	0.9985	0.9985	0.9986
3.2	0.9986	0.9987	0.9987	0.9988	0.9988	0.9988	0.9989	0.9989	0.9990	0.9990
3.3	0.9990	0.9991	0.9991	0.9991	0.9992	0.9992	0.9992	0.9992	0.9993	0.9993
3.4	0.9993	0.9994	0.9994	0.9994	0.9994	0.9994	0.9995	0.9995	0.9995	0.9995
3.5	0.9995	0.9996	0.9996	0.9996	0.9996	0.9996	0.9996	0.9996	0.9997	0.9997
3.6	0.9997	0.9997	0.9997	0.9997	0.9997	0.9997	0.9997	0.9998	0.9998	0.9998
3.7	0.9998	0.9998	0.9998	0.9998	0.9998	0.9998	0.9998	0.9998	0.9998	0.9998
3.8	0.9999	0.9999	0.9999	0.9999	0.9999	0.9999	0.9999	0.9999	0.9999	0.9999
3.9	0.9999	0.9999	0.9999	0.9999	0.9999	0.9999	0.9999	0.9999	0.9999	0.9999

A ±Z score of ±1.96 (across row 1.9 to intersect column 0.06) includes 0.9500 (95%) of all scores

Appendix: 6 – Values for the Mann Whitney U Distribution (2-tailed test).

0.05

n_2 \ n_1	8	9	10	11	12	13	14	15	16	17	18	19	20
1												0	0
2	0	0	0	0	1	1	1	1	1	2	2	2	2
3	2	2	3	3	4	4	5	5	6	6	7	7	8
4	4	4	5	6	7	8	9	10	11	11	12	13	13
5	6	7	8	9	11	12	13	14	15	17	18	19	20
6	8	10	11	13	14	16	17	19	21	22	24	25	27
7	10	12	14	16	18	20	22	24	26	28	30	32	34
8	13	15	17	19	22	24	26	29	31	34	36	38	41
9	15	17	20	23	26	28	31	34	37	39	42	45	48
10	17	20	23	26	29	33	36	39	42	45	48	52	55
11	19	23	26	30	33	37	40	44	47	51	55	58	62
12	22	26	29	33	37	41	45	49	53	57	61	65	69
13	24	28	33	37	41	45	50	54	59	63	67	72	76
14	26	31	36	40	45	50	55	59	64	67	74	78	83
15	29	34	39	44	49	54	59	64	70	75	80	85	90
16	31	37	42	47	53	59	64	70	75	81	86	92	98
17	34	39	45	51	57	63	67	75	81	87	93	99	105
18	36	42	48	55	61	67	74	80	86	93	99	106	112
19	38	45	52	58	65	72	78	85	92	99	106	113	119
20	41	48	55	62	69	76	83	90	98	105	112	119	127

0.01

n_2 \ n_1	8	9	10	11	12	13	14	15	16	17	18	19	20
1													
2												0	0
3		0	0	0	1	1	1	2	2	2	2	3	3
4	1	1	2	2	3	3	4	5	5	6	6	7	8
5	2	3	4	5	6	7	7	8	9	10	11	12	13
6	4	5	6	7	9	10	11	12	13	15	16	17	18
7	6	7	9	10	12	13	15	16	18	19	21	22	24
8	7	9	11	11	15	17	18	20	22	24	26	28	30
9	9	11	13	13	18	20	22	24	27	29	31	33	36
10	11	13	16	16	21	24	26	29	31	34	37	39	42
11	13	16	18	18	24	27	30	33	36	39	42	45	48
12	15	18	21	21	27	31	34	37	41	44	47	51	54
13	17	20	24	24	31	34	38	42	45	49	53	56	60
14	18	22	26	26	34	38	42	46	50	54	58	63	67
15	20	24	29	29	37	42	46	51	55	60	64	69	73
16	22	27	31	31	41	45	50	55	60	65	70	74	79
17	24	29	34	34	44	49	54	60	65	70	75	81	86
18	26	31	37	37	47	53	58	64	70	75	81	87	92
19	28	33	39	39	51	56	63	69	74	81	87	93	99
20	30	36	42	42	54	60	67	73	79	86	92	99	105

The example in chapter 8 has a sample sizes of n=6 and n=8 so at 0.05 level of significance the critical U value is 8

Appendix: 7 –   **Critical Values for the F Distribution** (at the 0.05 significance level).

Use df from greatest calculated mean square value here

df	1	2	3	4	5	6	7	8	9	10	11	12
1	161.4	199.5	215.7	224.6	230.2	234.0	236.8	238.9	240.5	241.9	243.0	243.9
2	18.5	19.0	19.2	19.2	19.3	19.3	19.4	19.4	19.4	19.4	19.4	19.4
3	10.1	9.55	9.28	9.12	9.01	8.94	8.89	8.85	8.81	8.79	8.76	8.74
4	7.71	6.94	6.59	6.39	6.26	6.16	6.09	6.04	6.00	5.96	5.94	5.91
5	6.61	5.79	5.41	5.19	5.05	4.95	4.88	4.82	4.77	4.74	4.70	4.68
6	5.99	5.14	4.76	4.53	4.39	4.28	4.21	4.15	4.10	4.06	4.03	4.00
7	5.59	4.74	4.35	4.12	3.97	3.87	3.79	3.73	3.68	3.64	3.60	3.57
8	5.32	4.46	4.07	3.84	3.69	3.58	3.50	3.44	3.39	3.35	3.31	3.28
9	5.12	4.26	3.86	3.63	3.48	3.37	3.29	3.23	3.18	3.14	3.10	3.07
10	4.96	4.10	3.71	3.48	3.33	3.22	3.14	3.07	3.02	2.98	2.94	2.91
11	4.84	3.98	3.59	3.36	3.20	3.09	3.01	2.95	2.90	2.85	2.82	2.79
12	4.75	3.89	3.49	3.26	3.11	3.00	2.91	2.85	2.80	2.75	2.72	2.69
13	4.67	3.81	3.41	3.18	3.03	2.92	2.83	2.77	2.71	2.67	2.63	2.60
14	4.60	3.74	3.34	3.11	2.96	2.85	2.76	2.70	2.65	2.60	2.57	2.53
15	4.54	3.68	3.29	3.06	2.90	2.79	2.71	2.64	2.59	2.54	2.51	2.48
16	4.49	3.63	3.24	3.01	2.85	2.74	2.66	2.59	2.54	2.49	2.46	2.42
17	4.45	3.59	3.20	2.96	2.81	2.70	2.61	2.55	2.49	2.45	2.41	2.38
18	4.41	3.55	3.16	2.93	2.77	2.66	2.58	2.51	2.46	2.41	2.37	2.34
19	4.38	3.52	3.13	2.90	2.74	2.63	2.54	2.48	2.42	2.38	2.34	2.31
20	4.35	3.49	3.10	2.87	2.71	2.60	2.51	2.45	2.39	2.35	2.31	2.28
21	4.32	3.47	3.07	2.84	2.68	2.57	2.49	2.42	2.37	2.32	2.28	2.25
22	4.30	3.44	3.05	2.82	2.66	2.55	2.46	2.40	2.34	2.30	2.26	2.23
23	4.28	3.42	3.03	2.80	2.64	2.53	2.44	2.37	2.32	2.27	2.24	2.20
24	4.26	3.40	3.01	2.78	2.62	2.51	2.42	2.36	2.30	2.25	2.22	2.18
25	4.24	3.39	2.99	2.76	2.60	2.49	2.40	2.34	2.28	2.24	2.20	2.16
26	4.23	3.37	2.98	2.74	2.59	2.47	2.39	2.32	2.27	2.22	2.18	2.15
27	4.21	3.35	2.96	2.73	2.57	2.46	2.37	2.31	2.25	2.20	2.17	2.13
28	4.20	3.34	2.95	2.71	2.56	2.45	2.36	2.29	2.24	2.19	2.15	2.12
29	4.18	3.33	2.93	2.70	2.55	2.43	2.35	2.28	2.22	2.18	2.14	2.10
30	4.17	3.32	2.92	2.69	2.53	2.42	2.33	2.27	2.21	2.16	2.13	2.09
50	4.03	3.18	2.79	2.56	2.40	2.29	2.20	2.13	2.07	2.03	1.99	1.95
75	3.97	3.12	2.73	2.49	2.34	2.22	2.13	2.06	2.01	1.96	1.92	1.88
100	3.94	3.09	2.70	2.46	2.31	2.19	2.10	2.03	1.97	1.93	1.89	1.85
150	3.90	3.06	2.66	2.43	2.27	2.16	2.07	2.00	1.94	1.89	1.85	1.82
∞	3.84	3.00	2.60	2.37	2.21	2.10	2.01	1.94	1.88	1.83	1.79	1.75

The example in chapter 9, df 2 (greatest mean square) and 12 gives a critical F value (0.05) of 3.89

Appendix: 7 – Critical Values for the F Distribution (at the 0.01 significance level).

Use df from greatest calculated mean square value here

df	1	2	3	4	5	6	7	8	9	10	11	12
1	4052	4999	5403	5625	5764	5859	5928	5981	6022	6056	6083	6106
2	98.50	99.00	99.17	99.25	99.30	99.33	99.36	99.37	99.39	99.40	99.41	99.42
3	34.12	30.82	29.46	28.71	28.24	27.91	27.67	27.49	27.35	27.23	27.13	27.05
4	21.20	18.00	16.69	15.98	15.52	15.21	14.98	14.80	14.66	14.55	14.45	14.37
5	16.26	13.27	12.06	11.39	10.97	10.67	10.46	10.29	10.16	10.05	9.96	9.89
6	13.75	10.92	9.78	9.15	8.75	8.47	8.26	8.10	7.98	7.87	7.79	7.72
7	12.25	9.55	8.45	7.85	7.46	7.19	6.99	6.84	6.72	6.62	6.54	6.47
8	11.26	8.65	7.59	7.01	6.63	6.37	6.18	6.03	5.91	5.81	5.73	5.67
9	10.56	8.02	6.99	6.42	6.06	5.80	5.61	5.47	5.35	5.26	5.18	5.11
10	10.04	7.56	6.55	5.99	5.64	5.39	5.20	5.06	4.94	4.85	4.77	4.71
11	9.65	7.21	6.22	5.67	5.32	5.07	4.89	4.74	4.63	4.54	4.46	4.40
12	9.33	6.93	5.95	5.41	5.06	4.82	4.64	4.50	4.39	4.30	4.22	4.16
13	9.07	6.70	5.74	5.21	4.86	4.62	4.44	4.30	4.19	4.10	4.02	3.96
14	8.86	6.51	5.56	5.04	4.69	4.46	4.28	4.14	4.03	3.94	3.86	3.80
15	8.68	6.36	5.42	4.89	4.56	4.32	4.14	4.00	3.89	3.80	3.73	3.67
16	8.53	6.23	5.29	4.77	4.44	4.20	4.03	3.89	3.78	3.69	3.62	3.55
17	8.40	6.11	5.18	4.67	4.34	4.10	3.93	3.79	3.68	3.59	3.52	3.46
18	8.29	6.01	5.09	4.58	4.25	4.01	3.84	3.71	3.60	3.51	3.43	3.37
19	8.18	5.93	5.01	4.50	4.17	3.94	3.77	3.63	3.52	3.43	3.36	3.30
20	8.10	5.85	4.94	4.43	4.10	3.87	3.70	3.56	3.46	3.37	3.29	3.23
21	8.02	5.78	4.87	4.37	4.04	3.81	3.64	3.51	3.40	3.31	3.24	3.17
22	7.95	5.72	4.82	4.31	3.99	3.76	3.59	3.45	3.35	3.26	3.18	3.12
23	7.88	5.66	4.76	4.26	3.94	3.71	3.54	3.41	3.30	3.21	3.14	3.07
24	7.82	5.61	4.72	4.22	3.90	3.67	3.50	3.36	3.26	3.17	3.09	3.03
25	7.77	5.57	4.68	4.18	3.85	3.63	3.46	3.32	3.22	3.13	3.06	2.99
26	7.72	5.53	4.64	4.14	3.82	3.59	3.42	3.29	3.18	3.09	3.02	2.96
27	7.68	5.49	4.60	4.11	3.78	3.56	3.39	3.26	3.15	3.06	2.99	2.93
28	7.64	5.45	4.57	4.07	3.75	3.53	3.36	3.23	3.12	3.03	2.96	2.90
29	7.60	5.42	4.54	4.04	3.73	3.50	3.33	3.20	3.09	3.00	2.93	2.87
30	7.56	5.39	4.51	4.02	3.70	3.47	3.30	3.17	3.07	2.98	2.91	2.84
50	7.17	5.06	4.20	3.72	3.41	3.19	3.02	2.89	2.78	2.70	2.63	2.56
75	6.99	4.90	4.05	3.58	3.27	3.05	2.89	2.76	2.65	2.57	2.49	2.43
100	6.90	4.82	3.98	3.51	3.21	2.99	2.82	2.69	2.59	2.50	2.43	2.37
150	6.81	4.75	3.91	3.45	3.14	2.92	2.76	2.63	2.53	2.44	2.37	2.31
∞	6.63	4.61	3.78	3.32	3.02	2.80	2.64	2.51	2.41	2.32	2.25	2.18

Appendix: 8 –   **Critical Values for the Studentized Range (q)** (at the 0.05 significance level).

df_E	\multicolumn{13}{c}{Number of means being compared}

df_E	2	3	4	5	6	7	8	9	10	11	12	13	14
1	18.0	27.0	32.8	37.2	40.5	43.1	45.4	47.3	49.1	50.6	51.9	53.2	54.3
2	6.09	8.33	9.80	10.89	11.73	12.43	13.03	13.54	13.99	14.39	14.75	15.08	15.38
3	4.50	5.91	6.83	7.51	8.04	8.47	8.85	9.18	9.46	9.72	9.95	10.16	10.35
4	3.93	5.04	5.76	6.29	6.71	7.06	7.35	7.60	7.83	8.03	8.21	8.37	8.52
5	3.64	4.60	5.22	5.67	6.03	6.33	6.58	6.80	6.99	7.17	7.32	7.47	7.60
6	3.46	4.34	4.90	5.31	5.63	5.89	6.12	6.32	6.49	6.65	6.79	6.92	7.04
7	3.34	4.16	4.68	5.06	5.35	5.59	5.80	5.99	6.15	6.29	6.42	6.54	6.65
8	3.26	4.04	4.53	4.89	5.17	5.40	5.60	5.77	5.92	6.05	6.18	6.29	6.39
9	3.20	3.95	4.42	4.76	5.02	5.24	5.43	5.60	5.74	5.87	5.98	6.09	6.19
10	3.15	3.88	4.33	4.66	4.91	5.12	5.30	5.46	5.60	5.72	5.83	5.93	6.03
11	3.11	3.82	4.26	5.58	4.82	5.03	5.20	5.35	5.49	5.61	5.71	5.81	5.90
12	3.08	3.77	4.20	4.51	4.75	4.95	5.12	5.27	5.40	5.51	5.61	5.71	5.80
13	3.06	3.73	4.15	4.46	4.69	4.88	5.05	5.19	5.32	5.43	5.53	5.63	5.71
14	3.03	3.70	4.11	4.41	4.64	4.83	4.99	5.13	5.25	5.36	5.46	5.56	5.64
15	3.01	3.67	4.08	4.37	4.59	4.78	4.94	5.08	5.20	5.31	5.40	5.49	5.57
16	3.00	3.65	4.05	4.34	4.56	4.74	4.90	5.03	5.15	5.26	5.35	5.44	5.52
17	2.98	3.62	4.02	4.31	4.52	4.70	4.86	4.99	5.11	5.21	5.31	5.39	5.47
18	2.97	3.61	4.00	4.28	4.49	4.67	4.83	4.96	5.07	5.17	5.27	5.35	5.43
19	2.96	3.59	3.98	4.26	4.47	4.64	4.79	4.92	5.04	5.14	5.23	5.32	5.39
20	2.95	3.58	3.96	4.24	4.45	4.62	4.77	4.90	5.01	5.11	5.20	5.28	5.36
30	2.89	3.48	3.84	4.11	4.30	4.46	4.60	4.72	4.83	4.92	5.00	5.08	5.15
40	2.86	3.44	3.79	4.04	4.23	4.39	4.52	4.63	4.74	4.82	4.90	4.98	5.05
120	2.80	3.60	3.69	3.92	4.10	4.24	4.36	4.47	4.56	4.64	4.71	4.78	4.84
∞	2.77	3.32	3.63	3.86	4.03	4.17	4.29	4.39	4.47	4.55	4.62	4.68	4.74

The example in chapter 9 has 3 means and 12 df for the error term (df_E) giving a critical q value (0.05) of 3.77

Appendix: 8 – Critical Values for the Studentized Range (q) (at the 0.01 significance level).

df_E	Number of means being compared												
	2	3	4	5	6	7	8	9	10	11	12	13	14
1	90.03	135.0	164.3	185.6	202.2	215.8	227.2	237.0	245.6	253.2	260.0	266.2	271.8
2	14.00	19.00	22.30	24.70	26.60	28.20	29.50	30.70	31.70	32.60	33.40	34.10	34.80
3	8.26	10.60	12.20	13.30	14.20	15.00	15.60	16.20	16.70	17.10	17.50	17.90	18.20
4	6.51	8.12	9.17	9.96	10.60	11.10	11.50	11.90	12.30	12.60	12.80	13.10	13.30
5	5.70	6.98	7.80	8.42	8.91	9.32	9.67	9.97	10.24	10.48	10.70	10.89	11.08
6	5.24	6.33	7.03	7.56	7.97	8.32	8.61	8.87	9.10	9.30	9.48	9.65	9.81
7	4.95	5.92	6.54	7.01	7.37	7.68	7.94	8.17	8.37	8.55	8.71	8.86	9.00
8	4.75	5.64	6.20	6.62	6.96	7.24	7.47	7.68	7.86	8.03	8.18	8.31	8.44
9	4.60	5.43	5.96	6.35	6.66	6.91	7.13	7.33	7.49	7.65	7.78	7.91	8.03
10	4.48	5.27	5.77	6.14	6.43	6.67	6.87	7.05	7.21	7.36	7.49	7.60	7.71
11	4.39	5.15	5.62	5.97	6.25	6.48	6.67	6.84	6.99	7.13	7.25	7.36	7.46
12	4.32	5.05	5.50	5.84	6.10	6.32	6.51	6.67	6.81	6.94	7.06	7.17	7.26
13	4.26	4.96	5.40	5.73	5.98	6.19	6.37	6.53	6.67	6.79	6.90	7.01	7.10
14	4.21	4.89	5.32	5.63	5.88	6.08	6.26	6.41	6.54	6.66	6.77	6.87	6.96
15	4.17	4.84	5.25	5.56	5.80	5.99	6.16	6.31	6.44	6.55	6.66	6.76	6.84
16	4.13	4.79	5.19	5.49	5.72	5.92	6.08	6.22	6.35	6.46	6.56	6.66	6.74
17	4.10	4.74	5.14	5.43	5.66	5.85	6.01	6.15	6.27	6.38	6.48	6.57	6.66
18	4.07	4.70	5.09	5.38	5.60	5.79	5.94	6.08	6.20	6.31	6.41	6.50	6.58
19	4.05	4.67	5.05	5.33	5.55	5.73	5.89	6.02	6.14	6.25	6.34	6.43	6.51
20	4.02	4.64	5.02	5.29	5.51	5.69	5.84	5.97	6.09	6.19	6.28	6.37	6.45
30	3.89	4.45	4.80	5.05	5.24	5.40	5.54	5.65	5.76	5.85	5.93	6.01	6.08
40	3.82	4.37	4.70	4.93	5.11	5.26	5.39	5.50	5.60	5.69	5.76	5.83	5.90
120	3.70	4.20	4.50	4.71	4.87	5.01	5.12	5.21	5.30	5.37	5.44	5.50	5.56
∞	3.64	4.12	4.40	4.60	4.76	4.88	4.99	5.08	5.16	5.23	5.29	5.35	5.40

Index